SOFTWARE PROJECT DYNAMICS

WITHDRAWN

SOFTWARE PROJECT DYNAMICS
AN INTEGRATED APPROACH

Tarek Abdel-Hamid
Naval Postgraduate School

Stuart E. Madnick
Massachusetts Institute of Technology

PRENTICE HALL
Englewood Cliffs, New Jersey 07632

Library of Congress Cataloging-in-Publication Data

Abdel-Hamid, Tarek K.
  Software project dynamics : an integrated approach / Tarek Abdel
-Hamid, Stuart E. Madnick.
     p.   cm.
  Includes bibliographical references and index.
  ISBN 0-13-822040-9
  1. Computer software--Development--Management.   I. Madnick,
Stuart E. II. Title.
QA76.76.D47A24 1990
005.1'068--dc20   90-47747
                                                       CIP

Editorial/production supervision: *Laura A. Huber*
Cover design: *Wanda Lubelska*
Manufacturing buyers: *Kelly Behr/Susan Brunke*
Acquisitions Editor: *Gregory Doench*

©1991 by Prentice-Hall, Inc.
A Division of Simon & Schuster
Englewood Cliffs, New Jersey 07632

The publisher offers discounts on this book when ordered
in bulk quantities. For more information, write:

Special Sales/College Marketing
College Technical and Reference Division
Prentice Hall
Englewood Cliffs, New Jersey 07632

Printed in the United States of America
10 9 8 7 6 5 4 3 2 1

ISBN 0-13-822040-9

Prentice-Hall International (UK) Limited, *London*
Prentice-Hall of Australia Pty. Limited, *Sydney*
Prentice-Hall Canada Inc., *Toronto*
Prentice-Hall Hispanoamericana, S.A., *Mexico*
Prentice-Hall of India Private Limited, *New Delhi*
Prentice-Hall of Japan, Inc., *Tokyo*
Simon & Schuster Asia Pte. Ltd., *Singapore*
Editora Prentice-Hall do Brasil, Ltda., *Rio de Janeiro*

To Nadia,
My wife and best friend.
  Tarek Abdel-Hamid

To my family:
My brothers, Ron and Jackson; and my children, Howard, Michael, and Lynne
Who share my life and give true meaning to it.
  Stuart E. Madnick

CONTENTS

PREFACE

Motivation for Book

Software is big business. It has been estimated that expenditures for software development and maintenance were $70 billion dollars in 1985. Even more impressive are the projections that computer software costs will grow to $450 billion worldwide by 1995.

The growth in the software industry has not, however, been painless. The record indicates that the development of software systems has been plagued by cost overruns, late deliveries, and users' dissatisfaction. The problems persist in spite of the significant software engineering advances that have been made over the last decade in tackling many of the technical hurdles of software production. In recent years, the management of software development has gained recognition as being at the cores of both the problem and the solution. This recognition has been accompanied by some serious concerns. Chief among them is the belief that we still lack the fundamental understanding of the software development process and that without such an understanding the likelihood of any significant gains in the management of software development is questionable.

Objective of Book

The objective of this book is to enhance systematically our understanding of and gain insight into the general process by which software development is managed. Through this improved understanding and insight, real progress towards overcoming the current ''software crisis'' will be possible.

Approach of Book

To achieve the above objective, we performed the following three tasks.

First, we developed an integrative model of software development project management. The model was developed on the basis of an extensive review of the literature supplemented by 27 focused field interviews of software project managers in five organizations. The model complements and builds upon current research efforts, which tend to focus on the micro components (e.g., scheduling, programming and productivity) by integrating the components of the software development process. This model divides the software development and management activities into four areas: (1) human resource management, (2) software production, (3) controlling, and (4) planning. Over 100 individual but interdependent phenomena were identified and represented using the systems dynamics modeling notation.

Second, a case-study in a sixth organization was conducted to test the model. The model was found to be highly accurate in replicating the actual development history of the software project selected (by the organization) for the case-study. Project variables tracked included: workforce level, schedule, cost, error generation and detection, and productivity.

Third, the model was used as an experimentation vehicle to study or predict the dynamic implications of an array of managerial policies and procedures. Four areas were studied: (1) scheduling, (2) control, (3) quality assurance, and (4) staffing. The exercise uncovered dysfunctional consequences of some currently adopted policies (e.g., the use of ''safety factors'' in the scheduling area), provided guidelines for managerial policy (e.g., on the allocation of quality assurance effort), and revealed new insights into software project phenomena (e.g., the applicability of Brooks' Law).

Organization of Book

This book is divided into four major parts. Part I serves as an introduction to the subject of software development management, its importance, and its complexity. Part II provides background material drawing upon the relevant literature and special interviews conducted for this book. Part III focuses on the software development process and the creation of a comprehensive model of the process. Finally, part IV presents a series of case studies and experiments conducted to provide a powerful basis for understanding important phenomena of software development and, thereby, help to derive critical lessons to be learned.

Uses and Users of Book

This book provides the reader with both a comprehensive understanding of the phenomena encountered in the software development process and a unique way of studying the dynamic interdependencies of these phenomena. This book is intended to be of use to managers, practitioners, researchers, and students of software development.

For managers and practitioners, this book provides insight into the complex problems that they often encounter. For these readers, Part II, which provides background material on previous research, may be skipped initially so that they can get directly to the discussion of software development issues (Part III) and the important lessons learned (Part IV).

For researchers and students, this book provides probably the most comprehensive study of the *dynamic* interactions in software development assembled to date. The background material of Part II provides a solid base to understand and organize the existing research literature and approaches. The model developed in Part III enables, for the first time, a systematic study of this complex field, the importance of which is demonstrated by the studies conducted in Part IV.

Tarek K. Abdel-Hamid
Stuart E. Madnick

SOFTWARE PROJECT DYNAMICS

PART ONE

INTRODUCTION TO
SOFTWARE DEVELOPMENT
MANAGEMENT

1

INTRODUCTION

1.1 The Symptoms of the "Software Crisis"

One measure of the impact of software is on the pocketbook. It has been estimated that U.S. expenditures for software development and maintenance were $70 billion in 1985 [51]. Even more impressive, Boehm projects that computer software costs are expected to grow to more than $225 billion by 1995 in the U.S. and more than $450 billion worldwide [50].

This growth in demand for software has not, however, been painless. Indeed, as the industry was making the transition in the 1970s, Pressman noted that " ...   we (grew) to recognize circumstances that are collectively called the 'software crisis,' ...   (a term that) alludes to a set of problems that are encountered in the development of software" [210].

The record shows that the software industry has been marked by cost overruns, late deliveries, poor reliability, and users' dissatisfaction. (For example, see [103, 182, 228, 249]).

As early as November 9, 1979, a report to Congress by the Comptroller General cited the dimensions of the "software crisis" within the federal government. The report's title summarizes the issue: "Contracting for Computer Software Development --- Serious Problems Require Management Attention to Avoid Wasting Additional Millions." The report concludes, "The government got for its money less than 2 percent of the total value of the contracts."

More than a decade later, the problems persisted. An article in the December 18, 1989 issue of *Defense News* described the software problems with the Peace Shield project which was then four years behind schedule and estimated to be up to $300 million over budget [29].

Big as the direct costs of the "software crisis" are, the indirect costs can be even bigger, because software is often on the critical path in overall system development (e.g., weapon systems, such as the B-1 bomber). That is, any slippages in the software schedule translate directly into slippages in the overall delivery schedule of the system.

Although many of the largest and most completely documented examples are found in military projects, the "software crisis" is by no means confined to software projects developed by or for the federal government. It is similarly prevalent within private sector organizations [275]. For example, DeMarco writes about such systems:

- Fifteen percent of all software projects never deliver anything; that is, they fail utterly to achieve their established goals.

- Overruns of one hundred to two hundred percent are common.

So many software projects fail in some major way that we have had to redefine ''Success'' to keep everyone from becoming despondent. Software projects are sometimes considered successful when the overruns are held to thirty percent or when the user only junks a quarter of the result. Software people are often willing to call such efforts successes, but members of our user community are less forgiving. They know failure when they see it [81].

Personal computer software development is not immune to these problems either. The headline in the May 11, 1990 issue of *The Wall Street Journal* says it explicitly: ''Creating New Software was Agonizing Task for Mitch Kapor Firm'' [63]. The article was sub-titled: ''Despite Expert's Experience Job Repeatedly Overran Time and Cost Forecasts.'' The issues cited in that article (e.g., ''... programmers spend 90% of their time on the first 80% of a project and 90% of their time on the final 20%'') have been repeated for decades in both public and private organizations, large and small companies (Kapor's company had less than 30 people), and computers from mainframes to PC's.

Due to the embarrassment and bad publicity associated with such problems, it is likely that only a small portion are ever publicly reported. Mitch Kapor, the founder of Lotus Development Corporation, agreed to describe the experiences in his new company ON Technology Inc. ''because he believes that software design must be improved and the development process better understood.''[63]   That nicely sums up the goal of this book.

1.2 The Challenge of Software Project Management

In an effort to bring discipline to the development of software systems, attempts have been made since the early 1970s to apply the more rigorous discipline of engineering to software production. This new discipline is called ''software engineering.'' It encompasses both the technical aspects of software development (e.g., design, testing, validation) as well as the managerial ones [33, 47, 246].

However, even though both technology and management were recognized early on as parts of both the problem and the solution, there was a huge disparity in the attention they received from the research community [149, 205].

On the technology side, many methodologies have evolved, over the last decade, that address technical problems experienced in software development. Articles addressing topics such as better coding style through ''structured programming,'' structured design, testing, formal verification, language design for more reliable coding, diagnostic compilers, and so forth have appeared in the literature.

... software engineers have progressed to the point where many major issues relevant to the *technology* of software production have been identified and considerable progress in addressing these issues has been made. Practical working tools to support improved software production are commonly available, and their design and generation have become a recognized topic for university instruction [249].

A comparable evolution in *management* methodologies, however, has not occurred [41, 127, 172, 208, 275].

In a special issue of the *IEEE Transactions on Software Engineering* devoted to project management, Dr. Richard E. Merwin, the guest editor, pointed out that an overall software engineering management discipline is missing. He stated:

> Programming discipline such as top-down design, use of standardized high level programming languages, and program library support systems all contribute to production of reliable software on time, within budget. ....   What is still missing is the overall management fabric which allows the senior project manager to understand and lead major data processing development efforts [176].

But what have been the consequences of this deficiency in our research repertoire?

First, our difficulties in producing software that is both on time and within budget and that meets user requirements are obviously still alive.

Second, because the problem persists in spite of substantial progress in the technological (vis-a-vis the managerial) aspects of software production, there is a decided shift in concern [59]. Consider the following quotes:

> There are more opportunities for improving software productivity and quality in the area of management than anywhere else. [46]
>
> Many of our technical and managerial leaders believe that the more effective management of a software development project (i.e., project management) would eliminate or reduce the severity of these software failures [246].
>
> The basic problem is management itself [112].
>
> A major barrier to the successful design and implementation of information systems has been the management of the software development activity itself [185].
>
> Poor management can increase software costs more rapidly than any other factor [261].
>
> A comprehensive study for the U.S. Air Force found that the problems of software productivity on medium- to large-scale projects are mostly problems of management: thorough organization, good contingency planning, thoughtful establishment of measurable project milestones, continuous monitoring whether the milestones are properly passed, and prompt investigation and corrective action if the milestones are not met. However, beyond these familiar concessions to classic management theory, the study group offered no novel approaches to finding out why they do not work for software development [208].
>
> We ran into problems because we didn't know how to manage what we had, not because we lacked the techniques themselves [253].

Along with the growing concern for software engineering project management, there are serious obstacles. Chief among them is that we still lack the fundamental understanding of the software development process [87, 96, 173] and that without such an understanding the likelihood of any significant gains in the management of software development front is questionable [36, 130, 161].

This is no trivial impediment. But it is not one unique to our young field:

Any worthwhile human endeavor emerges first as an art. . . .

Over the centuries, management as an art has progressed by the acquisition and recording of human experience. But as long as there is no orderly underlying scientific base, the experiences remain as special cases. The lessons are poorly transferable either in time or in space. . . . (And) in time (the art) ceases to grow because of the disorganized state of its knowledge. . . . .

The development of the underlying science (is then) motivated by the need to understand better the foundation on which the art rested. . . .

When the need and necessary foundation coincide, a science develops to explain, organize, and distill experience into a more compact and usable form. . . . Such a base of applied science would permit experience to be translated into a common frame of reference from which they could be transferred from the past to the present or from one location to another, (and) to be effectively applied in new situations. . . . [99].

To summarize:

- The record shows that the software industry continues to be plagued by cost overruns, late deliveries, poor reliability, and users' dissatisfaction — a set of difficulties that some refer to as the "software crisis."

- In an effort to bring discipline to the development of software, attempts have been made since the early 1970's to apply the more rigorous discipline of engineering to software production and management. The new discipline is called "software engineering."

- While significant inroads have been made in tackling the technical hurdles of software development, the management of software production has attracted much less attention.

- There is a growing concern that the next significant battle will be fought over management issues.

- The necessary first step is gaining a fundamental understanding of the general nature of the software project management process.

1.3 Unique Approach of this Book

The objective of this book is to develop and test an integrative view of software development project management in order to enhance our understanding of, provide insight into, and make predictions about the general process by which software development is managed.

Rather than present the various complex aspects of software project management as separate isolated issues, an integrated system dynamics model is developed in this book. This provides a consistent notation for discussing and formalizing the issues covered as well as enabling the development of a comprehensive model that spans the full range of interdependent management issues and serves several important purposes.

The first and primary purpose of the model is to enhance our understanding of the software development process. In general:

What is gained in understanding through the use of a scientific model to portray a portion of the real world is achieved by comprehending the law or laws built into the model. The locus of understanding in a scientific model is to be found in its laws of interaction (i.e., the modes of interaction among the variables of a model) [90].

There are hundreds of variables that affect software development. Furthermore, these variables are not independent; many of them are related to one another [119, 189]. So far:

The many studies on the subject emphasize the difficulty and complexity of the process, but have done little to reveal a well-defined methodology or to delineate precise relationships among project variables [200].

The second purpose of our model is to make predictions about the general process by which software systems are developed. As such, the model would serve as a framework for experimentation to test the implications of new managerial policies and procedures, especially where controlled manipulation of the system itself is impossible, or at least impractical or undesirable due to time, cost, inaccessibility, political or moral considerations, etc.

The two key features of this model that distinguish it from most others in the software engineering area are that: (1) it is integrative, and (2) it is a system dynamics model.

1.3.1 Why An Integrative Model The model is integrative in the sense that it integrates the multiple functions of the software development process, including the management-type functions (e.g., planning, controlling, and staffing) as well as the production-type functions that constitute the software development life cycle (e.g., designing, coding, reviewing, and testing).

A major defect in much of the research to date has been its inability to integrate our knowledge of the micro components such as project management, programming, and testing for deriving implications about the behavior of the organization in which the micro components are embedded [46, 77, 246]. As noted by Jensen and Tonies:

There is much attention on individual phases and functions of the software development sequence, but little on the whole life cycle as an integral, continuous process — a process that can and should be optimized [135].

Clearly, this ''micro-oriented'' work is a useful beginning in helping us obtain a better understanding of software development. However, before we can say that we have a *complete* understanding, it is necessary to show that our knowledge of the individual components can be put together in a total system.

Interactions and interdependencies are common in management systems [115, 152, 227, 259]:

The management system is a conglomerate of interrelated and interdependent functions. No one management subsystem can perform effectively without the others. Action taken by one subsystem can be traced throughout the entire management system and throughout the complex environment in which the management system exists. [66]

As a result:

The behavior of an individual subsystem in isolation may be different from its behavior when it interacts with other subsystems [68].

It is no wonder, then, that integrative-type models are viewed as useful and powerful aids in understanding management-type social systems and in trying to improve their functioning. The management of software development is certainly no exception:

... the solution to the (software management) problem involves more than just finding better tools and local optimization methods; it calls for an integrated approach. ... [135]

In addition to the benefit of helping us achieve overall understanding, an integrative perspective can be useful in two more "tactical" ways: problem diagnosis and solution evaluation [115].

A corollary of the above assertion is that the interactions and interdependencies that tend to characterize our management systems will similarly characterize the problems that beset such systems. This does indeed seem to be the case in software development, where " ... no one thing seems to cause the difficulty ... but the accumulation of simultaneous and interacting factors. ... "[57] An integrative perspective is useful since it would facilitate the search for the multiple and potentially "diffused" set of factors that are interacting to cause our software problems.

The second benefit of our integrative perspective derives from its ability to trace the chain of effects in going from a particular managerial intervention (e.g., to solve a perceived problem) to immediate consequences *and then* to second- and third-order consequences and newly created problems [67, 259].

Such a comprehensive world view helps to assess more fully such second- and third-order consequences of management policies and procedures.

... consequences are not given much attention, and apparently logical solutions may prove faulty as their consequences ramify. Furthermore, since the consequences of a decision often occur much later than the decision itself, it is difficult for the members to trace backward from the disruptive consequences to determine precisely what caused them. The members cannot make such an analysis, simply because there are too many competing explanations. Thus, the only thing members can do when a new problem arises is to engage in more localized problem-solving [259].

Notice that this statement highlights two "new" complicating factors, namely, that the consequences are *dynamic* and that they are *complex*. The system dynamics modeling approach addresses both of these issues.

1.3.2 Why A System Dynamics Model "System Dynamics is the application of feedback control systems principles and techniques to managerial, organizational, and socioeconomic problems." [224]

The system dynamics philosophy is based on several premises:

1. The behavior (or time history) of an organizational entity is principally caused by its structure. The structure includes not only the physical aspects, but more importantly the policies and procedures, both tangible and intangible, that dominate decision-making in the organizational entity.

2. Managerial decision-making takes place in a framework that belongs to the general class known as information-feedback systems.

3. Our intuitive judgment is unreliable about how these systems will change with time, even when we have good knowledge of the individual parts of the system.

4. Thorough model experimentation is possible to fill the gap where our judgment and knowledge are weakest — by showing the way in which the known separate system parts can interact to produce unexpected and troublesome over-all system results.

Based on these philosophical beliefs, two principal foundations for operationalizing the system dynamics technique were established. These are:

1. The use of information-feedback systems to model and understand system structure (Premises 1 and 2).

2. The use of computer simulation to understand system behavior (Premises 3 and 4).

In the remaining part of this section we would like to discuss these two important concepts in more detail to find out what they mean and why they are useful.

The use of information feedback systems

Feedback is the process in which an action taken by a person or thing will eventually affect that person or thing. A feedback *loop* is a closed sequence of causes and effects, a closed path of action and information. Feedback loops divide naturally into two categories, which are labeled deviation-amplifying feedback (DAF) or positive loops and deviation-counteracting feedback (DCF) or negative loops. An interconnected set of feedback loops is a feedback *system* [221].

The significance and applicability of the feedback systems concept to managerial systems has been substantiated by many studies in the system dynamics field (e.g., [225]).

Recognition of the feedback concept can seen in the software engineering literature [159, 214, 258, 274]. For example:

Discussion and research into the framework of software development and support, by dividing such efforts into phases of work, has overemphasized the discrete nature of that work. ... The ever-present and controlling feedback among action, results, information, and new action is overlooked by such an approach [175].

A point that is particularly important to the application of deviation-amplifying feedback (DAF) to management concerns the distinction between (1) the initial event (from outside a loop), which starts the deviation amplifying process in motion, and (2) the dynamics of the feedback process, which perpetuates it. While the initial event is important in determining the direction of the subsequent deviation amplification, the feedback process is *more important to an understanding of the system.* The initial event sets in motion a cumulative process, which can have final effects out of proportion to the magnitude of the original push. The push might even be withdrawn after a time, and still a permanent change will remain or even the process of change will continue without a new balance in sight. A further problem is that after some period of time has elapsed, it may be difficult, if not impossible, to discover the initial event. An interesting example of this has been provided by Wender:

> a fat and pimply adolescent may withdraw in embarrassment and fail to acquire social skills; in adulthood, acne and obesity may have disappeared but low self-esteem, withdrawal, and social ineptitude may remain. Social withdrawal and low self esteem are apt to stay fixed because the DAF chain *now* operates: social ineptitude leads to rejection, which leads to lowered self-esteem, greater withdrawal, less social experience, and greater ineptitude. *What has initiated the problem is no longer sustaining it. ...* Furthermore, in some instances the initial event may have left no traces of its existence and may be undiscovered [267].

Weick has noted that ''most managers get into trouble because they forget to think in circles. I mean this literally. Managerial problems persist because managers continue to believe that there are such things as unilateral causation, independent and dependent variables, origins, and terminations'' [259].

The use of computer simulation

So far we have argued for an *integrative* model of software development, which in addition captures its information feedback systems. To stop here is not enough. We need a tool for handling the high *complexity* of such a model. There are two sources of high complexity; and computer simulation can be an effective tool to handle both.

First,

> Managerial systems contain as many as 100 or more variables that are known to be relevant and believed to be related to one another in various nonlinear fashions. The behavior of such a system is complex far beyond the capacity of intuition. Computer simulation is one of the most effective means available for supplementing and correcting human intuition [225].

And second,

> The behavior of systems of interconnected feedback loops often confounds common intuition and analysis, even though the dynamic implications of isolated loops may be reasonably obvious. The feedback structures of real problems are often so complex that the behavior they generate over time can usually be traced only by simulation [221].

Simulation's particular advantage is its greater fidelity in modeling processes, making possible both more complex models and models of more complex systems. It also allows for vicarious experimentation.

Using the simulation model as an experimentation vehicle is important to the software engineering community. Several authors have "complained" about the lack of tested "ideas" in the software engineering field [246, 264]. For example, Weiss commented:

> ... in software engineering it is remarkably easy to propose hypotheses and remarkably difficult to test them. Accordingly, it is useful to seek methods for testing software engineering hypotheses [265].

Unfortunately, controlled experiments in the area of software development tend to be costly and time-consuming [190]. Furthermore, those who try it often find that " ... the isolation of the effect and the evaluation of impact of any given practice within a large, complex and dynamic project environment can be exceedingly difficult" [117].

In addition to permitting less costly and less time-consuming experimentation, simulation models make possible "perfectly" controlled experiments that address the desire expressed by Forrester:

> The effects of different assumptions and environmental factors can be tested. In the model system, unlike real systems, the effect of changing one factor can be observed while all other factors are held unchanged. Such experimentation will yield new insights into the characteristics of the system that the model represents. By using a model of a complex system, more can be learned about internal interactions than would ever be possible through manipulation of the real system. Internally, the model provides complete control of the system organizational structure, its policies, and its sensitivities to various events. Externally, a wider range of circumstances can be generated than are apt to be observable in real life [99].

Finally, the process of constructing the simulation can be useful in several ways [229]:

1. Confrontation — vague generalizations crumble when put to the test of modeling.

2. Explication — assumptions must be made explicit, logical, and precise in order to build a simulation model.

3. Expansion — the tendency to a holistic approach in simulation forces a broadening of one's horizon, a looking into other relevant fields for ideas.

4. Communication — problem-oriented simulation leads to crossing disciplinary boundaries and to less parochialism.

5. Involvement — it can be fun: the construction process motivates the modeler to attempt to fill in the knowledge gaps.

1.4 Key Contributions

The unique approach of this book is made possible through three key activities performed in the preparation of this book:

1. Development of an integrative model of software development project management.

2. Performance and analysis of a detailed case study to apply and test the model.

3. Use of the model as an experimental vehicle to study or predict the dynamic implications of an array of managerial policies and procedures.

In the remaining part of this section, these three accomplishments are elaborated.

Model Development

The development of the integrative system dynamics model accomplishes the following:

1. The mathematical formulation of a system dynamics model forces explication, i.e., structural relationships between variables must be explicitly and precisely defined. As such, the model sets the foundation for the development of a theory of software project management.

2. The model complements and builds upon current research efforts, which tend to focus on the micro components (e.g., project management, programming, testing and productivity), by *integrating* our knowledge of these micro components into an integrated, continuous view of the software development process, which in turn allows us to identify and capture a richer set of interactions and interdependencies between the variables of software project management.

3. The model identifies feedback mechanisms and uses them to structure and clarify relationships in software project management. While the significance and applicability of the feedback systems concept to the study of managerial systems has been substantiated in many studies outside software engineering, the concept remains largely foreign to the software engineering project management community.

4. The high degree of explication required in the model helped us ferret out "knowledge gaps" in the literature. Our 27 interviews with software development managers in 5 organizations helped us fill these knowledge gaps. The model, therefore, incorporates new findings about the management of software project management (e.g., on manpower acquisition policies under different scheduling considerations).

Case Study

A case study was conducted to test the model. The model was found to be highly accurate in replicating the actual development history of the software project selected (by the organization) for the case study. Project variables tested included the work force level, the schedule, and the cost.

Experimentation

If "understanding" is the intellectual outcome of a theoretical model, then "prediction" is its practical outcome [90]. The model was used as an experimental vehicle to study or predict the dynamic implications of an array of managerial policies and procedures. Four areas were studied: scheduling; quality assurance, control, and staffing. The exercise uncovered dysfunctional consequences of some currently adopted policies (e.g., in the scheduling area), provided guidelines for managerial policy (e.g., on the allocation of quality assurance effort), and provided new insights into software project phenomena (e.g., "90 % syndrome").

1.5 Book Outline

This book is divided into four parts. Part I (chapters 1 and 2) serves as an introduction to the subject of software development management. Chapter 2 provides an overview of our modeling approach and a summary of the system dynamics concepts and notations used.

Part II (chapters 3 and 4) provide background material. Chapter 3 contains a survey of the relevant literature, broken into two sections. First the system dynamics literature is surveyed. Then the software engineering literature is surveyed to see what has been proposed to understand and solve the problems of software project management. Chapter 4 summarizes the 27 interviews held in 5 software development organizations that reinforce or supplement the literature.

Part III (chapters 5-11) focuses on the development of the comprehensive integrative model of software development management. This part is divided into the four major areas of software project management: human resource management (chapter 5), software production (chapters 6-9), project control (chapter 10), and project planning (chapter 11).

Part IV (chapters 12-20) presents a series of case studies and experiments used to study the implications of various management actions. In chapter 12 a detailed case study is conducted to test the model's ability to replicate the development history of a completed software development project. Chapter 13 presents an example project environment that can be used as a vehicle to study and predict the dynamic implications of an array of managerial policies and procedures. Four areas are studied: scheduling (chapters 14-16), control (chapter 17), quality assurance (chapter 18), and staffing (chapter 19). Finally, chapter 20 concludes the book with a summary of findings and suggestions for further investigation.

2

KEY COMPONENTS OF

SOFTWARE DEVELOPMENT

2.1 Management Aspects of Software Development

The impressive improvements that are continually being made in the cost-effectiveness of computer hardware are causing an enormous expansion in the number of applications for which computing is becoming a feasible and economical solution. This, in turn, is placing greater and greater demands for the development and operation of computer software systems. In an effort to bring discipline to the development of software systems, developers have attempted since the early 1970s to apply the rigors of science and engineering to the software production process. This led to significant advances in the *technology* of software production (e.g., structured programming, structured design, formal verification, language design for more reliable coding, and diagnostic compilers).

The *managerial* aspects of software development, on the other hand, have attracted much less attention from the research community [41, 249, 275]. Cooper provides an insightful explanation:

> Perhaps this is so because computer scientists believe that management per se is not their business, and the management professionals assume that it is the computer scientists' responsibility [71].

This "deficiency" in the field's research repertoire is being blamed by a growing number of researchers and practitioners for the persistence of the difficulties in producing software systems [208, 253, 262]. A chief concern expressed is that we lack a fundamental understanding of the software development process. Without such an understanding the likelihood of any significant gains in the management of software development is questionable [36, 173].

This chapter introduces a system dynamics model of the software development process that enhances our understanding of, provides insight into, and makes predictions about the process by which software development is managed. The following examples illustrate some of the critical management decisions that have been addressed:

1. A project is behind schedule. Possible management actions include revising the completion date, holding to the planned completion date but hiring more staff, and holding to the planned completion date but working current staff overtime. What are the implications of the alternatives?

2. How much of the development effort should be expended on quality assurance and how does that affect completion time and total cost?

3. What is the impact of different distributions of effort among project phases (e.g., should the division of effort between development and testing be 80:20 or 60:40 percent)?

4. What are the reasons for and implications of the differences among *potential* productivity, *actual* productivity, and *perceived* productivity?

5. Why does the "90% completion syndrome," whereby a project appears to get stuck when it reaches the 90% completion point, chronically occur?

In the remaining parts of this chapter we present our approach to modeling the software development process. We start by presenting a simple model to illustrate the process.

2.2 A Simple Model of the Software Development Process

Software development and its related project management activities are often based on the simple "mental picture" captured by the single-loop model shown in Figure 2.1 [225].

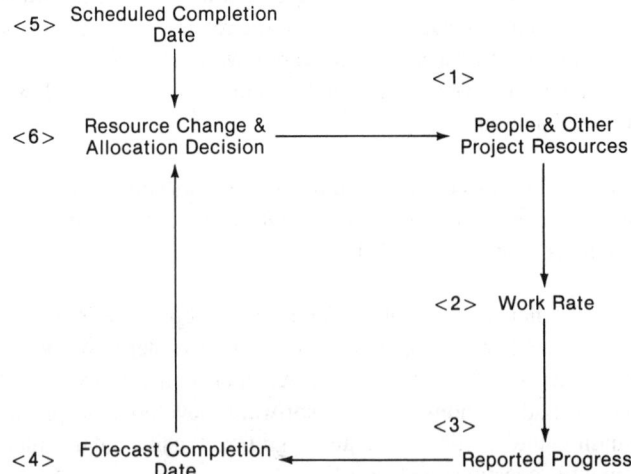

Figure 2.1 A simple model of software development

The model portrays how project work is accomplished through the use of project resources <1> (e.g., manpower, facilities, equipment). As work <2> is accomplished on the project, it is reported <3> through some project control system. Such reports accumulate and are processed to create the project's forecast completion time <4> by adding to the current date the indicated time remaining on the job. Assessing the job's remaining time involves figuring out the magnitude of the effort (e.g., in man-days) that management believes remains to complete the project, the level of manpower working on the project, and the perceived productivity of the project team. The feedback loop is closed as the difference, if any, between the scheduled completion date <5> and the forecast completion date <4> causes adjustments <6> in the magnitude or allocation of the project's resources.

This model is attractive because it is reasonable, simple, and manageable. But is it an adequate model of the dynamics of software project management?

The software project management system is a far more complex conglomerate of interdependent variables that are interrelated in various nonlinear ways. By excluding vital aspects of the real environment, the above model could seriously misguide the unsuspecting software manager. To see how, let us consider just a few of the many typical decisions that arise in a software project environment.

2.2.1 Adding More People to a Late Project Figure 2.1 suggests a direct relationship between adding people resources and increasing the rate of work on the project, i.e., the higher the level of project resources the higher the work rate. This ignores one vital aspect of software project dynamics, namely that adding more people often leads to higher communication and training overheads on the project, which can in turn dilute the project team's productivity. Lower productivity translates into lower progress rates, which can, therefore, delay the late project even more. Delays in turn can trigger an additional round of workforce additions and another pass around this vicious cycle. These dynamic forces create the phenomenon often referred to as "Brooks' Law," i.e., that adding more people to a late software project makes it later [57].

In Figure 2.2(a) we amend Figure 2.1 by incorporating the linnk between the workforce level and productivity.

2.2.2 Adjusting the Schedule of a Late Project Another part of the real system that is ignored by Figure 2.1 concerns the impact of intangible project pressures (e.g., schedule pressures) on the software developers' actions and decisions. For example, when faced with schedule pressures as a project falls behind schedule, software developers typically respond by putting in longer hours and by concentrating more on the essential tasks of the job [131]. In one experiment, Boehm [49] found that the number of man-hours devoted to project work increased by as much as 100%. This additional link between schedule pressure and productivity is captured in Figure 2.2(b).

The impact of schedule pressures on software development is not limited to the direct role referred to above. Schedule pressures can also play less visible roles. For example, as Figure 2.2(c) suggests, schedule pressures can increase the error rate of the project team and thus the amount of rework on the project [215, 181]. For example, DeMarco noted that

> People under time pressure don't work better, they just work faster. ... In the struggle to deliver any software at all, the first casualty has been consideration of the quality of the software delivered [81].

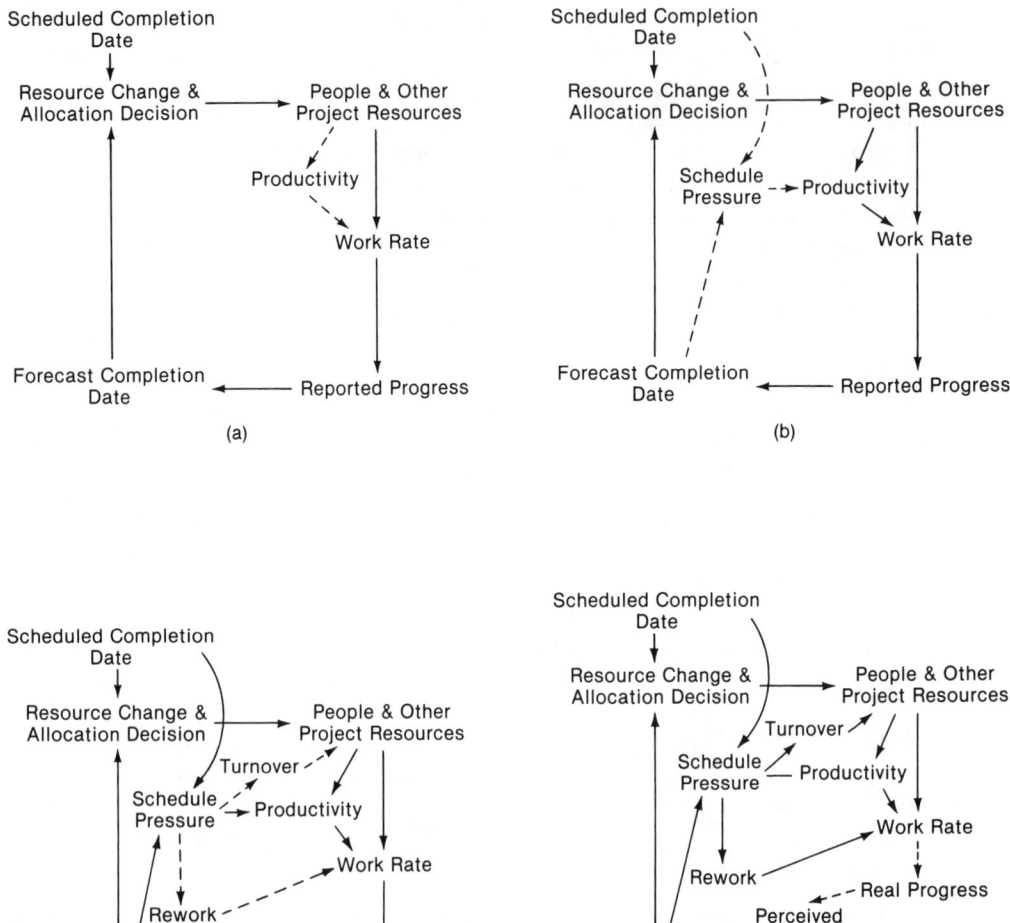

Figure 2.2 Amendments to the project management model

The rework necessary to correct such software errors obviously diverts the project team's effort from making progress on new project tasks and thus can have a significant negative impact on the project's progress rate.

Also, consider the impact of schedule pressure on the workforce turnover rate shown in Figure 2.2(c). There is evidence to suggest that workforce turnover increases when scheduling pressures persist in an organization [104]. This can be costly, since a higher turnover rate translates into lower productivity on the project.

2.2.3 How Late is a Late Software Project?   Because software remains largely intangible during most of the development process [28], it is often difficult for project managers to assess real progress on the project. To the extent that the perceived progress rate differs from the real progress rate, an error in perceived cumulative progress will gradually compound as shown in Figure 2.2(d). Furthermore, bias, often in the form of overoptimism, and delay in gathering and processing control information additionally distort the reported progress. This undoubtedly poses yet another complication that is too real for the software project manager to exclude from a model of the process.

2.2.4 Need for a Comprehensive Model   Although the above discussion has introduced many important aspects of the software development process, it is clear that an effective investigation needs two elements: (1) significantly more depth and detail and (2) a systematic way to organize the information. Both of these points are addressed in the rest of this chapter.

2.3 An Integrative System Dynamics Perspective

The above discussion illustrates that there are many variables, both tangible and intangible, that affect the software development process. Furthermore, these variables are not independent but are related to one another in complex ways. Understanding the behavior of such systems is complex far beyond the capacity of human intuition [225].

As was mentioned in chapter 1, a major deficiency in much of the research on software project management has been the inability to draw inferences about the behavior of the total socio-technical system from our knowledge of the micro components such as scheduling, productivity, and staffing [246]. In this book we build upon and extend what has been learned about the micro components in order to construct a holistic model of the software development process. It integrates the multiple functions of software development, including both managerial functions (e.g., planning, controlling, and staffing) as well as software production activities (e.g., designing, coding, reviewing, and testing).

A unique feature of our model is its use of the feedback principles of system dynamics to structure and clarify the complex web of dynamically interacting variables. Examples of such feedback systems in the software project environment have already been demonstrated in the above discussion and are evident in Figures 2.1 and 2.2.

The significance and applicability of the feedback systems concept to managerial systems has been substantiated by a many studies [225]. For example, Weick observed that

> The cause-effect relationships that exist in organizations are dense and often circular. Sometimes these causal circuits cancel the influences of one variable on another, and sometimes they amplify the effects of one variable on another. It is the network of causal relationships that impose many of the controls in organizations and that stabilize or disrupt the organization. It is the patterns of these causal links that account for much of what happens in organizations. Though not directly visible, these causal patterns account for more of what happens in organizations than do some of the more visible elements such as machinery, time clocks ... [259].

2.4 Model Boundary

As stated in chapter 1, the primary purpose of our model is to help us understand the
process by which software systems are developed and managed.

Notice that the focus is confined to the *development* phases of software production,
extending only until the last phase of software development, namely, the testing phase.
Not included in our model are the subsequent maintenance activities.

It was also indicated that the model would integrate the managerial functions of
planning, controlling, and human-resource management as well as the software
production activities of design, coding, and testing. Notice that the model's boundary
extends from the beginning of the design phase of the software life cycle, excluding the
requirements definition phase. There were two reasons for this. First,

> Analysis to determine requirements is ... distinguished as an activity apart from
> software development. Technically, the product of analysis is non-procedural (i.e.,
> the focus is functional) while the prime development is the basis for mutual
> agreement between the customer and the developer as to what the system must
> accomplish [170].

Second, our focus in this study is on the software development organization, i.e.,
project managers and software development professionals, and how *their* policies,
decisions and actions affect the success or failure of software development. The
definition of user requirements is therefore excluded from the model's boundary for the
additional reason that it lies beyond the control of the software development group. Such
arguments have also been the basis for excluding the software requirements phase from
the "boundaries" of quantitative software cost-estimation models such as COCOMO
[49].

In addition to excluding the requirements definition phase, we will assume that
once requirements are fully specified and the architectural design phase is initiated, there
will be no significant subsequent changes in the users' requirements. We realize that
changes in users' requirements are frequently blamed for cost and budget overruns in
software projects [23, 47, 276] and for which users are often found "guilty" [86, 246,
254]. However, the focus in this book is on the software development group members
and *their* policies, decisions and actions. Investigating the policies, decisions, and actions
that can cause cost and budget overruns *in spite of* stable user requirements is a more
interesting and challenging endeavor than answering the question "do changes in users'
requirements negatively affect the development process?"

Looking within the model's boundary (e.g., at the actions of the software
development team) for the causes and cures of problematic behavior rather than outside it
(e.g., the actions of the users) is a characteristic of the system dynamics approach.
Richardson and Pugh called it the "Endogenous Point of View."

> ... the system dynamics approach tends to look *within* a system for the sources of
> its problem behavior. Problems are not seen as being caused by external agents
> outside the system ... The internal view creates a dramatically different problem
> focus. The external view places an individual, a firm, a city, or whatever, at the
> mercy of exogenous events ... . The external view is frequently predisposed to

search for blame: "instabilities in our work force and inventory are caused by erratic and seasonal customer orders" (or software projects overrun schedules merely because of changes in user requirements). ... The internal view searches (instead) for structures within (the system), which can create or exacerbate the system's problem behavior [221].

Our focus is on the decisions and actions of the software development group including both project management as well as software development professionals (e.g., designers and programmers). In addition to excluding users, it also excludes computer center operators, personnel department personnel, secretaries, higher management, janitors, and so on.

Furthermore, our focus is not small one-programmer projects, nor super-large projects involving hundreds of software professionals over a period of several years. Instead, our primary focus is that of medium-sized projects. Jones defined medium-sized software projects as follows:

> ... (they) range between 16K and 64K lines in size, (and in which) development teams or departments are the norm. ... Below the "medium" size range, programming as a business endeavor is often successful: at least the programs tend to work fairly well and insurmountable problems are not often encountered. At the "medium" size and above, cost and schedule overruns pop up more frequently, and are more serious when they do occur [137].

2.5 Model Structure

The model consists of four major subsystems: human resource management, planning, controlling, and software production, together with the various flows that connect them. The various assumptions and propositions behind the model are supported by references to the literature described in chapter 3 and to the interviews of chapter 4.

A documented listing of each subsystem's DYNAMO equations is included in Appendix A. DYNAMO is a computer simulation language specifically designed to handle non-linear feedback models of the sort associated with the system dynamics method. (For an introduction to DYNAMO see Pugh [211].)

2.6 Model Subsystems

Figure 2.3 is an overview of the model's four subsystems: The Human Resource Management Subsystem; The Software Production Subsystem; The Controlling Subsystem; and The Planning Subsystem. The figure also illustrates the interrelatedness of the four subsystems.

The Human Resource Management Subsystem comprises the hiring, training, assimilation, and transfer of the project's human resources. Such actions are not carried out in a vacuum; as Figure 2.3 suggests, they both affect and are affected by the other subsystems. For example, the project's "hiring rate" is a function of the "work force needed" to complete the project on a *planned* completion date.

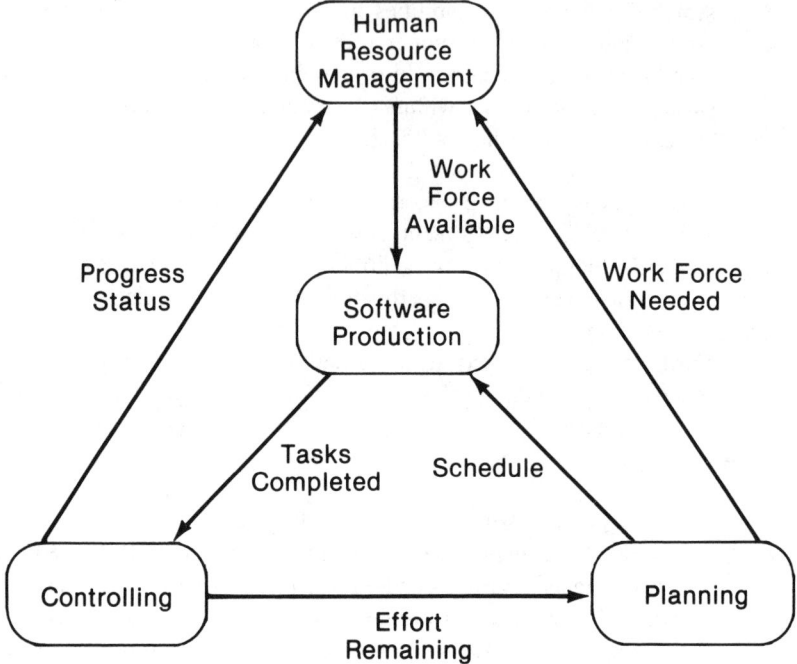

Figure 2.3 Software development subsystems

Similarly, the "work force available" has a direct bearing on the allocation of manpower among the different software production activities in the Software Production Subsystem. The four primary software production activities are development, quality assurance, rework, and testing. The development activity comprises both the design and coding of the software. As the software is developed, it is also reviewed to detect any design or coding errors. Errors detected through quality assurance are then reworked. Not all errors will be detected and reworked; some will "escape" detection until after development, i.e., until the testing phase.

As progress is made, it is reported. A comparison of where the project is versus where it should be (according to plan) is a control activity captured within the Controlling Subsystem. Determining where a software project *really* is, such as in terms of the percentage of tasks completed, is not always possible. Software is basically an intangible product during most of the development process; there are no visible milestones to measure progress and quality like a physical product would. Once an assessment of the project's status is made, it becomes an important input to the planning function.

In the Planning Subsystem, initial project estimates are made to start the project, and then those estimates are revised, when necessary, throughout the project's life. For example, to handle a project that is perceived to be behind schedule, a manager can hire more people, extend the schedule, or do a little of both.

Since all the subsystem diagrams used in the detailed descriptions will be in terms of the schematic conventions used in system dynamics, it is useful to introduce these conventions. As an illustration of the usage of these conventions, the model for the Human Resources Management Subsystem is shown in Figure 2.4; a detailed explanation of this subsystem is provided in chapter 5.

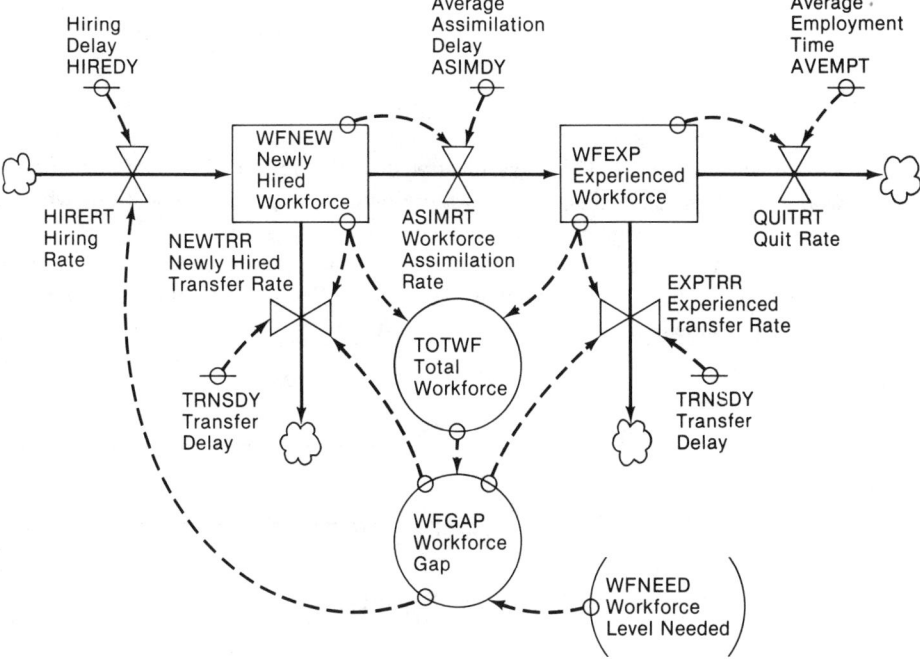

Figure 2.4   Human resources management subsystem

2.7 System Dynamics Schematic Conventions

From a system dynamics perspective all systems can be represented in terms of "level" and "rate" variables, with "auxiliary" variables used for added clarity and simplicity.

A *level* is an accumulation, or an integration, over time of flows or changes that come into and go out of the level. The term "level" is intended to invoke the image of the level of a liquid accumulating in a container. The system dynamicist takes the simplifying view that feedback systems involve continuous, fluid-like processes, and the terminology reinforces that interpretation.

The flows increasing and decreasing a level are called *rates*. Thus, a manpower pool would be a level of people that is increased by the rate of hiring and decreased by the rate of firing and quitting.

Rates and levels are represented as stylized valves and tubs, as shown in Figure 2.5, further emphasizing the analogy between accumulation processes and the flow of a liquid.

Flows will always, of course, originate somewhere and terminate somewhere. Sometimes, the origin of a flow is treated as essentially limitless, or at least outside the model-builder's concern. In such a case the flow's origin is called a *source*. Similarly, when the destination of a flow is not of interest, it is called a *sink*. Both sources and sinks

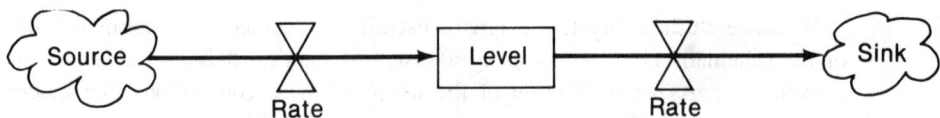

Figure 2.5 Representation of rates and levels

are shown as little "clouds," as illustrated in Figure 2.5. For example, for a level of workforce these cloud-like symbols represent where people come from when they are hired and where they go after leaving the project.

The flows that are controlled by the rates are usually diagramed differently, depending on the type of quantity involved. We will use the two types of arrow designators shown in Figure 2.6.

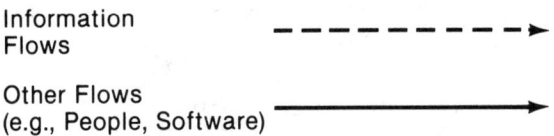

Figure 2.6 Representation of flows

Tangible variables are either levels or rates i.e., they are either accumulations of previous flows or are presently flowing. Usually, however, it is difficult to write a rate equation without doing some computation. These additional algebraic computations are termed *auxiliaries*. Auxiliary variables are combinations of information inputs into concepts e.g., "*desired* work force," or policies e.g., "*training* policy." Auxiliaries are represented by a circular symbol as shown in Figure 2.7. For example, in Figure 2.4 the "hiring rate" equals the "workforce gap" divided by the "hiring delay" where the "workforce gap" is defined to be the difference between the "workforce level needed" and the current "total workforce."

A few other symbols complete the designation of items included in formal system dynamics diagrams. In addition to the variable symbols shown above, models also include constant terms, i.e., parameters of the model whose values are assumed to be unchanging throughout a particular computer simulation. Constants are depicted in Figure 2.8; the name of the constant being underlined, with an information arrow going to the variable that is affected by the constant.

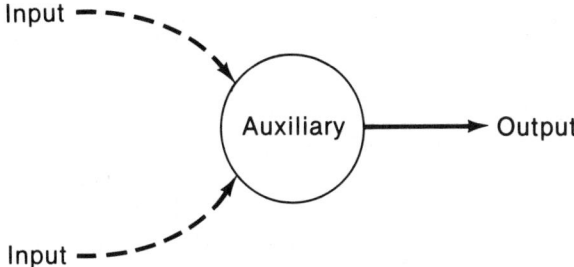

Figure 2.7   Representation of auxiliaries

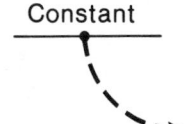

Figure 2.8   Representation of a constant

Finally, because complex models are often diagrammed in multiple displays, situations arise in which variables pictured on one diagram are used in another diagram. These variable cross-references are shown by including the name of the other diagram's variable in parentheses as shown in Figure 2.9.

Figure 2.9   Variable cross-reference

2.8 Transition to Part II and Part III

Part II, consisting of chapters 3 and 4, provides a summary of the literature sources and system developer sources, respectively, that were used to inspire and develop the models that are described in subsequent chapters. These chapters can be read now or the reader can skip directly to the description of the subsystems presented in Part III, starting in chapter 5, and come back to Part II at a later time.

PART TWO

SOURCES

OF

INFORMATION

3

REVIEW OF RELEVANT LITERATURE

In this chapter we review the System Dynamics literature that addresses the general area of modeling and analyzing project management, and the software engineering literature in the area of software development project management.

3.1 System Dynamics Modeling of Project Management

Professor Edwards B. Roberts' doctoral dissertation, ''The Dynamics of Research and Development,'' [223] completed in 1962, was the first scholarly effort to apply System Dynamics methodology to project management within an R&D environment. Since then, especially as a thesis advisor, he has continued to play an active ''guiding'' role in System Dynamics, advancing the field through studies of R&D projects. Roberts' work, and that of his students at MIT's Sloan School of Management, constitute the bulk of this research in System Dynamics.

We briefly digress to explain how and why this body of research first attracted our attention. Frustrated by the lack of innovative activity in the area of software management, we decided to look into other more established fields for new ideas. The management of R&D was the obvious first choice. It is the area most often likened in the software engineering literature to software production. For example, Gehring and Pooch noted:

> The stages of research and development are similar in many respects to the stages of software analysis and design. First, the determination of what the system is to do (specification of outputs and inputs) is ill-defined, making the estimation of the time and cost of its development uncertain (like the research stage). Second, the specification of how inputs (file specification, programming) is easier to estimate (like the development state). These similarities suggest that a good many managerial practices and procedures from the latter may be applied to the former [112].

Wolverton, in his highly referenced 1974 paper [270], writes: ''The general principles involved in pricing large R&D efforts of any kind ... apply to large software development as well.''

Putnam's celebrated SLIM model for software cost estimation is based on the *R&D* work of Peter Norden [214]. Norden had showed that R&D projects have a well-defined manpower pattern of the Rayleigh form [198]. When Putnam ''adapted'' Norden's findings on R&D projects to the software environment, he found that here too manpower application follows the same Rayleigh pattern.

Roberts' System Dynamics model of R&D project management continues to be the most comprehensive work published in the area. The model traces the full life cycle of a single R&D project. It incorporates the interactions between the R&D product, the firm, the customer, and the processes relating to the nature of the work itself. Figure 3.1 (from Roberts' thesis) is an overview of the model's sectors, and their interrelationships.

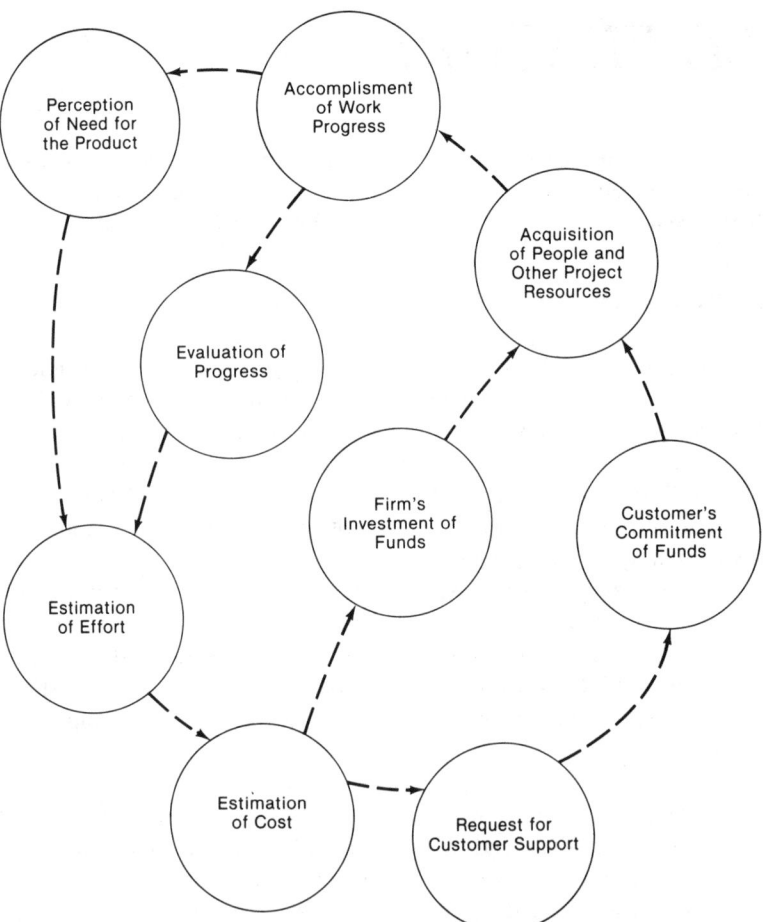

Figure 3.1 Over-all organization of R&D project [223]

3.1.1 Similarities Between R&D Management and Software Project Management

Rather than delve into a detailed discussion of Roberts' R&D model, we will present excerpts of his work and relevant corresponding excerpts from the software engineering literature.

On **project planning**:

Roberts:

> No unerring formula can be used to estimate the total number of man-years required to carry out a given (R&D) project. This kind of general statement reflects the inherent nature of research and development: The exact character of a specific task is indefinite, (and) the specific technical requirements are uncertain. ... [223]

The Software Engineering Literature:

> - ... quantitative software engineering has not progressed to the point that we can even begin to provide (software sizing) formulas. And it is not clear that we will ever get very close to such an ideal [49].
>
> - (We lack the means) ... to provide clear, concise, and unambiguous statements of user requirements. ...   The problem here again has to do with the "absence" of a clear understanding on the part of both software users and developers as to what can be accomplished with software [83].
>
> - The production of software is not a deterministic activity. Product specifications are liable to be shifted [255].

Roberts:

> Two factors significantly influence the initial estimate of the job size: (1) the firm's previous experience; and (2) the general over-all tendency to underestimate the job size [223].

The Software Engineering Literature:

> - ... when methods of estimating are ranked, the list is headed by the *Experience Method.* ...   This approach takes advantage of experience on a similar job. ...   The major problem in the method is that it does not work on systems larger than the base used for comparison. System complexity grows as the square of the number of system elements; therefore, experience with a small system cannot account for all the things that will have to be done in a large system. Neither will the Experience Method apply to systems of totally different content [23].
>
> - The software undersizing problem is our most critical road block to accurate software cost estimation ...   there are no magic formulas that we can use to overcome the software undersizing problem. In the absence of any such formula, it is important to understand the major sources of the software undersizing problem. ...   A major (reason) is a strong tendency to underestimate the size of support software (e.g, compilers, tools, utilities), which for large operational systems is generally three to five times as large as the operational software [49].

On **management of human resources**:

Roberts:

> Whatever the know-how developed in solving the R&D project problems, some time is required for it to be adequately absorbed. Then, as the experiences accumulate, the firms' engineers supplement their nonproject skills with these new, more specific insights and approaches to the task [223].

The Software Engineering Literature:

> Programmers become more effective during larger programming operations because of "learning." The programmer gains familiarity with program logic, coding notation, testing restrictions, and other requirements as he progresses through each major activity in the programming methods [234].

Roberts:

> Above a certain level, the assignment of additional personnel to a large project may not only reduce total time proportionality, but in fact may increase total time to accomplishment [223].

The Software Engineering Literature:

> Increasing the size of a software team increases the amount of software produced per unit time, up to a point. Then the problems of communication among the programmers begin to dominate the project and reduce the amount of software being produced [44]

And finally, on the **control of progress**:

Roberts:

> (Control) problems ...   result from lack of tangible, precise measurement in R&D. ...

The Software Engineering Literature:

> Abstraction, or intangibility, is a management challenge for such rudiments as recognizing process, exhibiting results, and communicating between packets of work. And compounding this is lack of hardware-like measures ...   ." [226].

> It is difficult to measure performance in programming ...   . (And) it is difficult to evaluate the status of intermediate work such as undebugged programs or design specifications and their potential value to the completed project [181].

Roberts:

One particular difficulty is that, during the very early phases of a project, milestones have a tendency to be less precisely definable, and hence less accurately measurable, than during later phases of the project ... . The shortcomings of the concept, ''percent complete,'' were sufficiently great to negate its value. While projects tended to make rapid progress towards completion when work first began, it took an inordinately long time to get from 90 percent to 100 percent.

The Software Engineering Literature:

- In the early stages of a project, it is difficult to distinguish between 5% completion and 10% completion, yet the resultant projection can vary 100% based on which number is chosen [88].

- One frequent difficulty stems from an over-reliance on individual percent-complete estimates as indicators of project progress [49].

- (This) method of estimating progress typically leads to estimates of the fraction of work completed which increase as originally planned until a level of about 80-90% is reached. The programmers' individual estimates then increase only very slowly until the task is actually completed [28].

Clearly some of the problems that Roberts addresses resemble some of those we are struggling with today in software engineering. It is no wonder then, that we felt that Roberts' model would be an effective tool for addressing the problems of project management in software development.

3.1.2 Extensions to Roberts' Original Work Roberts' work was extended to multi-project environments by Nay (a four-project model) [195] and Kelly (a two-project model) [143]. In a multi-project environment, competition for company resources becomes a significant dimension. For both Nay and Kelly, the focus remained, as for Roberts, on project life cycle behavior. Edelman's work, while building on Nay's model, focused instead on the allocation and utilization of manpower resources and the effects of the management system on effectiveness [91].

Richardson took still a different tack. Rather than focusing on a *project*, he focused on the development *group*. His model does not trace the life cycle(s) of one or more projects; rather, it reproduces the dynamics of a development group over an eight-year period as a continuous stream of products are developed and placed into production. The model focuses on the number of products under development, the use of resources required, and the aggregate average product development time [220].

Finally, several more recent models have emphasized the role of rework in project management. Rework can result from errors that escape detection until later in a project's life cycle. Of course, the longer an error goes undetected, the more extensive the necessary rework and the greater the cost. Changing design specifications after development begins also results in rework. Cooper describes a large system dynamics study of cost overruns in a shipbuilding contract. The study showed that the rework required by frequent design changes imposed by the Navy was the major reason for a 500 million dollar overrun [73]. Rework caused by undetected errors is also the focus of the simple R&D project models in Roberts [224] and Richardson and Pugh [221].

3.2 Software Engineering Project Management Literature Review

As we stated in chapter 1, the focus of this book is on software project management, and our objective is to improve our understanding of it. In the following sections we review the software engineering literature on project management to assess the current state of understanding.

We will begin with overview models and frameworks and continue with separate discussions of software project planning, human resource management, and control — the three project management subsystems that together constitute the project management activities in our detailed model. We present our model in chapters 5 through 11.

3.3 Overview of Models and Frameworks

3.3.1 Thayer's Work Richard Thayer's 1979 Ph.D dissertation at the University of California at Santa Barbara, "Modeling a Software Engineering Project Management System," is a fitting starting point for this discussion. For one, it probably was indeed "the first attempt to completely model a software engineering project management system" [246]. But, perhaps more important, if we judge from the number of publications it has generated (one in *IEEE Transaction on Software Engineering* [249], two in *Computer* [248, 250] and several conference papers), it has had a significant impact on the software engineering community.

Thayer's goal was twofold: (1) to develop and verify "a generalized descriptive management model of a software engineering project management system" and (2) to "identify and verify the major issues of software engineering project management." Although Thayer considered the development of the model to be his most important contribution, it was his issues findings that generated all of the above publications.

To develop his model, he first surveyed the literature and examined his personal experience to identify the various functions, actions, procedures, and tools used or proposed for use in managing a software engineering project. He then superimposed the functions, actions, procedures, and tools on the classic management model, which breaks management activity into five functions: planning, organizing, staffing, directing, and controlling.

The skeleton of Thayer's model is shown in Table 3.1. Each of the eight general management and production models he later expanded. For example, his detailed Planning Model is shown in Table 3.2, together with the set of assumptions he used to formulate it (in Figure 3.2).

To identify the major issues of software engineering project management, Thayer first reviewed the literature for software engineering problems. Then, by using the software engineering delivery and success model shown in Figure 3.3, he hypothesized which problems would most affect the success of software delivery. These problems, he believed, were the major issues.

He reworded the issues as problems from the project manager's point of view. Then he classified them on the basis of the classic management model of planning, organizing, staffing, directing, and controlling. He found that "By far, the two dominant (problematic) activities are planning and controlling, which together (accounted) for 80% of the issues, with planning alone involving ten issues." The 20 issues he identified are shown in Figure 3.4.

TABLE 3.1   OVERVIEW MODEL OF A SOFTWARE ENGINEERING PROJECT
MANAGEMENT SYSTEM [246]

GENERAL MANAGEMENT AND PRODUCTION MODEL(S)	SOFTWARE ENGINEERING PROJECT MANAGEMENT AND PRODUCTION MODEL
Project Identification	Program Identification
	Hardware Identification
	Customer Identification
	Contract Identification
	Cost & Schedule Identification
	Software Identification
	Complexity Identification
	Data Base Identification
Requirements & Constraints	Requirement Specifications
	Document Requirements
	Customer Constraints
Planning	Planning and Scheduling
	Quality Assurance Program
Organizing	Preorganization Function
	Project Management Organization
	Software Engineering Project Team
Staffing	Project Manager Staffing
	Software Development Staff
	Staff Support
	Training
Directing/Monitoring	Responsibility and Authority
	Management Techniques
	Assignment of Work
Controlling	Project Control
	Reporting
	Formal Reviews
	Configuration Management
	Informal Reviews and Walkthroughs
Deliveries & Successes	Schedule
	Cost
	Meets Requirements
	Meets Reliability Standards
	Meets Maintainability Standards
	Meets Usability Standards

TABLE 3.2 PLANNING MODEL[246]

GENERAL MANAGEMENT FUNCTIONS	PROJECT MANAGEMENT ACTIVITIES
Analyze Requirement	Analyze inputs and output requirements, functions of the system, and deliverables.
	Determine hardware and system software restrictions.
	Determine user identification and type of contract.
	Determine size, complexity, and user or company constraint.
Set Objectives	Determine and establish success criteria.
	Determine attributes of delivered software: reliable, maintainable, usable, etc.
Forecast	Determine cost and schedule to deliver software.
Set Procedures	Select planning and project control tools and techniques.
	Develop quality assurance plan.
	Select design, programming, and testing tool, technique, and methods.
Develop Strategies	Same
Develop Policies	Same
Program	Determine priority and milestones for events.
Budget and Resources	Budget, locate and secure resources: funds, programmer/analyst, computer time, etc.

A separate organization from the development organization would perform the planning and scheduling (this is also an element of the organizing model).

Planning would be accomplished through the use of formal planning guides, methods, and tools.

The plan, no matter how well accomplished by the planning group, would be modified either the senior manager or the customer.

Planning documentation would be prepared.

The planning function would be a formal function with time allocated for planning.

Modular planning design and delivery techniques would be used on the software development project.

The planning function would include a software quality assurance program.

Each project would use some of the tools, techniques and procedures known as "modern programming techniques."

Software development tools, techniques and aids would be used on the software development project.

Software test tools, techniques, and methods would be used in the software development project.

Figure 3.2   Assumptions used to formulate Thayer's Planning Model

To verify his assertion he did two things. First he conducted an opinion survey with a selected sub-set of the computer community: technical leaders in computer science, software engineering authors, project managers, R&D personnel, and software engineering educators. (He received 294 replies.) Those surveyed were asked to weigh the importance of the hypothesized problems as critical, important, not important, or not problematic at all. They also were invited to disagree with the hypothesis completely and the way it was stated. Those surveyed were, in addition, asked to state how they would (or did) solve each problem.

The 13 starred (*) issues in Figure 3.4 were the problems verified in the survey. Verification meant that at least 70% of the respondents felt that the issue was either "critical" or "important." Most of Thayer's surveyees either came from large companies or obtained their knowledge from data processing in large companies.

The second verification step was through a separate survey of 60 software development projects in the aerospace industry. He checked to see that "the condition described in the major issue existed, and (that) the existence of the condition was a problem to the project manager. ... If the data substantiates (this) the hypothesized issue is labelled a problem."

    · Deliveries:

       — Software

       — Documentation

    · Success Attributes:

       — On time

       — Within resources

       — Meets requirements

       — Useable

       — Reliable

       — Maintainable

Figure 3.3   Software Development Delivery and Success Model

Nine of the 20 major issues (marked with + in Figure 3.4) were verified as problems, two were inconclusive, and nine were verified not to be problems. Six major issues concerning planning and one concerning controlling were judged conclusively as problems in both surveys.

Thayer noted with interest, though, that "there is some disagreement between the general data processing community and the project managers and developers. ... The fact that these two groups do not, in general, agree on the major issues is in itself a fundamental problem of project management."

In addition:

> Similar to the problem in identifying the major issues, the computing community is divided on the solutions to the major problems. There are no well defined software management techniques to guarantee a successful software delivery.

Finally, we conclude our discussion of Thayer's work with some of his own concluding remarks:

> Future research should continue to "refine" this model. ... This model, as a first attempt, has many omission and frequent generalizations. Similar research projects, using a different approach, could fine-tune this model and find more elements with a full range of values for each element.

> This research identified several major issues of software engineering project management and proposed a number of solutions. What is needed is a good definitized experimentation method that can be used as a test bed for validating new project management tools, techniques, and procedures. ... etc.

> There is still a long way to go; this is only the beginning [246].

Planning

*+   1. *Requirements:* Requirement specifications are frequently incomplete, ambiguous, inconsistent, and/or unmeasurable.

*   2. *Success:* Success criteria for a software development are frequently inappropriate, which result in "poor-quality" delivered software; i.e., not maintainable, unreliable, difficult to use, relatively undocumented, etc.

*+   3. *Project:* Planning for software engineering projects is generally poor.

*+   4. *Cost:* The ability to estimate accurately the resources required to accomplish a software development is poor.

*+   5. *Schedule:* The ability to estimate accurately the delivery time on a software development is poor.

*+   6. *Design:* Decision rules for use in selecting the correct software design techniques, equipment, and aids to be used in designing software in a software enginering project are not available.

*+   7. *Test:* Decision rules for use in selecting the correct procedures, strategies, and tools to be used in testing software developed in a software engineering project are not available.

     8. *Maintainability:* Procedures, techniques, and strategies for designing maintainable software are not available.

*   9. *Warranty:* Methods to guarantee or warranty that the delivered software will "work" for the user are not available.

\+   10. *Control:* Procedures, methods, and techniques for designing a project control system that will enable project managers to successfully control their project are not readily available.

Organizing

     11. *Type:* Decision rules for selecting the proper organizational structure: e.g., project, matrix, function, are not available.

*   12. *Accountability:* The accountability structure in many software engineering projects is poor, leaving some question as to who is responsible for various project functions.

Staffing

*   13. *Project manager:* Procedures and techniques for selection of project managers are poor.

Directing

     14. *Techniques:* Decision rules for use in selecting the correct management techniques for software engineering project management are not available.

Controlling

\+   15. *Visibility:* Procedures, techniques, strategies, and aids that will provide visibility of progress (not just resources used) to the project manager are not available.

*   16. *Reliability:* Measurements or indexes of reliability that can be used as an element of software design are not available and there is no way to predict software failure; i.e., there is no practical way to show the delivered software meets a given reliability criteria.

*   17. *Maintainability:* Measurements or indexes of maintainability that can be used as an element of software design are not available; i.e., there is no practical way to show that a given program is more maintainable than another.

     18. *Goodness:* Measurements or indexes of "goodness" of code that can be used as an element of software design are not available; i.e., there is no practical way to show that one program is better than another.

*+ 19. *Programmers:* Standards and techniques for measuring the quality of performance and the quantity of production expected from programmers and data processing analysts are not available.

     20. *Tracing:* Techniques and aids that provide an acceptable means of tracing a software development from requirements to completed code are not generally available.

Figure 3.4   Twenty hypothesized problems in SEPM [218]

3.3.2 Riehl's Work   In his doctoral thesis, Riehl developed a "planning and control framework to assist in the management of computer-based information systems development in large organizations" [218]. The research included: (1) an extensive literature survey to compile "those concepts and practices that are advanced by authorities in the field of computer-based information systems and electronic data processing management" and (2) a determination of those policies and procedures actually employed in practice by companies "judged to be effective managers of computer-based information systems."

His model, termed the "Composite-Working Model," consisted of 25 "principles" and 50 "issues." Principles are those "specific concepts, policies, and procedures upon which general agreement was found to exist in the literature and in the observed practices of the (5) companies investigated." Issues, on the other hand, "identify those proposed practices about which disagreement or uncertainty exists within the literature or which are the subject of clear divergences between the concepts advanced in the literature and the majority practices of the firms in the research." The principles and issues were classified into four categories: strategic planning, project planning, project control, and organizational behavior considerations.

A summary of the major categories of the Composite-Working Model is presented in Figure 3.5. We included as an illustration the "Consensus Principle V (PP): Project Plan," within the "project planning" category.because "the importance of a project plan is widely recognized in the source literature ... (and) the research findings supported the principle." Furthermore, "A single issue was generated concerning the degree of detail that should be included in the project plan. Brandon, for example, proposes a comprehensive scheme based on an automated system. Other writers generally provide considerably fewer details on the subject." A similar disagreement was observed among the companies studied.

Riehl concluded that he has met his research goal, namely, to develop "a planning and control framework to assist in the management of computer-based information systems development in large organizations, by identifying those practices and procedures which are both advocated in the literature as well as used by (selected) large business organizations with a reputation for effective computer-based information systems management."

3.3.3 McFarlan's Work   Instead of focusing, as Riehl and Thayer did, on *common* issues among software development projects, McFarlan focused on the *differences*. "One conclusion from my research stands out," he wrote, and that was:

> A monolithic approach to systems and programming project management is unlikely to produce the most satisfactory results. There are critical differences in project composition ... which influence the mix of tools that should be brought on by its management [167].

He identified three "important" dimensions for characterizing software development projects: (1) the degree of predetermined structure inherent in the project (he defined a highly structured project to be "one where the processing routines and outputs of the system are so determined by the project's environment in advance that there are little or no design options open to the system architect or user"); (2) the degree of company-relative computer technology implicit in the project (a high "company-relative technology" project is "one which involves complex hardware-software features which have not been dealt with previously in the organization"); and (3) project size, measured as man-years of effort or manpower dollars of expenditures ("In this context a

Strategic Planning

    Consensus Principle I(SP): Master Systems Planning
        Issue A: Structure for Planning
        Issue B: Type of Planning
    Consensus Principle II(SP): Management Involvement
        Issue A: Top Management Involvement
        Issue B: User-Management Involvement
        Issue C: Chief Executive Officer Involvements
    Consensus Principle III(SP): Master Systems Plan
        Issue A: Planning Details
    Consensus Principle IV(SP): Planning Coordination
        Issue A: Planning Integration
    Consensus Principle V(SP): Provision for Change
        Issue A: Means for Achieving Change

Project Planning

    Consensus Principle I(PP): System Development Life Cycle
        Issue A: Description of the system Development Life Cycle
    Consensus Principle II(PP): Feasibility Study and Project Proposal
        Issue A: Analysis of Alternative Designs
        Issue B: Feasibility Study
    Consensus Principle III(PP): Economic Analysis
        Issue A: Treatment of Reliability
        Issue B: Present Value Discounting
        Issue C: Estimating Intangible Benefits
        Issue D: Approval Criteria
    Consensus Principle IV(PP): Project Management
        Issue A: Assignment of Project Manager
        Issue B: Project-Status Audit
        Issue C: Project Thresholds
        Issue D: Project Establishment
    Consensus Principle V(PP): Project Plan
        Issue A: Project Plan Detail
    Consensus Principle VI(PP): Project Control Reporting
        Issue A: Reported Information
        Issue B: Management Review
    Consensus Principle VII(PP): Estimation Process
        Issue A: Estimating Methods
        Issue B: Reliability of Estimates
    Consensus Principle VIII(PP): Change Control
        Issue A: Review of Changes
        Issue B: Limiting Impact of Changes
    Consensus Principle IX(PP): System Development Standards
        Issue A: Form of Standards
    Consensus Principle X(PP): Cost Allocation
        Issue A: Method of Cost Allocation
        Issue B: Influence on User Behavior

Figure 3.5   Summary of the Composite-Working Model

Project Control

    Consensus Principle I(PC): User-Management Control

        Issue A: Level of Management Control

        Issue B: Key Check-Points

        Issue C: Form of Check-Point Reviews

    Consensus Principle II(PC): Information Requirements Definition

        Issue A: Methods of Requirements Identification

        Issue B: Requirements Validation

    Consensus Principle III(PC): Functional Specifications

        Issue A: User Participation

        Issue B: Conversion Plan

    Consensus Principle IV(PC): Performance Criteria

        Issue A: Performance Criteria Specifications

    Consensus Principle V(PC): Detailed Design Specifications

        Issue A: User Participation

    Consensus Principle VI(PC): System Implementation

        Issue A: User Participation

    Consensus Principle VII(PC): System Testing

        Issue A: User-Management Involvement

        Issue B: User Representative Participation

    Consensus Principle VIII(PC): Conversion and Cut-Over

        Issue A: Conversion Organization

        Issue B: Management Control

    Consensus Principle IX(PC): Post-Implementation Audit

        Issue A: Conduct of Audit

        Issue B: Documentation of Audit

Organizational Behavior Considerations

    Consensus Principle I(BC): User Acceptance

        Issue A: Intergroup Communications

        Issue B: Personnel Management

        Issue C: User-Management Involvement

        Issue D: User Participation and Control of Change

        Issue E: Awareness of User Attitudes

Figure 3.5 (cont)   Summary of the Composite-Working Model

$50,000 project will be considered small while a $1 million project will be considered large'').

Table 3.3 shows how McFarlan classified projects in one of eight different categories.

As stated above, McFarlan felt that a project's classification should influence the mix of tools that should be brought on by its management. To show how, he divided project management tools into four main groups: (1) formal integration procedures with users of the project's output, who are located outside the EDP department (e.g., a formal User-EDP project advisory committee); (2) formal integration procedures within the EDP design team and among the various units of the EDP department (e.g., formal flow charts and other documentation to highlight interfaces between key systems components); (3) formal planning tools (e.g., PERT or CPM); and (4) formal control tools (e.g., regular use of formal post-audit procedures).

TABLE 3.3   CLASSIFICATION OF SYSTEMS AND PROGRAMMING PROJECT TYPES

		Degree of Structuredness	
		High	Low
Degree of Company-Relative Technology	Low	I. Large Project	V. Large Project
		II. Small Project	VI. Small Project
	High	III. Large Project	VII. Large Project
		IV. Small Project	VIII. Small Project

The final step was to put the two pieces together into what he called a "contingency theory" of EDP systems and programming project-management. The outcome is exhibited in Table 3.4.

TABLE 3.4   CONTINGENCY THEORY OF PROJECT MANAGEMENT [167]

Project Types	Project Description[*]	External Integ[**]	Internal Integ[***]	Formal Planning	Formal Control
I	HS, LT, Large	Low	Medium	High	High
II	HS, LT, Small	Low	Low	Medium	High
III	HS, HT, Large	Low	High	Medium	Medium
IV	HS, HT, Small	Low	High	Low	Low
V	LS, LT, Large	High	Medium	High	High
VI	LS, LT, Small	High	Low	Medium	High
VII	LS, HT, Large	High	High	Low	Low
VIII	LS, HT, Small	High	Medium	Low	Low

[*] HS = High Structure; LS = Low Structure; HT = High Tech; LT = Low Tech.

[**] No attempt is made here to suggest how external integration may shift over time as the user becomes more sophisticated through experience. My research suggests this may be important. This table highlights the importance of external integration in getting user commitment to a project structure. It does not explicitly address his important role in enabling the EDP technicians to adequately understand the process to be automated. This appears to be important even in highly structured situations. Thus even these projects that are ranked low in the above table in external integration, may involve considerable user liaison of the fact finding sort.

[***] This does not identify the sharp split in the mix of the tools in internal integration identified in the text. Later work may split this into two categories.

3.3.4 The Life Cycle Model   At still a higher level of specificity are the research efforts to distinguish differences among phases *in* the life of a *single* project. According to McKeen:

> The dominant organizing framework for application system development is the life cycle concept. This methodology apportions the total developmental effort into identifiable stages — each stage representing a distinct activity characterized by a starting point, an ending point, and deliverables in concert with an express purpose [171].

The life cycle model was formally acknowledged as an important element in systems development by its inclusion in the information system curricular proposed by the ACM Curriculum Committee on Computer Education for Management [26]. In recent years, many books and papers on the life cycle concept have been published (e.g., [49, 107, 130, 177, 253, 272]).

According to Davis, application systems all need to undergo a similar process — the life cycle — when they are conceived, developed and implemented. If any portion of the life cycle is neglected, there may be serious consequences. Davis describes the contribution of the life cycle concept to systems development:

> Information system development involves considerable creativity, the use of the life cycle is the means for obtaining more disciplined creativity by giving structure to a creative process. The life cycle is important in planning, management, and control of information system application development [80].

The steps or phases in the software development life cycle are described differently by different authors, but the differences are primarily in amount of detail and number of categorizations. A common breakdown is given by Glass [116]:

Requirements/Specifications

Design

Implementationes in concert with an express purpose [171].

Checkout

Maintenance

A mere list of the phases is not, however, an adequate model of the software life cycle because it "conceals" the *iterative* nature of the software development process [25]. The life cycle does not proceed linearly; rather "the process is iterative so that, for example, the review after the system design phase may result in going back to the beginning to prepare a new design" [80]. Boehm's "waterfall" model, shown in Figure 3.6, emphasizes this highly iterative nature of software development, represented by the feedback arrows from each phase to its predecessor(s) [49].

Moreover, to put the overall process in perspective, we must evaluate the percentages of resources consumed in each phase. Numerous authors have reported on resource consumption by phase. Table 3.5 compares three authors' results. McKeen, who made the comparison, stated that:

> Substantial differences do exist particularly in the coding and testing phases of development. These differences may be due to the inherent attributes of the systems being developed, or to terminological variations, or to a combination of both of these. In the absence of a careful description of the systems and the environment in which they were developed ... the generalization of results beyond the immediate environment is not possible [171].

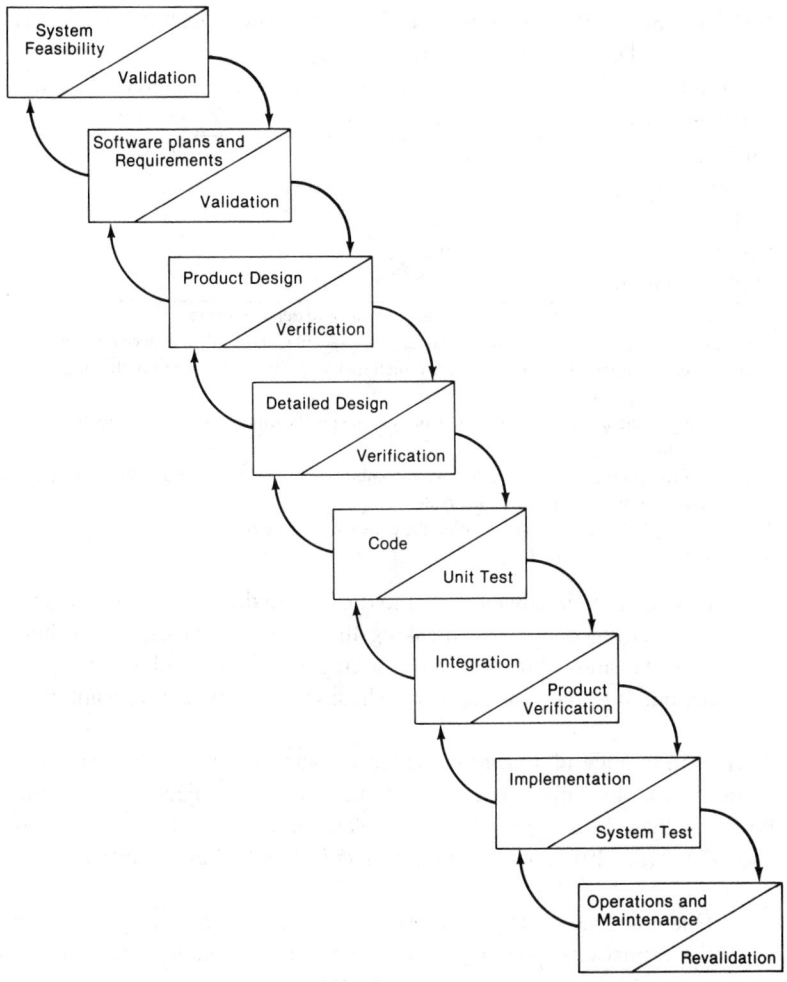

Figure 3.6   The waterfall model of the software life-cycle [49]

The above views are shared by others in the literature. For example, Kustanowitz supports the notion that system size affects the distribution of resources as shown in Figure 3.7 [153]. Myers reported on a study at Boeing, which showed that "the costs were shifted into earlier stages (of the life cycle) by the use of modern programming practices" [190].

The life-cycle model of the distribution of resources plays an important role in enabling project managers to estimate the allocation of resources for software development. This role will be discussed in some detail in our review of the literature on project planning, which follows.

3.4 Planning

In his "IEEE Tutorial on Software Management," Reifer defined planning as follows:

TABLE 3.5 COMPARISON OF EFFORT BREAKDOWN BY ACTIVITY FOR DIFFERENT AUTHORS [172]

Life Cycle Phase/Activity	Percentage Resource Allocation		
	Davis	Zelkowitz	Shaw
Analysis[1]	25	20^2	25
Design	20	15	10^3
Coding	25	45^4	30
System Test	n/a[5]	20	5
Implementation	15	n/a[6]	19

1. Analysis encompasses all development activity prior to detailed design.
2. The analysis effort is probably understated. If, as speculated, this data is derived from system developments in a military environment, then initial activity such as feasibility analysis and preliminary systems study has been excluded.
3. According to the authors, the activities of system specifications and technical requirements constitute detailed design activities.
4. Coding effort and module test effort were combined. Programmers are typically responsible for testing each unit or module of the system they have coded.
5. This activity has been subsumed within the conversion stage by Davis.
6. This activity is not reported.

It is deciding in advance what to do, how to do it, when to do it, and who is to do it. It is setting objectives, breaking the work into tasks, establishing schedules and budgets, allocating resources, setting standards, and selecting future courses of action. It bridges the gap from where we are to where we want to be [217].

3.4.1 Importance of Planning There is abundant support in the software engineering literature for the importance of planning software projects [169, 246]. Unfortunately, however, there is ample evidence that planning is inadequate or absent entirely [47, 136, 142, 177, 210, 249]. Pooch and Gehring corroborate those assertions:

One universal management principle, for example, has been called the "principle of the primacy of planning." In other words, planning has primacy over the other managerial functions of organizing, staffing, directing, and controlling. Thus, the degree of control over a programming project can be *no greater than* the extent to which adequate plans have been made for the project ... Inadequate planning is the primary reason for loss of control on many computer programming projects. It is not the comparative newness of the computer programming process, difficulties with programmers, or technical factors — it is simply that programming projects are not adequately planned in the first place [208].

When Thayer surveyed the software engineering literature to identify the major problems of software engineering project management, he ended up with 20 hypothesized problem areas [246]. Of these, a full fifty percent (or 10 problems) were identified as being planning problems (see Figure 3.4). When he proceeded to verify his list, the dominance of planning problems was even more impressive: of the seven problem-areas that were verified, six were planning problems (the seventh was in the control area).

In addition, Thayer's work, which incorporated a survey of 60 software projects (in the aerospace industry), sheds some light on the planning activity. For example, he reported that:

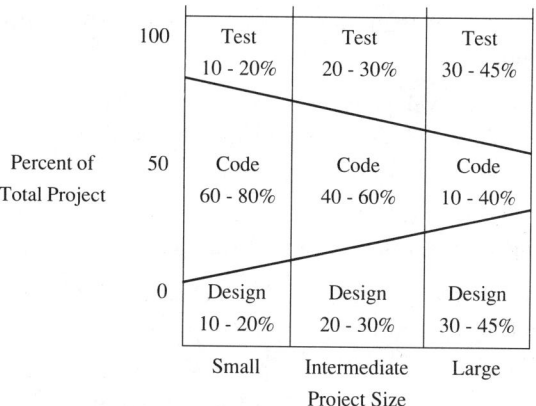

Figure 3.7 System life cycle varies with project size.[153]

- The primary tools or techniques used in planning a software development project were workload charts, work break-down structure (WBS), and the subdivision of the software development into phases or tasks.

- About one-fourth of the (planning) time was spent in developing an overall project plan. An equal amount of time was devoted to planning for the (project) organization, planning on how to staff the organization, and developing control procedures.

- (Contrary to Thayer's initial assumption) a separate planning group does *not* normally perform the planning and scheduling functions. The data showed that in 92% of the cases, planning was done by the future manager of the project.

- The predominant estimation method was "estimation based on a similar project" (used in 67% of the projects), followed by "use of a formula" (40%), "expert opinion" (17%), and "crystal ball" (12%). [Note: Some projects combined methods.]

A further analysis of the data suggested that " ... it makes little difference what type of technique is used in estimating delivery schedule and project cost. None of the used techniques significantly improved the project manager's ability to deliver the project on time and within cost" [246].

Software estimation historically has been and continues to be a major difficulty in managing software development [85, 86, 130, 180, 208, 272, 274, 275]. Farquhar articulated the significance of the issue:

Unable to estimate accurately, the manager can know with certainty neither what resources to commit to an effort nor, in retrospect, how well these resources were used. The lack of a firm foundation for these two judgments can reduce programming management to a random process in that positive control is next to impossible. This situation often results in the budget overruns and schedule slippages that are all too common today [95].

3.4.2 Difficulty of Planning Several reasons for the difficulty have been suggested in the literature:

1. Software development is a process that is not yet fully understood by "estimators" [188, 200, 208, 242, 207]. This often leads to the overlooking of significant cost factors [49, 62, 188].

2. The phases and functions that comprise the software development process are influenced by many ill defined variables [23, 85, 86, 208, 200, 210].

3. Most of the activities within the process are still primarily human rather than mechanical, and therefore prone to all the subjective factors which affect human performance [200, 208, 210].

4. The lack of a historical data base of cost measurements [65, 81, 102, 188, 200, 274].

5. Little penalty is often associated with a poor estimate [275].

Over the years, estimating project size, development time, and cost has been an intuitive process [162]. Experience and the prevailing industry norms have been used as a basis to develop estimates for any given project [111, 172, 184, 200]. Myers has identified several "traps" in the experience method (i.e., basing estimates on actual costs of similar past projects), namely:

1. The relationship between cost and system size is not linear. In fact, cost increases approximately exponentially as size increases. Therefore, the experience method should only be applied when the sizes of the current project and past projects are equivalent.

2. Products with similar names are normally dissimilar. For instance, chances are slim that two products titled "Payroll System" have the same development costs.

3. Frequent budget manipulations by management to avoid overruns make historical cost data questionable. For example, the movement of cost from an over-budget account to an under-budget account disguises the real costs and makes future use of this data dangerous [188].

3.4.3 Quantitative Software Estimation Models In the last two decades, several quantitative software estimation models have been developed. They range from highly theoretical ones, such as Putnam's model [212], to empirical ones, such as the Walston and Felix model [257], and Boehm's COCOMO model [49]. An empirical model uses data from previous projects to evaluate the current project and derives the basic formulae from analysis of the particular data base available. A theoretical model, on the other hand, uses formulae based on global assumptions, such as the rate at which people solve problems and the number of problems available for solutions at a given time. However,

Even today, almost no model can estimate the true cost of software with any degree of accuracy. (Furthermore,) it is highly unlikely, that any two will produce the same cost estimate for a given project ... The variations in cost estimations are influenced by both the many factors involved and the quantization of these factors by the users of the models. Therefore, to estimate a software project and develop appropriate manpower guidelines, it is essential to know the factors that influence the software development process at a given facility [184].

Finally, we conclude this discussion by Pietrasanta's frequently quoted insights into the estimation problem and its solution:

> ...   Many of the problems of resource estimating are symptoms of an underlying ignorance of the program system development for which the estimates are being made. The serious student of estimating must first be willing to probe deeply into the fascinating and complex system development process, to uncover the phases and functions of the process, to highlight the subtle interrelationships of the program system being developed and the project organization doing the developing ... examining the influence variables and their causal relationships is precisely what is required if estimates are ever to be improved. Only then can we do meaningful quantitative research and scientific analysis of resource requirements [207].

3.5 Management of Human Resources

People and organizational issues have gained recognition in recent years for being at the core of effective software development project management [52, 82, 233]. There are several reasons:

> Personnel costs are skyrocketing relative to hardware costs. Chronic problems in software development and implementation are more frequently traced to personnel shortcomings. Information systems staff sizes have mushroomed with little time for adequate selection and training. It is little wonder that Information Systems (IS) managers find themselves focusing increasing amounts of attention on human resource issues [35].

In this section we will review the human resource issues of software project management at two levels: individuals (e.g., selection and motivation) and groups (e.g., organization and communication).

3.5.1 Individual Dimensions

On Motivation: A major challenge to managers is to motivate employees. The few studies that have focused on motivational issues among data processing personnel have mainly concerned themselves with rankings of various job factors [35]. The findings have generally supported the notion that work, achievement, and growth are all important to data processing personnel [75].

For example, Fitz-enz's study provides rankings of the job factors considered most important by 1500 data processing professionals. The items' rankings were as follows: (1) Achievement, (2) Possibility for growth, (3) Work itself, (4) Recognition, (5) Advancement, (6) Technical supervision, (7) Responsibility, (8) Interpersonal relations with peers, (9) Interpersonal relations with subordinates, (10) Salary, (11) Personal life, (12) Interpersonal relations with superiors, (13) Job security, (14) Status, (15)

Company policy and administration, and (16) Working conditions [97].

A mechanism for motivation, which is attracting interest in the software engineering field, is "goal setting" [49]. An experiment by Weinberg and Schulman investigated the motivational value of setting clear goals in a programming environment [263]. In the experiment, five teams were given the same programming assignment, but each team was given a different objective: one team was asked to complete the job with the least possible effort, another team to minimize the number of statements in the program, another to minimize the amount of memory required by the program, another to produce the clearest possible program, and the last team to produce the clearest possible output. When the programs were completed and evaluated, the researchers found that each team finished first (or, in one case, second) with respect to their objective. They also found that none of the teams performed consistently well on the *other* objectives.

On Selection: Programmer aptitude tests are available, but their effectiveness is widely questioned [235]. Instruments such as the IBM Programmer Aptitude Test (PAT) or the Test on Sequential Instructions (TSI) for measuring programming ability and the Strong Vocational Interest Blank (SVIB) for measuring interest or motivational level have at best produced weak correlations with analyst or programmer capability) [49, 260].

On Performance Appraisal: The *general* literature on performance appraisal suggests that overall, global judgments regarding individual performance are an inferior means of measuring and appraising performance [35]. Instead, performance in most jobs consists of a number of different dimensions (e.g., quality versus quantity or efficiency of program execution versus ease of alteration by another programmer).

Gilb has suggested a several possible metrics of performance [114]. Jones has pointed to the difficulties in using certain standard measures, such as lines of code per programmer-month, and has suggested other approaches, such as separating quality measurements into "defect removal efficiency" and "defect prevention" [138].

On Turnover: Turnover continues to be a chronic problem for software project managers [155]. Willoughby estimates that the annual turnover in the DP field ranged between 15 and 20% during the 1960s, declined to about 5% in the early 1970s, and began to rise again by the end of the decade [268]. More recent studies place the annual turnover rate at 25.1% [243], 30% [222], and even as high as 34% [55]. As McLaughlin points out, at such rates the equivalent of a work unit turns over every three to four years — no minor matter in a profession where it frequently takes 12 to 18 months before a new employee makes significant contributions [174].

There are few predictive studies of DP turnover. In one such study, Bartol investigated the relative importance of two individual factors, personality and professional attitude, versus two organizational factors, professional reward system and tenure, in predicting turnover among computer professionals [34]. Only the variables of professional rewards and tenure were found to predict turnover variable, both in the expected negative direction.

3.5.2 Group Dimensions There are two basic issues involving the use of groups in software development. One concerns structural factors (i.e., how the groups are formulated), and the other involves process factors relevant to the ongoing operations and interrelationships of group members.

On Structural Factors: Software development projects are structured in one of three basic organizational forms: (1) Functional form; (2) Matrix form; or (3) Project form [79, 246]. Youker [271] suggests that these three organizational forms may be represented as a continuum ranging from functional on one end to project on the other end; matrix falls in between and includes a wide variety of structures from a weak matrix near functional to a strong matrix near project. Several authors have presented proposed guidelines or checklists for choosing the "appropriate" organizational form. (See [79, 121, 271]).

In a survey of 60 software development projects in the aerospace industry, Thayer found that the matrix organization is predominant; 58% of the projects used a matrix organization, 38% used a project organization, and 4% used a functional organization [246]. He also found that small projects were split between project and matrix organizations, medium priced projects (between 1 and 5 million dollar) were slightly biased in favor of project organization, while expensive projects (5 million to 50 million) are almost always matrix. As for "on time" and "within budget" delivery of the software, "it made little difference as to what kind of project (organization) type is used."

Thayer's data also showed that the team concept is much in use. About 95% of the projects were handled by teams under the direction of technical leaders of some sort.

Two philosophies for organizing programming teams have achieved a moderate amount of popularity in the data processing field. These are the egoless programming team proposed by Weinberg [260] and the chief programmer team proposed by Mills [179] and implemented by Baker [32].

Little experimental work on programming team and task interaction has been carried out [164]. Weinberg's suggestions are anecdotal and Baker's conclusions are confounded by the team personnel and the programming methods selected.

On Process Factors: The attention here has focused on the communication processes between members of a programming team. In what is probably the most cited reference on the topic, Brooks suggests that human communication in a software development project is the most significant cause of overhead — i.e., slowdowns and obstacles. [57]. Brooks also suggests that overhead results from training and communication. Each worker must be trained in the technology, the goals of the effort, the overall strategy, and the plan of work. Training cannot be partitioned, so the amount of effort training adds varies linearly with the number of workers. Communication among team members, Brooks further suggests, is worse. It increases by a factor of n(n-1)/2, where n is the number of team members.

The implication is that increasing the size of a software team increases the amount of software produced per unit time but *only* to a point. Then the problems of communication among the programmers begin to dominate the project and reduce the amount of software being produced [44]. Or in Brooks' words, "Oversimplifying outrageously, we state Brooks' Law: Adding manpower to a late software project makes it later" [57].

The relationship between human communication and programmer productivity was investigated by Scott and Simmons. First, using the Delphi survey technique to identify project variables that influence programmer productivity, they found the "effect of project communication" to be one of the "eight consensus variables which have an important influence on productivity" [230]. In a later study, they used computer simulation to evaluate the communication overhead as a function of a team's communication structure [231].

Finally, taking a different tack, Parnas considered the impact of human communication on the *product* of software development [204]. He suggested that too much communication between the members of a programming team could negatively affect modularity because team members would tend to use informal information to bypass structured interfaces.

3.6 Control

Once a plan becomes operational, control is necessary to measure progress, to uncover deviations from the plan, and to indicate corrective action [151]. While in most production environments, control is a *standard* business practice [181], in the production of software, control is a "perilous activity" [24, 46, 102, 111, 110, 111, 158, 177, 178, 208, 246]:

It is difficult to measure performance in programming. It is difficult to diagnose trouble in time to prevent it. It is difficult to evaluate the status of intermediate work such as undebugged programs or design specification and their potential value to the complete project [181].

Such a state of affairs has stirred not only self-criticism within the profession [83, 135, 158, 177] but also open criticism from the user community:

You software guys are too much like the weavers in the story about the Emperor and his new clothes. When I go out to check on software development the answers I get sound like, 'we're fantastically busy weaving this magic cloth. Just wait a while and it'll look terrific.' But there's nothing I can relate to, no way to pick up signals that things aren't really all that great. And there are too many people I know who have come out at the end wearing a bunch of expensive rags or nothing at all. (A U.S. Government spokesman quoted in Pooch and Gehring [208]).

The manifestation of poor software project control has more than one form. For example:

1. The "90% Syndrome" [28, 49, 81, 88].

2. The production of inadequate software, e.g., which doesn't meet user requirements [117, 244].

3. Systems that are inordinately expensive [172, 270], e.g., because of unconstrained goldplating [49, 145, 215, 270].

4. Lack of historical software cost data bases [49, 246].

3.6.1 Difficulty of Control   Why is it difficult to control software development projects? Two classes of explanations have been proposed in the literature: product-type and people-type factors.

Product-Type Factors:

1. Intangibility of the product during most of the development process, for which
    there are no visible milestones to measure progress and quality as there are for a
    physical product [44, 58, 74, 111, 124, 136, 178, 219, 258, 270]. "This invisibility
    is compounded for *large* software, for which logical complexity cannot be
    maintained in one person's mind, and for which development must be partitioned
    into a number of tasks assigned to different people" [275].

2. High complexity [74, 172]. "In an overly ambitious project, managers who do not
    understand the details of what they are managing are easily blustered and misled by
    subordinates. Conversely, low-level staff may be unable to appreciate the
    significance of details and fail to report serious problems" [74].

3. Volatility of requirements [86, 177, 254, 255, 275]. "Since software system
    modules are not visibly connected, in contrast to hardware systems, the impact of a
    change is often not readily apparent even to the designers of the system" [111].

People-Type Factors:

1. The "software wizard syndrome" [44]. Management sometimes abdicates its
    responsibility to a highly trusted software specialist, whose pronouncements are *ex
    cathedra*. Unfortunately, software wizards, unlike the mythical kind, are both
    fallible and mortal.

2. Inaccurate reporting [44, 111, 139]. In software development, "The employee has
    control of the resource, his time, and he accounts for the resource on his time sheet.
    The employee knows that his time sheet is a performance evaluation factor and is a
    written record. He knows the estimated time for the project serves as a recorded
    budget. This combination of written records makes a pressure device and 'adjusted
    amounts' often result" [216], e.g., to hide problems or embarrassing situations
    [139]. Another explanation was given by Boebert:

    > Programmers are paid to program, not to pay attention to progress. ...
    > Management should not expect to get progress or status information by
    > asking programmers; the typical programmer doesn't know or care, and will
    > usually give whatever answer is needed to end the meeting and get back to
    > programming [44].

3. Optimism [74, 123, 136, 172, 200, 238]. "All programmers are optimists," Brooks
    remarked. They always assume that " 'This time it will surely run' or 'I just found
    the last bug' " [57].

3.6.2 Approaches of Control

The persistence of the industry's difficulties in controlling
software development does not seem to be the result of either a scarcity of advice from the
research community or a reluctance on the industry's part to heed that advice.

Numerous techniques, often adapted from other industries, have been proposed in
the literature. These include: Work Break Structure (WBS) [245], PERT [49], Gantt
Charts [148], Formal Reviews [105], and Unit Development Folder (UDF) [133].

Furthermore, evidence indicates that most of these proposed solutions have been
disseminated throughout the industry, albeit to varying degrees [117]. For example,

Thayer's survey of techniques used in software projects in the aerospace industry is shown in Table 3.6

TABLE 3.6 TECHNIQUES USED IN AEROSPACE INDUSTRY [248]

Technique	% of Projects Using it
Formal Reviews	97 %
WBS	60 %
Automated Project Management System	57 %
PERT	38 %
Gantt	32 %

Thayer further investigated whether the above ''state-of-the-art'' techniques were effective in resolving the control difficulties in the aerospace firms he surveyed. (Note: Thayer [246] and others [158] believe that the aerospace industry is the most advanced and experienced in employing software project management techniques.) His results indicated that they were not.

Lehman's survey of software development projects in the aerospace industry were more surprising:

> ... 17% of the projects had no project control mechanism. And more surprisingly yet, that group fared better than average relative to on-time delivery. ... [158].

A similar finding was reported by Powers and Dickson. In a study of 20 MIS projects, they found that:

> With respect to the project control techniques used for the projects in the study, they tended to be dysfunctional to project success. The use of project control methods was not significantly related to any criterion of success, and, indeed, had a negative relationship to the reported quality of project documentation. ... In general, project leaders appeared to feel an implicit pressure from tight project reporting requirements, to which they responded by cutting corners on documentation and preparations for implementation [209].

So, what is the prognosis on the status of software project control? Bauer put it this way:

> We are able to identify the sources of our troubles, but in many cases we have nothing to offer but good advice. We are in the situation of a physician who keeps trying out different pills on his patient in the hope that some will finally cure him [40].

4

SOURCES OF
INFORMATION

4.1 Information Gathering Steps

To build our model of software project management, we took three information-gathering steps:

Step 1: A series of interviews were conducted with software development project managers in several organizations. Our purpose was to provide a first-hand account of how software projects are currently managed in software development organizations. The information collected in this phase complemented our own software development experience and became the basis for a "skeleton" model.

Step 2: An extensive review of the literature was conducted, part of which was presented in chapter 2. The "skeleton" model served as a useful "road-map" in carrying out this literature review.

> A model should come first. And one of the first uses of the model should be to determine what formal data need to be collected [99].

The review filled in many gaps in our knowledge of software development, giving rise to a more detailed version of the model.

Step 3: Another series of interviews was conducted to refine the model.

> The model is exposed to criticism, revised, exposed again and so on in an iterative process that continues as it proves to be useful. Just as the model is improved as a result of successive exposures to critics a successively better understanding of the problem is achieved by the people who participated in the process [224].

4.2 Step 1: First Set of Interviews

An initial series of 10 interviews were conducted with software project managers at Digital Equipment Corporation (DEC), MITRE, and SofTech.

Our objective was to increase our familiarity with the software development process — in particular, ''the concepts and information on which software project managers are already acting'' — in order to formulate an initial model of the process.

The technique used was the ''focused interview.'' In the focused interview, as described by Selltiz, Wrightsman, and Cook:

> ... the main function of the interviewer is to focus attention on a given (list of topics). Interviewers know in advance what topics, or what aspects of a question, they wish to cover. This list of topics or aspects is derived from a formulation of the research problem. ... This list constitutes a framework of topics to be covered, but the manner in which questions are asked and their timing are left largely to the interviewer's discretion [232].

This type of interview, according to Green and Tull, ''is useful in obtaining a clear understanding of the problem and determining what areas should be investigated (further)'' [122].

Before each interview, two things were done. First the interviewee was briefed, in a telephone conversation, about the objectives of the research. The interviewee was also told that the primary objective of the interview is to find out how software projects are managed in his or her organization. The list of topics shown in Figure 4.1 was read to each. Second, each interviewee was mailed a copy of an internal report describing our project.

Environment:	• Project types, sizes
	• Hardware environment
	• Organizational structure
Software Production:	• Software tools
	• Standards
	• Error rates
	• QA policy
Planning:	• Estimating
	• Effort Distribution
Control:	• Control tools
	• Milestones
	• Reporting frequency
Human Resources:	• Hiring/firing policies
	• Training
	• Turnover
	• Overtime policy

Figure 4.1 Interview topics

Ten interviews were conducted with each interviewee taking, on the average, two hours. The titles of the initial interviewees and their organizations are shown in the first part of Table 4.1.

TABLE 4.1.

Interview #	Title	Organization
	INITIAL INTERVIEWS	
1	Group Leader	MITRE
2	Member of Technical Staff	MITRE
3	Principal Consultant	Softech
4	Project Manager	DEC
5	Project Leader	DEC
6	Project Leader	DEC
7	Project Manager	DEC
8	Project Leader	DEC
9	Lead Designer	SofTech
10	Group Leader	MITRE
	FINAL INTERVIEWS	
11	Mgr. of Planning	DEC
12	Mgr. of Business Systems	MIT
13	(same as 11)	DEC
14	Project Leader	GM
15	Sr. Supervisor	GM
16	Mgr. of Revenue Disbursement	DEC
17	(same as 16)	DEC
18	Systems Manager	DEC
19	(same as 12)	MIT
20	(same as 14)	GM
21	(same as 15)	GM
22	(same as 11)	DEC
23	(same as 11)	DEC
24	(same as 12)	MIT
25	(same as 18)	DEC
26	(same as 15)	GM
27	(same as 18)	DEC

Each of the interviewees was currently managing one or more software development projects, had been a software project manager or leader for at least two years, and had managed at least two completed software projects. Those were the criteria we decided would insure us that the interviewee had a sufficient level of managerial experience and maturity to offer insights into the management of software projects.

As is shown in Table 4.1, three organizations were represented, namely, Digital Equipment Corporation (5 interviewees), MITRE (3 interviewees), and SofTech (2 interviewees). Their software development environments differed considerably. At DEC, all five interviewees were involved in developing software for in-house use (e.g., order administration systems). At MITRE, the projects involved the development of software for the Air Force. At SofTech, the projects involved a wide range of systems developed on contract for client organizations, both private and public.

The outcome of the above exercise was the formulation of an initial model of software project management. The model is discussed in detail elsewhere [9]. This initial model, in addition to serving as a road-map for the succeeding literature reviewing step, was also the "skeleton" for developing a more detailed version. References to these interviews that appear in later chapters will be in the form: (interview number).

4.3 Step 2: Literature Review

Starting the extensive review of the literature using the initial model as a road-map had several important advantages. It was helpful in organizing and integrating the findings. The integrative nature of the model "prompted" us to look into other relevant fields for ideas: for example, Management Control [21, 156], Cybernetics [27], Organizations [152, 227, 259], Project Management [163], and Psychology [132, 157, 240].

In discussing the final model's structure and formulation in later chapters, we will make extensive use of the massive amount of information gathered in this literature review.

4.4 Step 3: Final Set of Interviews

There were two reasons to conduct the second set of interviews. First, there were still unanswered questions that had to be addressed. Second, it helped us to study the more detailed model and, in Roberts' words, to "criticize it, revise it, expose it again and so on in an iterative process that would continue as long as it proves to be useful" [224].

The second set of 17 interviews were conducted with software project managers at Digital Equipment Corporation (DEC), MIT's Administrative Information Systems group (MIT), and General Motors (GM). The model's structural components became a core around which the interviews was constructed. The interviews were thus more structured in terms of content than those in Step 1. However, the interviews were unstructured in the sense that no standardized set of questions was used. Such a format, according to Isaac and Michael, allows the interviewer to adjust the interview so as to take advantage of an interviewee's personal areas of expertise [134].

As in Step 1, before each interview, interviewees were contacted by telephone and briefed on the objectives of the research. Interviewees were mailed copies of "A Model of Software Project Management Dynamics" [9] and "System Dynamics — An Introduction" [224]. It was necessary that this group of interviewees have some understanding of the systems dynamics methodology, since one of our objectives was to have them critique the model. All they really needed was to have a basic understanding of the feedback concept and its representation in causal loop diagrams. In the interviews, we referred only to pieces of the model, and these were always in the form of causal loop diagrams. The diagram on the effects of "schedule pressure" on "productivity" and "error generation," is shown in Figure 4.2.

The second set consisted of seventeen additional interviews. (See the second part of Table 4.1.) None of the interviewees of Step 1 were among those interviewed in Step 3. This had two positive results. First, it provided a larger and more varied pool of experiences and ideas to draw upon, and second, it decreased the possibilities for bias in the interviewees' critiques of the model.

Again, each of the interviewees was currently managing one or more software development projects, had been a software project manager or leader for at least two years, and had managed at least two completed software projects.

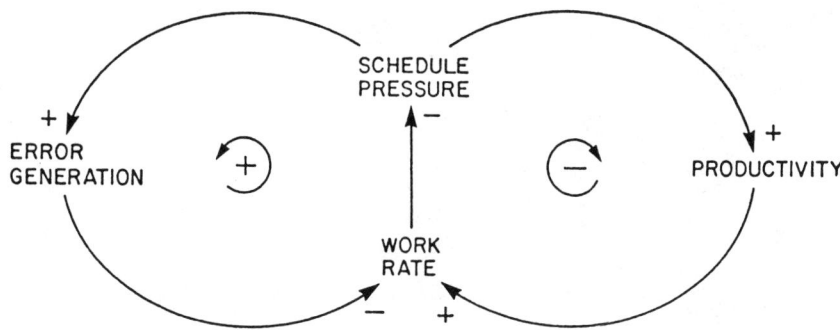

Figure 4.2   Effects of schedule pressure on productivity and error generation

Because the discussions at this stage were at a more detailed level than those of Step 1, more time was needed per interviewee. On average, three two-and-half-hour-long interviews were conducted per interviewee.

This battery of seventeen interviews constituted the third and final information gathering step that led to the formulation of the final model, presented in Part III (chapters 5 through 11).

PART THREE

THE SOFTWARE

DEVELOPMENT

PROCESS

5

HUMAN RESOURCE

MANAGEMENT

Our study of the dynamics of software project management is divided into four major activities: human resource management, software production, controlling, and planning. We turn our attention first to human resource management, which includes hiring, training, assimilation, and transferring a project's human resources.

5.1 Characterizing the Work Force

The model of the Human Resource Management Subsystem that we will be using is depicted in Figure 5.1. As the figure shows, a project's total work force is assumed to consist of two work force levels, namely, "Newly Hired Work Force" and "Experienced Work Force." We divided the work force into these two categories for two reasons.

First, newly hired project members pass through an orientation during which they are less than fully productive [75, 243] (1), (16), and (26).† Orientation has both technical as well as social dimensions. On the technical side,

> ... (newly hired) personnel often require considerable training to become familiar with an organization's unique mix of hardware, software packages, programming techniques, project methodologies and so on [269].

Schein noted that social orientation

> ... refers to the processes of teaching the new recruit how to get along in the organization, what the key norms and rules of conduct are, and how to behave with respect to others in the organization. The new recruit must learn where to be at specified times, what to wear, what to call the boss, whom to consult if he or she has

---

† Remember, a reference citation in the form (i) where "i" is a number between 1 and 27, refers to one of the 27 interviews of Table 4.1.

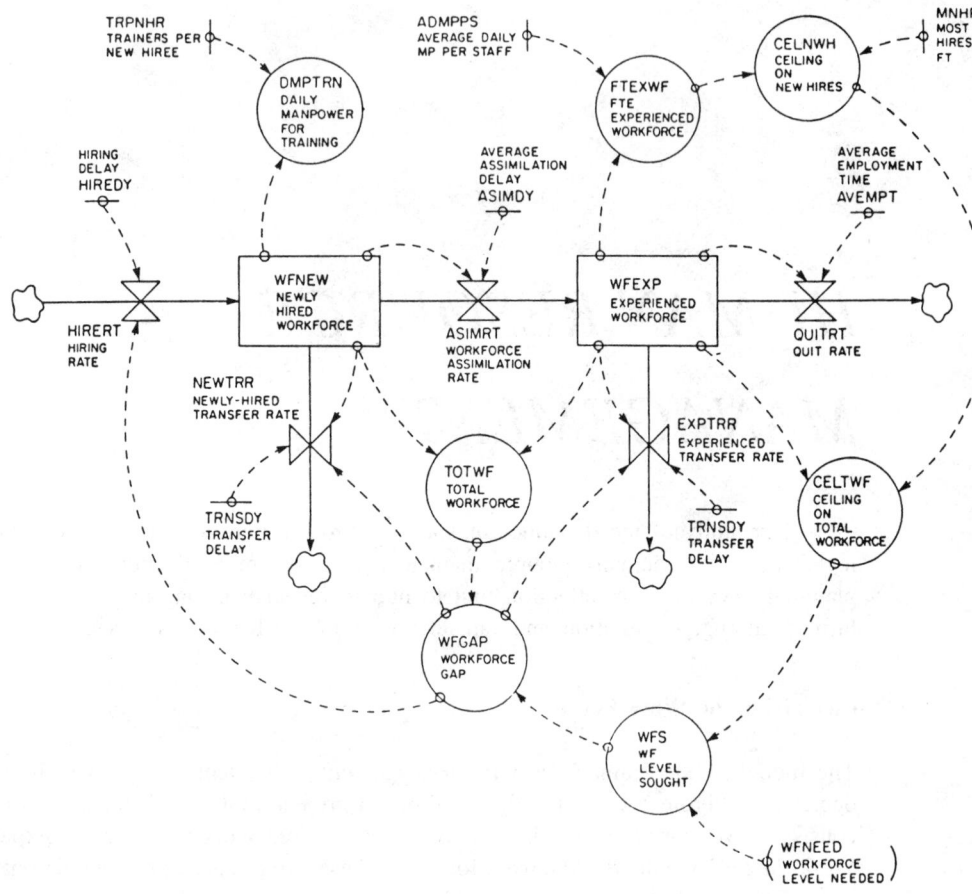

Figure 5.1 Human Resource Management Subsystem

a question, how carefully to do a job, and endless other things which insiders have learned over time [227].

Of course, not all new project members are necessarily recruited from *outside* the organization; some might be recruited from within, e.g., transferred from other projects. For the transferred employee, there will still be a period of orientation [57] to learn the project's ground rules, the goals of the effort, the plan of work, and all the details of the system [113, 251]. Although obviously less costly than the full orientation needed by an out-of-company recruit, orientation can still be a significant drag on productivity, especially when a project lacks adequate documentation [62]. A GRC (1977) report noted that when work force additions are made to ''rescue'' a project that is behind schedule, such a project often suffers also from sparse and outdated documentation [113].

5.2 Productivity Differential and Training Overhead

The important point is that, because of orientation, the ''Newly Hired Work Force'' is, on average, less productive than the ''Experienced Work Force.'' Later, in our discussion on ''Productivity'' within the Software Production Subsystem in chapters 6 through 9, we will take a closer look at this issue to quantify the productivity differential.

5.2.1 Training of Newly Hired Work Force
The productivity differential was the first reason to distinguish between work forces. The second reason was to capture the training overhead involved in adding new members to a software development project. The training of newcomers, both technical and social, is usually carried out by the ''old-timers'' [55, 74, 77] (16). This is costly because ''while (the old-timer) is helping the new employee learn the job, his own productivity on his other work is reduced'' [62].

Determining how much effort to commit to training new employees is generally a result of managerial intuition and organizational custom. There are no proposed formulas in the literature, nor were any found in the organizations interviewed. However, rules-of-thumb ranged from 15% (21) to 25% (18). In the model, the value of the parameter ''Trainers per New Hire''is set at 0.20. That means on the average each new employee consumes in training overhead the equivalent of 20% of an experienced employee's time for the duration of the training or assimilation period.

5.2.2 Assimilation of Newly Hired Work Force
Estimates for the average assimilation period vary between 2 months (16) and 6 months [56, 74]. In the model, the ''Average Assimilation Delay'' is set at 80 days. (Note: ''Days'' in the model represent *working* days. One week is five working days, and one year is 48 working weeks.)

The assimilation delay is formulated in the model as a first-order exponential delay. Such delays are primary building-blocks of system dynamics models, and they are extensively used in ours. In Figure 5.2, we show how a first-order exponential delay looks schematically, how it is formulated mathematically, and how it behaves over time. Thus, if a number $L(0)$ of project members are recruited at time (0), they will be assimilated into the experienced work force pool at a rate similar to the one in Figure 5.2. That is, some will be assimilated quickly — e.g., those recruited from within the company; others will take a much longer time — e.g., new hirees fresh from school. The average new employee will be assimilated at the ''Average Assimilation Delay,'' i.e., in 80 days.

5.3 Determining Work Force Level

In deciding the level of the ''Total Work Force'' (i.e., newly hired plus experienced work force), project management considers many factors. One important factor is the *current* scheduled completion date of the project. As part of the planning function (see chapter 11 for details), management determines the work force level that it believes is necessary to complete, within the scheduled completion time, the project tasks *perceived* to be remaining. In addition, management also assesses the ''stability of the work force.'' Thus, before hiring new project members, management tries to estimate how long new members will be needed. Different firms weigh stability differently. In general, however, the desire for stability and the desire for timeliness change in intensity with the stage of project completion. For example, toward the end of the project there is likely to be

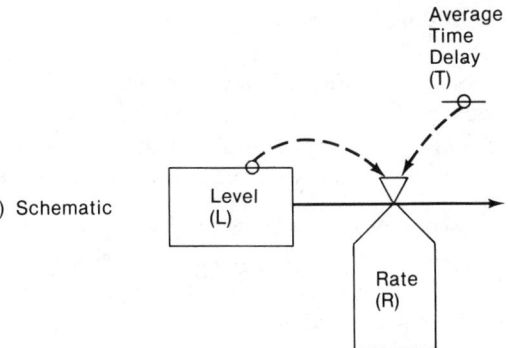

(A) Schematic

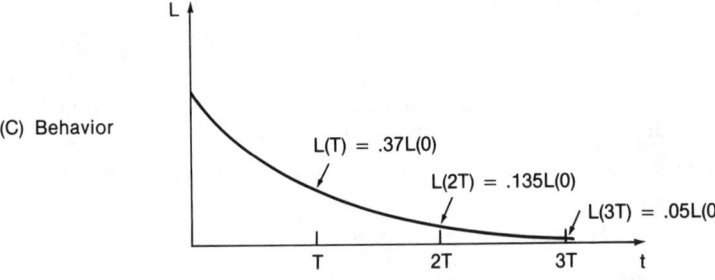

(B) Mathematical
    Information

At any time (t),

$$R(t) = L(t)/T$$

Also,

$$\frac{d}{dt} L(t) = -R(t) = -L(t)/T$$

Separating variables and integrating both sides yields,

$$L(t) = L(0) e^{-t/T}$$

And it can be shown that the average time spent in the delay $= T$

(C) Behavior

$$L(T) = .37L(0)$$

$$L(2T) = .135L(0)$$

$$L(3T) = .05L(0)$$

Figure 5.2   Modeling assimilation delay

reluctance to bring in new people, even though the time and effort perceived to be remaining imply that more people are indeed needed. It would take too much time to acquaint new people with the mechanics of the project, integrate them into the project team, and train them in the necessary technical areas.

5.3.1 Ability to Absorb New People   The "Work Force Level Needed" does not automatically translate into a hiring goal for human resource management. Management must assess the project's *ability to absorb* new people, i.e., train them and make them an part of a productive team [57]. We shall here recognize a policy, formal or more usually implicit, that the rate of hiring of new project members be restricted to the number that project management feels its fully integrated staff can handle (20) (22).

This restriction is formulated in the model using the variable "Ceiling on New Hires," which simply equals the "Full-Time-Equivalent Experienced Work Force" level multiplied by the largest number of new hires that a single full-time experienced staff can be expected to handle effectively. In the model, the value of "Most New Hires per Full-Time Experienced Staff" is set at 3.

In some organizations software developers are assigned to more than one project (i.e., the "Average Daily Manpower per Staff" per project would be less than 1 man-day); thus the "Full-Time-Equivalent Experienced Work Force" level can be less than the "Experienced Work Force" level. So, for example, if there are only 2 experienced project members, each of whom allots 50% of his or her time to the project (i.e., "Average Daily Manpower per Staff" = .5) then we have $0.5 \times 2 = 1$ "Full-Time-Equivalent Experienced Staff." In that case the "Ceiling on New Hires" will be $1 \times 3 = 3$.

The summation of "Ceiling on New Hires" and the value of the current "Experienced Work force" level establish the "Ceiling on Total Work Force." The value of this variable represents the maximum number of employees management wish to hire. That is, "Work Force Level Sought" would be set to the value of "Work Force Level Needed" as long as this is less than or equal to the "Ceiling on Total Work Force." Otherwise, "Work Force Level Sought" is set to the value of the "Ceiling."

5.3.2 Time for Work Force Adjustment   Thus, the three factors: schedule completion time, work force stability, and training requirements, all affect management's determination of the "Work Force Level Sought." Once the determination is made, management will face one of three situations. First, the "Work Force Gap" between the "Work force Level Sought" and the current "Total Work Force Level" could be zero if the two levels are exactly equal. In that case no further action is necessary.

Second, and more likely, the "Work Force Level Sought" is larger than the current "Total Work Force Level." In this case, new employees will be hired. This, of course, takes time. The delay in hiring software professionals, is often several months [174]. Usually, some recruits are available in a short period from elsewhere in the organization, whereas others (especially when the project management is seeking special skills, or new college recruits) will not be available for a much longer time. Averaging the estimates of these variables, we set the "Hiring Delay" at 40 days [174] (9) (26).

The third and final possibility is for the "Work Force Level Sought" to be less than the current "Total Work Force Level." In this case, project members will be transferred out of the project. We will assume that if there are new recruits still in training in the "Newly Hired Work Force" level, then these will be the first to be transferred out. If still more transfers are needed, they would then be made from the "Experienced Work Force" pool.

Those who are being transferred require some period of time for paper work and transfer arrangements before they actually leave the project. The average transfer delay is set in the model at 10 days (22).

5.3.3 Turnover Finally, there is the effect of turnover on the project's work force. Turnover continues of course to be a chronic problem for software project managers. Willoughby estimates that annual turnover in the DP field ranged between 15 and 20% during the 1960s, declined to about 5% in the early 1970s, and began to rise again by the end of the decade [268]. More recent studies place the annual turnover rate at 25.1% [243], 30% [222], and even as high as 34% [55].

Turnover is captured in the model, through the "Quit Rate" of "*Experienced* Work Force." That is, we are assuming no turnover among the "Newly Hired Work Force," since it is unlikely for a new recruit to quit within 80 days of joining the project (i.e., during the assimilation period).

The annual turnover rate is set in the model at 30%. The "Quit Rate" of Figure 5.1 is a first-order exponential decay, as was the "Work Force Assimilation Rate." Using the equation of Figure 5.2, we can calculate the average employment time:

$$L(t) = L(0) \times e^{-1/T} \tag{5.1}$$

where,

$$L = Experienced\ WorkForce\ (men)$$

$$t = time\ (years)$$

$$T = Average\ Employment\ Time\ (years)$$

For a 30% annual turnover rate,

$$0.70L(0) = L(0) \times e^{-1/T} \tag{5.2}$$

Thus,

$$T = \frac{-1}{ln(0.70)} = 2.8\ years \tag{5.3}$$

Which translates into 673 working days, since it is assumed that one year is 240 working days.

6

SOFTWARE PRODUCTION

6.1 Software Production Sectors

Software production is the major activity of a software development project. In our model there are four primary activities in the Software Production Subsystem: development, quality assurance, rework, and system testing. The development activity includes both the design and coding of the software. As the software is being developed, it is also reviewed using, for example, structured walk-throughs to detect any design/coding errors. Errors detected through such quality assurance (QA) activities are then reworked. Not all errors will be detected during the development phase; however, some will "escape" and remain undetected until the testing phase.

This subsystem is too complex to explain as one piece. We break it into four sectors:

1. Manpower Allocation

2. Software Development

3. Quality Assurance & Rework

4. System Testing

These sectors will be connected, not only through information variables, but also through flows; for example, software will flow from the "Software Development" sector to the "QA & Rework" sector and from there to the "System Testing" sector. To diagram such inter-sector flows, we use a new symbol, a "sector symbol." The symbol was proposed by Morecroft [186], and is shown in Figure 6.1.

The shape of the symbol has been selected to avoid ambiguity or overlap with the standard system dynamics symbols. Figure 6.2 shows an example of how the symbol is used to depict the flow of software into and out of the "QA & Rework" sector [186].

6.2 Manpower Allocation Sector

The "Total Daily Manpower" available for the project is simply a function of the "Total Workforce" level and the "Average Daily Manpower per Staff." In some organizations,

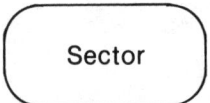

Figure 6.1   Sector symbol

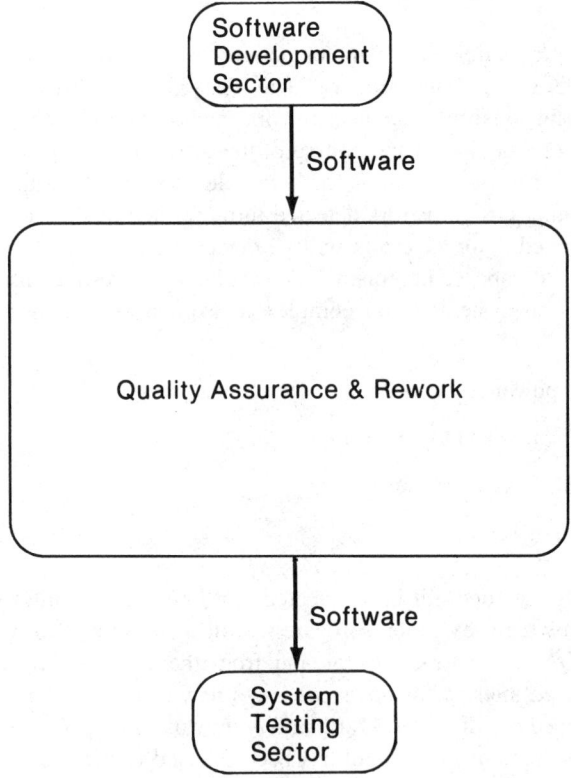

Figure 6.2   Software flow using sector symbols

software professionals are assigned to one project at a time. In such a case the "Average Daily Manpower per Staff" would be one Man-Day since each staff member contributes one man-day every day on the project. In other organizations, however, software professionals are assigned to more than one project. So, for example, if on the average each staff member is assigned to two projects on a 50-50 basis, then the "Average Daily Manpower per Staff," for *each* of the projects, would be 1/2 man-day.

Part of the available manpower will be consumed in training, as explained in Chapter 5. The "Daily Manpower Available *after* Training Overhead" is what is then allocated to quality assurance, rework, software development and testing.

6.2.1 Manpower Allocation for Quality Assurance   Quality assurance is defined in Pressman as a set of activities

> ...   performed in conjunction with (the development of) a software product to guarantee the product meets the specified standards. These activities reduce doubts and risks about the performance of the product in the target environment [210].

Several techniques are used including walk-throughs, reviews, inspections, code reading (a process where code logic and code format are scrutinized by a programmer other than the original designer), and integration-testing [78, 141]. Not included in this activity is unit or module testing, which is commonly considered to be part of the coding process [172].

There is a lack of data in the literature on quality assurance expenditures. There are instead estimates; for example 6% of development effort [146], and 15-20% of development effort [49]. Within the organizations interviewed, *estimates* for the QA effort included 10% (27), 15% (22), and in one case as high as 25% (26).

In the model, the "*Planned* Fraction of Manpower for QA" will be set at a uniform 15% level. Notice that in the manpower allocation sector model, depicted in Figure 6.3, the variable "Planned Fraction of Manpower for QA" is shown as a function of "the percentage of job worked." This will allow us to experiment later with other QA policies in which the QA effort is *not* uniformly distributed throughout the life cycle.

6.2.2 Impact of Schedule Pressure on Manpower Allocation for Quality Assurance
As indicated in Figure 6.3, the "*Actual* Fraction of Manpower for QA" can be different from the "*Planned* Fraction of Manpower for QA" because of schedule pressures. Several authors have observed that as schedule pressures mount, quality assurance activities are often relaxed [115, 236]. For example, Glass notes:

> Modules and changes were initially inspected in depth but with less severity as work pressure increased and greater risks were taken to meet delivery schedules [117].

Walk-throughs and inspections are usually the greatest casualties. Under schedule pressures, they are not only relaxed but often suspended altogether [94]. Hart provides an explanation:

> As the project progressed, there were the usual pressures to meet the project deadline. The walk-throughs were a natural area of concern in the schedule, since they represented a significant time commitment before their effectiveness was obviously demonstrated... .

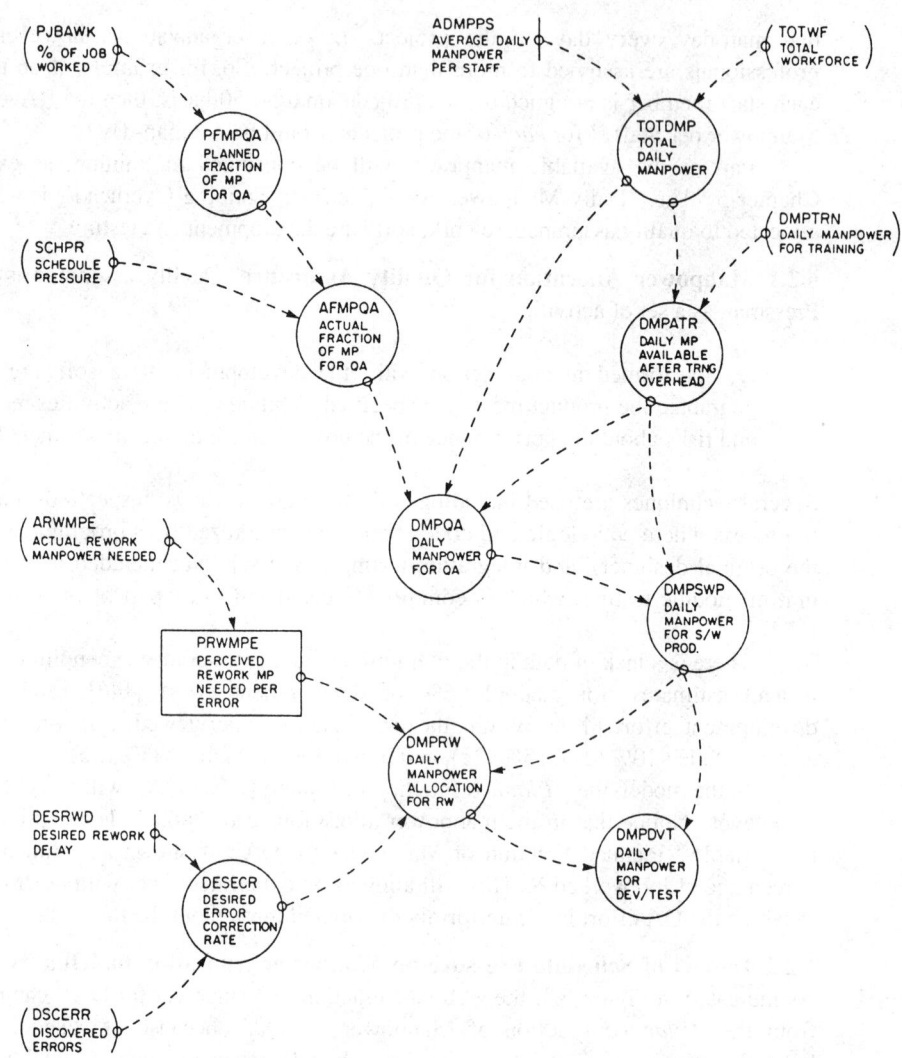

Figure 6.3 Manpower allocation sector

As the deadline neared, there were pressures to hurry the walk-through and, eventually, to 'temporarily suspend' them [125].

In the model, the "schedule pressure" variable SCHPR is formulated as follows:

$$Schedule\ Pressure = (TMDPSN-MDRM)/MDRM \tag{6.1}$$

where

>   TMDPS = Total Man Days Perceived to be Still Needed to complete
>   the project

and

MDRM = Total Man Days Remaining in current plan.

Thus, when the project is perceived as being completely on target and the effort still needed is exactly equal to the effort actually remaining in the project's budget, schedule pressure will be zero. But if the effort perceived still needed is 150 man-days, while the project's budget has only 100 man-days left, then schedule pressure is 0.5. Conversely, if perceived need is *less* than what is remaining, then schedule pressure will be less than zero, i.e., there is a slack.

The effect of schedule pressure on "Actual Fraction of Manpower for QA" is assumed to be as shown in Figure 6.4. To model such a nonlinear relationship between two variables in a system dynamics model requires a "table function."

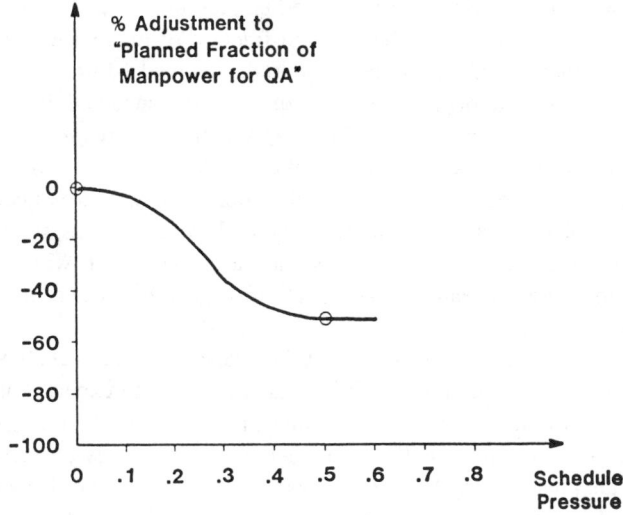

Figure 6.4 Effect of schedule pressure on QA manpower

A table function would be based on measurements, if such measurements are available. In many cases (including this one), however, measurements are not available since there are no published data on the effect of schedule pressure on the QA effort.

> There seems to be a general misunderstanding to the effect that a mathematical model cannot be undertaken until every constant and functional relationship is known to high accuracy. This often leads to the omission of admittedly highly significant factors (most of the 'intangible' influences on decisions) because these are unmeasured or unmeasurable. To omit such variables is equivalent to saying they have zero effect ...   probably the only value that is known to be wrong ... .
> A mathematical model should be based on the best information that is readily available, but the design of a model should not be postponed until all pertinent

parameters have been accurately measured. That day will never come. Values
should be estimated where necessary. . . . [99]

Because of the lack of published measurements, it was necessary to *estimate* the
relationship between schedule pressure and the QA effort. To give a flavor of how both
judgment and available information are used to formulate a table function, the formulation
of Figure 6.4 will be discussed in some detail.

    There are three potential considerations in formulating a table function: slope, one
or more specific points, and shape.

    The slope of the relationship between schedule pressure and adjustments to QA
effort is easy to determine. It must be negative, since, as schedule pressure increases, QA
effort decreases.

    At least one point on the graph can be identified straight forwardly. It is the point
(0,0) since in the absence of any schedule pressure (i.e., "Schedule Pressure" is zero), the
percentage adjustment to the planned fraction of manpower effort for QA will be zero;
that is, actual QA effort will be equal to the planned effort.

    As schedule pressure mounts, quality assurance activities are relaxed; i.e., cuts are
made into the *planned* QA effort. QA activities are *not* eliminated completely. For
example while walk-throughs might be decreased or even temporarily suspended,
integration testing might not. In the judgment of the project managers interviewed,
planned quality assurance activities could be cut by as much as 50% under severe
schedule pressures, which were defined as situations in which "Schedule Pressure" is
equal to or greater than 0.5 (4) (9) (25) (26). On the basis of their judgments, we identify
the point (.5, -50) of Figure 6.4.

    The final step is to figure out the shape of the negatively sloping curve connecting
the two points (0,0) and (.5, -50). It is reasonable to expect that the curve flattens out at
the two extreme points. As schedule pressure starts to rise, people react not only by
cutting corners but also by working harder [49]. This absorbs some of the effects of
schedule pressure on QA effort allocations at the vicinity of point (0,0). Additionally, as
schedule pressure increases, it gradually reaches a saturation point at which it ceases to
affect *further* adjustments to the QA effort and the curve flattens at (.5, -50). Finally,
these two extreme flat parts of the curve are connected by a negatively sloping *smooth*
curve: "Any sharply bent or kinked curve is probably not realistic. A bend or kink
implies something special about the exact conditions at which the bend or kink occurs"
[120].

6.2.3 Manpower Allocation for Rework So far we have accounted for manpower
resources consumed in training and quality assurance activities. The remaining bulk of
the manpower resource, labelled in Figure 6.3 as the "Daily Manpower for Software
Production," is to be allocated to software development (i.e., design and coding), testing,
and rework.

    As software errors are detected through the quality assurance activities, manpower
effort is allocated to correct them. The amount of *daily* effort allocated is a function of
both the "Desired Error Correction Rate" (the daily rate at which these discovered errors
are to be corrected) and the "Perceived Rework Manpower Needed per Error." In other
words, the effort is allocated based on the rework job to be done, and the perceived
rework productivity.

The "Perceived Rework Manpower Needed per Error" is diagrammed in Figure 6.3 as a special kind of level, one with an input that is *not* a rate. This is a "shorthand notation" for an exponential smoothing operation. That is, "*Perceived* Rework Manpower Needed per Error" is the "exponential smooth" of its input, the "*Actual* Rework Manpower Needed per Error." (Because smoothing or averaging of information accumulates that information, a smoothed variable is represented by a level's rectangular symbol.)

Why smooth? Because, "Full and immediate action is seldom taken on a change of incoming information (e.g., on the sudden drop in yesterday's rework productivity). ... (There is a) tendency to delay action until the change is insistent. ... " [99].

A full schematic representation of the smoothing operation is shown in Figure 6.5 together with its mathematical formulation. (Readers familiar with smoothing formulations may want to observe that the equation for a smoothed variable can be written in the familiar weighted-average form for exponential smoothing.) Figure 6.5 also shows the behavior of the "smoothed variable" in response to a spike in the "variable to be smoothed." Thus, a sudden increase, for example, in the "*Actual* Rework Manpower Needed per Error," will not initially affect the project member's rework-manpower allocation decisions. If, however, the increase persists over a period of time, the change will be perceived as permanent (i.e., "*Perceived* Rework Manpower Needed per Error" catches up with the actual) and thus incorporated in the allocation decision making process. The smoothing time is set in the model at 10 days.

The amount of daily effort allocated for rework activities is a function of not only the "Perceived Rework Manpower Needed per Error" but also the "Desired Error Correction Rate," which is the daily rate at which discovered errors are to be corrected. For example, if it is desired to correct one error a day and it is perceived that one Man-Day is needed on average to correct an error, then one Man-day will be allocated daily for rework activities.

The "Desired Error Correction Rate" is the value of the total number of discovered errors divided by a "Desired Rework Delay." When an error is detected usually, it is *not* immediately corrected. Some time elapses before a software professional "deals" with it. In a TRW study this delay was found to be between 8-19 days [247]. The "Desired Rework Delay" is set in the model at 15 days (1) (16).

Figure 6.3 shows that after manpower is allocated to rework activities, the remaining (often larger) portion of the "Daily Manpower for Software Production" is devoted to development (i.e., design and coding) and testing activities, which are discussed in detail in Chapters 7 and 9 respectively.

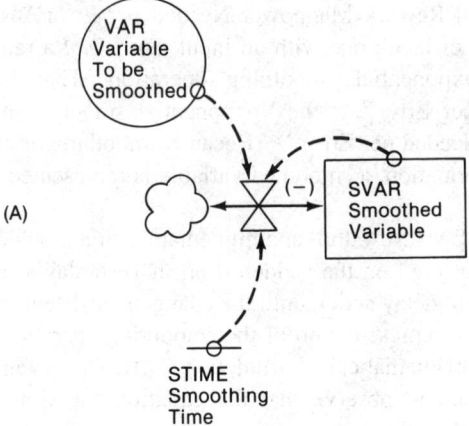

(A)

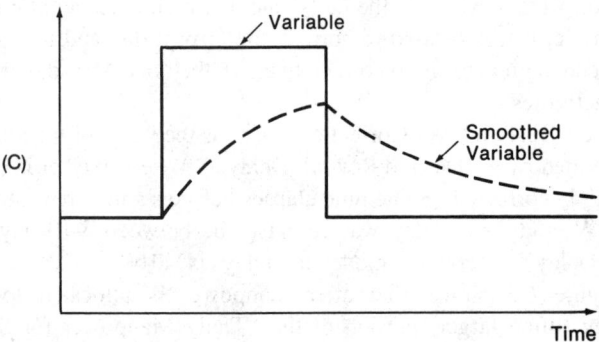

(B) $SVAR_T = SVAR_{T-1} + \dfrac{\Delta T}{STIME}(VAR_{T-1} - SVAR_{T-1})$

(C)

Figure 6.5 Modeling smoothing operation

7

SOFTWARE DEVELOPMENT

7.1 Software Development Sector

The software development process consists of the design and coding of the software product. A software project is defined as a number of "Tasks." Thus, the software development rate is a function of "Tasks per day," software developed of "Tasks" developed, and software development productivity of "Tasks per man-day." (A precise definition of a "Task" will be provided shortly, when nominal productivity is discussed.) The model of the software development sector is shown in Figure 7.1.

As indicated earlier, after manpower allocations are made for training, quality assurance, and rework activities, the remaining bulk of the available manpower resource is allocated to the development of the software product. This allocation continues until it is perceived that most of the software development tasks are completed, at which point the System Testing phase begins and manpower is allocated to testing. The switch in manpower allocation is quantified in the model through the variable "Fraction of Effort for System Testing." The value of "Fraction of Effort for System Testing" is initially set at zero. When all development tasks are perceived to be completed, the value of the "Fraction of Effort for System Testing" becomes a 1, that is, 100% of the effort available for software development and testing is used in system testing activities. The switch is not abrupt, however. There is usually some overlap between the development and testing phases [78, 126, 252]. For example, the design of test cases usually begins towards (not at) the end of the software development phase [18]. The overlap of the phases is captured in Figure 7.2. It shows the assumed gradual increase in the value of the "Fraction of Effort for System Testing" as the fraction of development tasks perceived remaining decreases.

7.2 Software Development Productivity

During the software development phase, the *rate* at which the software is developed is a function not only of how much manpower is used, but also of how productive the software developers are (as is shown in Figure 7.1).

"Software Development Productivity" is a function of a complex set of factors. Our formulation of the productivity of the software development group is based on a

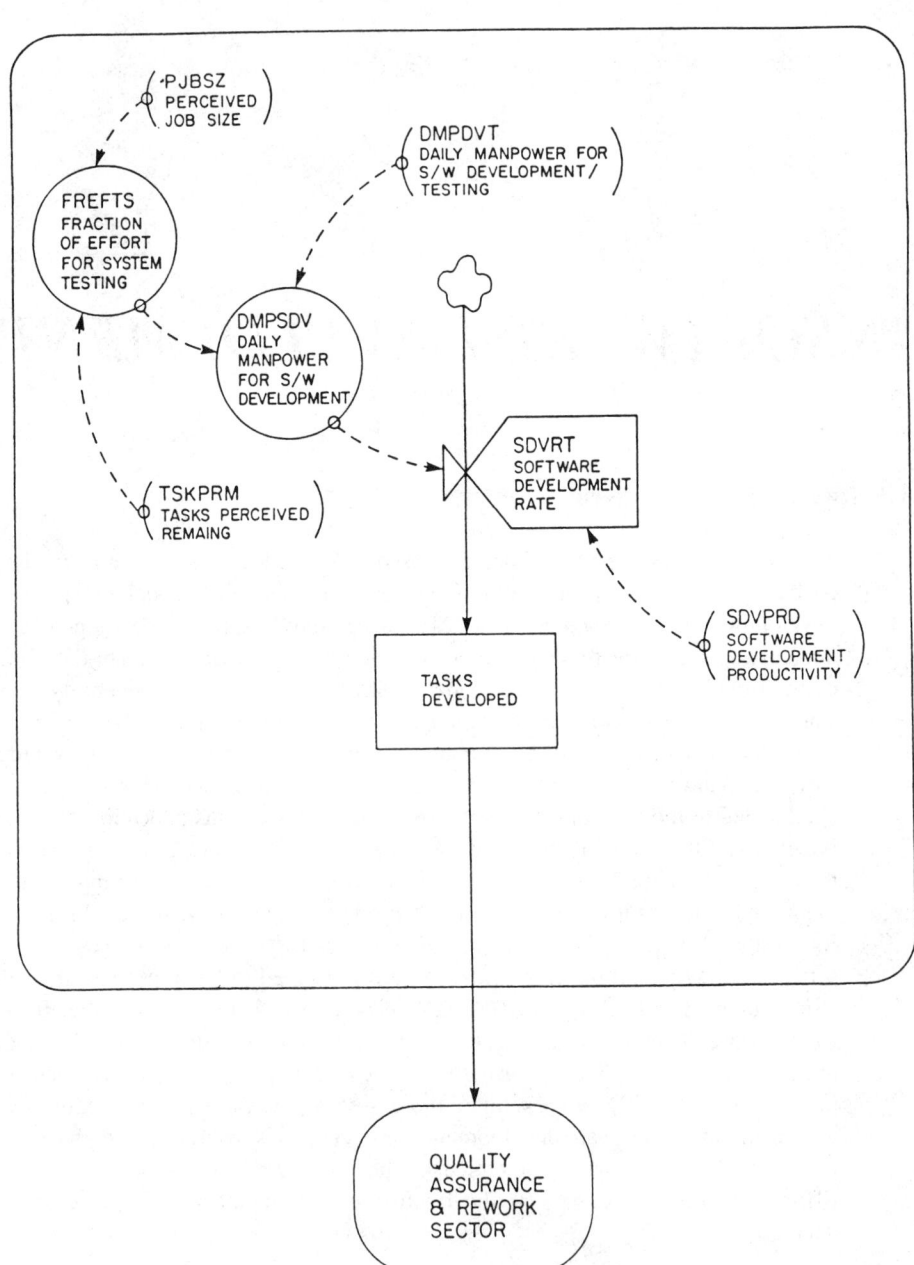

Figure 7.1 Software development sector

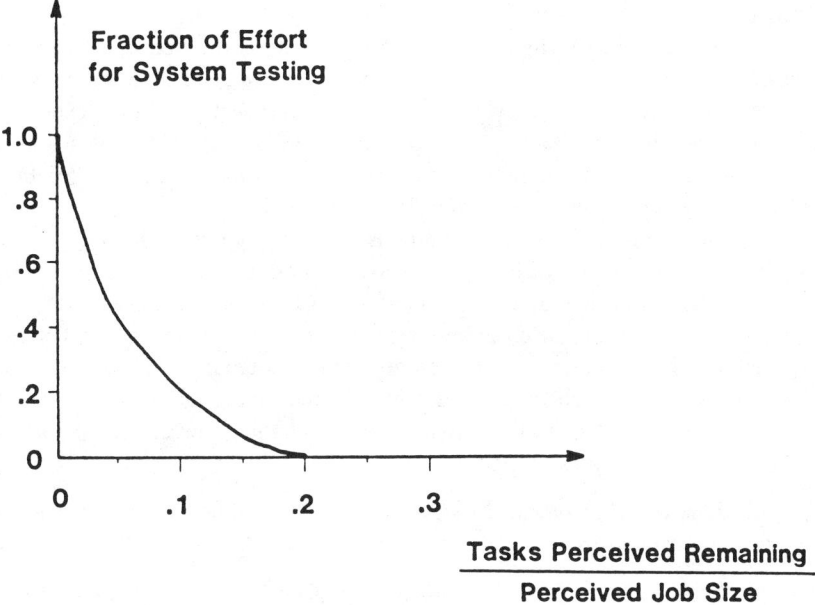

Figure 7.2 Fraction of effort for system testing

psychological model of group productivity proposed by Ivan Steiner [240]. The model can be stated as follows:

$$Actual\ Productivity = Potential\ Productivity$$
$$- Losses\ Due\ to\ Faulty\ Process \qquad (7.1)$$

Where losses due to faulty process refer basically to communication and motivation losses:

> Potential productivity is defined as the maximum level of productivity that can occur when an individual or group employs its funds of resources to meet the task demands of a work situation. It is the level of productivity that will be attained if the individual or group makes the best possible use of its resources (that is, if there is no loss of productivity due to faulty process). Potential Productivity can be inferred from a thorough analysis of task demands and available resources, for it depends only on these two types of variables. Actual productivity, what the individual or group does accomplish, rarely equals potential productivity. Individuals and groups usually fail to make the best possible use of their available resources. Problems of coordination and/or motivation are responsible for inadequacies in process and for consequent losses in productivity [240].

The three pieces of Steiner's model — namely, actual productivity, potential productivity, and communication/motivation losses — are all incorporated in the formulation of the software development productivity subsystem shown in Figure 7.3. Their structures fall in the middle part, the left part, and the right and bottom parts of the figure.

According to Steiner, potential productivity is a function of two determinants, the nature of the task and the group's resources. The effects of these two factors on the productivity of software development have been investigated in the software engineering literature. However, actual and potential productivity are not distinguished in the software engineering literature. In all such studies the dependent variable is always the *actual* productivity of software development.

For example, Scott and Simmons used the Delphi technique "to determine what programming project variables have the greatest impact on programmer productivity" [230]. They identified three "resource-type" variables — the availability of programming tools, the availability of programming practices, and programmer experience — and two "task-type" variables — the programming language and the quality of external documentation — as having significant influence on productivity.

Boehm's COCOMO software cost estimation model incorporates the following determinants of productivity:

1. *Task-type Variables:* Product complexity, required reliability, memory constraint, and database size.

2. *Resource-type Variables:* Software tools available, turnaround time, and personnel experience [49].

Finally, Chrysler mapped several research findings into a model that categorizes the determinants of software productivity into six categories. Three of the categories were of task factors: "Programming Problem Characteristics," "Source Language," and "Computer Hardware Characteristics." The other three categories were resource factors: "Programmer Characteristics," "Organizational Characteristics," and "Programming Mode." [64]

While most of the above factors would vary from organization to organization (e.g., availability of software tools, personnel capability, and computer-hardware characteristics) and from project to project within a single organization (e.g., programming language, database size, and product complexity), they would remain constant within a single project. From our viewpoint, this observation is significant. It means that in a *single* software development project, most of the above variables would remain constant and can therefore be captured by a single constant parameter in the model. Such a parameter would need adjustments only when modeling different projects and/or different organizations. Since our concern is with the *dynamics* of software development, we must look further to identify additional factors.

7.3 Potential Productivity

7.3.1 Nominal Potential Productivity
The "Nominal Potential Productivity" parameter represents the maximum level of software development productivity that can occur when an individual employs the available resources to perform the tasks for a specific project within a specific organization.

The "Nominal Potential Productivity" parameter is defined in terms of a number of "Tasks/man-day" which means that its value depends on how "Task" is defined. We can define "Task" as a constant against which the value of "Nominal Potential

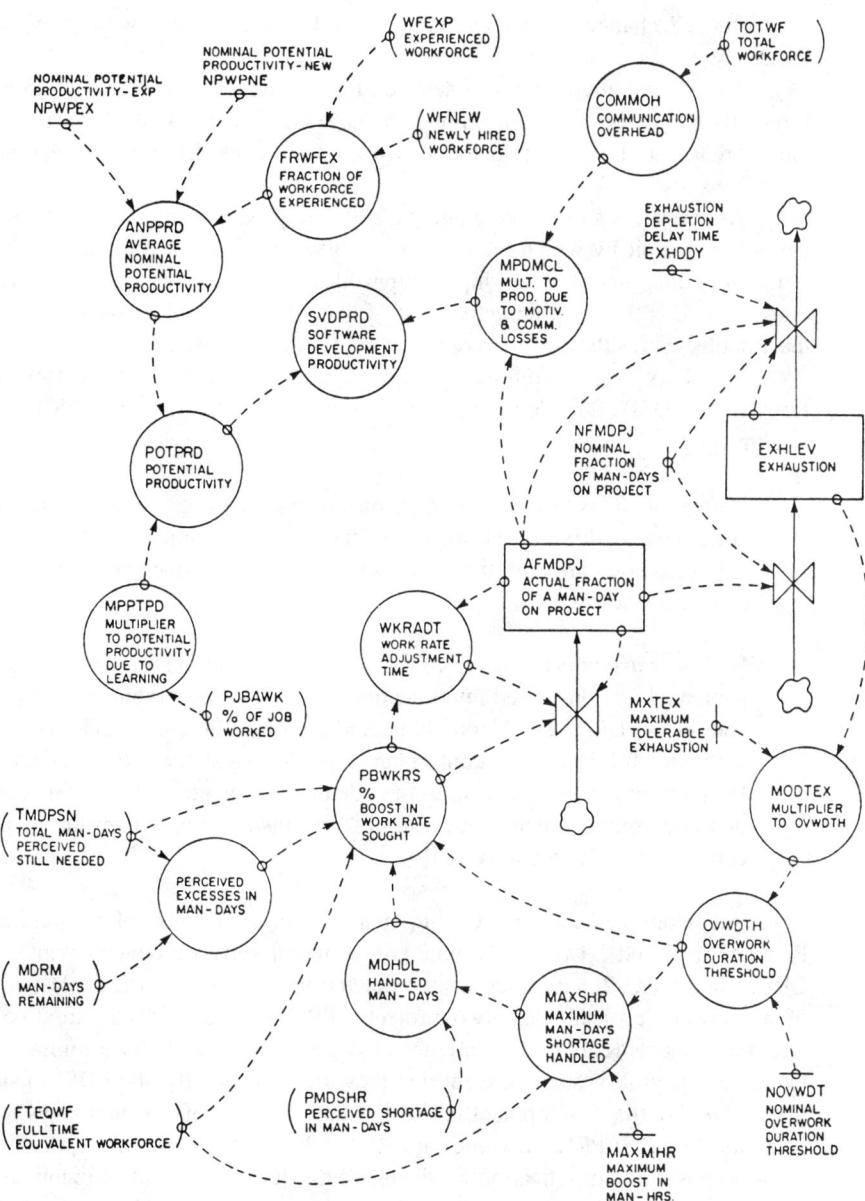

Figure 7.3 Software development productivity subsector

Productivity'' changes, or we can define "Task" as a variable with "Nominal Potential Productivity" as a constant.

The second alternative was selected for our model. We *define* "Nominal Potential Productivity" to be a certain number of tasks/man-day; "Task" is a parameter in the model that can be set at different values to reflect different project and resource characteristics.

A "Task" is a unit for sizing up a software product. In principle, a "Task" can be any arbitrary unit by which we measure a software project's size, such as lines of code, function-points, modules, and input/output files. From a practical point of view, though, lines of code is the most attractive unit. Lines of code provides us with direct access to most published results on software productivity measurements.

A "Task" is, therefore, defined in terms of a number of Delivered Source Instructions (DSI). The definition of Delivered Source Instructions (DSI) is provided by Boehm:

> *Delivered.* This term is generally meant to exclude nondelivered support software such as test drivers. However, if these are developed with the same care as delivered software with their own review, test plans, documentation, etc., then they should be included.

> *Source Instructions.* This term includes all program instructions created by project personnel and processed into machine code by some combination of preprocessors, compilers, and assemblers. It excludes comment cards and unmodified utility software. It includes job control language, format statements, and data declarations. Instructions are defined as lines of code or card images. Thus, a line containing two or more source statements counts as one instruction; a five-line data declaration counts as five instructions. [49]

An example should help to clarify the concepts of "Nominal Potential Productivity" and "Task." Assume two different software development organizations, ORG-1 and ORG-2, have each just completed the development (i.e., design and coding) of a software project. The two projects, PROJ-1 and PROJ-2, are two completely different projects (e.g., one is an embedded piece of software for a military satellite and the other a payroll system), except that they are both exactly 8000 DSI in size. Assume that in ORG-1 the development effort consumed a total of 400 man-days to design and code the 8000 DSI PROJ-1, while for PROJ-2 the development effort was 200 man-days. If for purposes of simplification we disregard the communication and motivation losses in both organizations, i.e., assume that actual productivity = potential productivity, we could then conclude that the potential productivity in ORG-1 is half that of ORG-2. This distinction would be realized in the model as follows: The "Nominal Potential Productivity" parameter would be defined in both runs of the model at the same value, say, 1 Task/Man-day, but in the PROJ-1 run we would define a "Task" to be 20 DSI, while in the PROJ-2 run a "Task" would be set at 40 DSI. That is, the 8000 DSI project PROJ-1 will be defined as a 400 Task project, while the 8000 DSI project PROJ-2 would be defined as a 200 Task project.

7.3.2 Impact on Potential Productivity Due to Experience and Learning We have thus far addressed only one set of factors that affect the potential productivity of a software development project, namely, those factors that remain constant throughout a particular project. While most of the factors listed in the literature are constants, at least two are not: work force experience level [64] and increases in project familiarity due to learning-curve effects [76, 77, 261].

To integrate the effect of experience in the model, we used two nominal potential productivity parameters, one to represent the nominal potential productivity of the average experienced staff member and the other to represent that of the average newly hired employee. At any time in the project the "Average Nominal Potential Productivity" for the work force as a whole is the weighted average of the two parameters (in which each parameter is weighted by the fraction of its corresponding employee-type in the total work force). Thus, while the two nominal potential productivity parameters for the two types of employees remain constant throughout a project, the project's "Average Nominal Potential Productivity" may not, since the mix of experienced and new employees could (and probably would) change.

We take the nominal potential productivity of an average *experienced* staff member to be our reference point and define it to have a value of 1 Task/Man-day. The value of the nominal potential productivity of the average employee within the newly-hired work force pool is then determined relative to that 1 Task/Man-day reference point. In the literature, estimates for the productivity of a newly hired staff member relative to that of an experienced staff member included 0.45 [266], 0.5 [199], 0.6 [254], and 0.64 [43, 49]. Estimates provided from interviews ranged from 0.33 (26) to 0.5 (16). It should be noted, however, that all the estimates are for *actual* productivities and not potential productivities. But since there is no evidence that there are significant differences in the communication and motivation losses between the two groups of employees, we consider the estimates a "reasonable" approximation for the ratio between the *potential* productivities of the two groups. The value of the nominal potential productivity for the average newly hired employee is accordingly set in the model to 0.5 Task/Man-day.

The second factor affecting potential productivity is the increased project know-how due to the learning-curve effect [76, 234, 261]. "As a project proceeds, the implementers learn their job better. The 'learning curve' is the rate of improvement" [23]. Several authors have suggested that an S-shaped learning-curve characterizes "rate of improvement" in the software development environment [76, 261]. Reflecting on his experience at IBM, Aron estimates that the total improvement for a medium-sized project (e.g., 12-24 months long) would be a 25% improvement in productivity [23].

In the model the learning curve effect is formulated as the variable "Multiplier to Potential Productivity Due to Learning." As Figure 7.4 shows, it is S-shaped and a function of progress in the project, starting with a value of 1 at the beginning of the project, and peaking at a value 25% higher (i.e., at 1.25) towards the end of the development period.

7.4 Actual Productivity

Potential productivity is the level of productivity that will be attained if the individual or group makes the best possible use of the available resources. However, due to losses caused by communication and motivation problems, actual productivity — what the

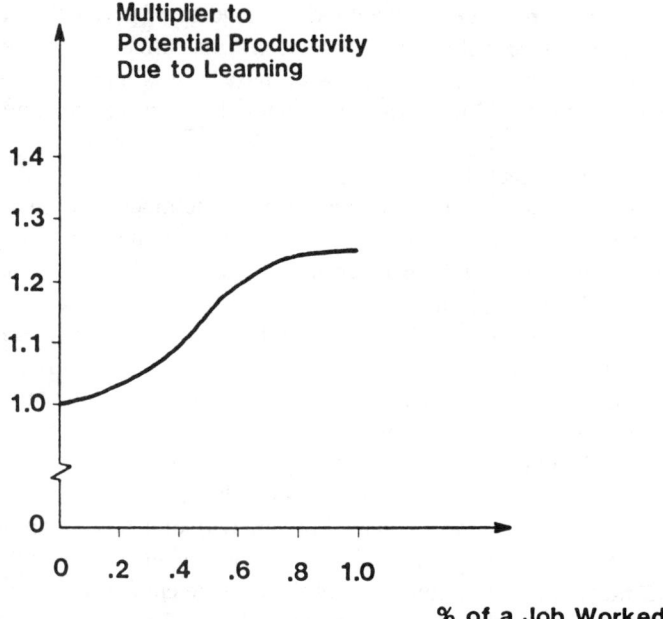

Figure 7.4 Multiplier to potential productivity due to learning

individual or group does in fact accomplish — rarely equals potential productivity [240].

"Software Development Productivity" is a product of "Potential Productivity" and the "Multiplier to Productivity Due to Communication and Motivation Losses." In the absence of any communication and motivation losses, the multiplier assumes a value of 1; actual productivity is thus equal to potential productivity. However, losses will occur, and these will drive the multiplier to values that are less than 1, thus depressing the value of actual productivity to levels below that of potential productivity.

The "Multiplier to Productivity Due to Communication and Motivation Losses" has the following interpretation. It represents the average *productive* fraction of a Man-Day. In other words, if the nominal man-day for a full-time employee is 8 hours, his or her daily contribution to the project will be less than 8 man hours because of communication and motivation losses. For example, if, on average, the communication and motivation losses amount to a 4 man-hour loss per day, then the value of the multiplier would be a 0.5.

The effects of communication and motivation are multiplicative. Motivation factors first determine the fraction of a man-day devoted to *project* work. The fraction usually has a value less than 1, since time is often lost on reading mail, coffee-breaks, personal matters, and other miscellaneous non-project related activities. Communication losses refer to project-type communication losses, and are thus formulated as a fraction of the "project hours" devoted to *project* work, hence the multiplicative formulation of the two components of productivity loss. The detailed formulation of the effects of both communication and motivation losses on productivity are shown in Figure 7.3.

7.5 Impact on Actual Productivity Due to Motivation

A distinction must be made between factors that remain constant during a *single* project and those that change throughout the life of the single project. The review of the literature on motivation in chapter 3 indicates that most motivational factors — e.g., possibility for growth, advancement, responsibility, salary, company policy and administration — tend to characterize the overall organizational setting and climate. Such invariant factors would therefore be "implicitly" incorporated within the definition of the potential productivity parameters.

It has been suggested that project goals and schedules can play a significant motivational role throughout the life of a software development project. "Another motivation approach which is particularly appropriate to the data processing area is goal setting" [35].

Boehm went a step further and provided the means to "operationalize" this idea [48]. He suggests that the motivational role of schedule pressures and project deadlines is to expand or contract the project members' "slack time." Slack time is the fraction of project time *lost* on non-project activities, e.g., coffee-breaks, personal business.

7.5.1 Slack Time The motivation mechanism in the model is designed to capture the motivational impact of schedule pressures on "slack time." That is why motivation losses are formulated in terms of *man-hour* losses.

In the absence of schedule pressures, which can be either positive (i.e., when the project is perceived to be behind schedule) or negative (i.e., when the project is perceived to be ahead of schedule), the fraction of daily hours allocated to project-related work by the average full-time team member is defined by the parameter "Nominal Fraction of a man-day on Project." In designating a value for this parameter, we were able to draw on the experiences of our interviewees as well as on those of many authors. Most of the estimates were clustered within the 50-70% range, e.g., 50% [57] (25), 50-60% [112, 208], 60% [39], and 70% [49]. In addition, in a study based on over 7000 observations of a group of production programmers, Stalnaker reported that 35% of the time was lost on "personal activities," "being away or out," and other "miscellaneous" non-project related activities [239]. In the remaining 65% of available working time, there were further losses spent on mail, non-project related company business, and so on.

Consequently, we set the value of the parameter "Nominal Fraction of a Man-Day on Project" at 60%. This means that in the absence of schedule pressures, a full-time employee would allocate, on the average, $0.6 \times 8 = 4.8$ hours to the project (assuming an 8-hour day). Under these *nominal* conditions, therefore, the "contribution" of motivation losses to the "Multiplier to Productivity Due to Motivation and Communication Losses" amounts to a 40% cut in potential productivity.

The loss in productivity due to motivational factors does not, of course, remain constant at the 40% level throughout the life of the project. The motivational effects of schedule pressures can push the "*Actual* Fraction of a Man-Day on Project" to higher (under positive schedule pressure) or lower (under negative schedule pressure) values.

As shown in Figure 7.3, the "Actual Fraction of a Man-Day on Project" in the model is a level variable. Its value is set, at the initiation of the project, at the value of "Nominal Fraction of a Man-Day on Project," i.e., at 60%. It maintains that nominal value in the absence of any schedule pressures.

To see how schedule pressures influence the "Actual Fraction of a Man-Day on Project," consider the effects of *positive* schedule pressures. Schedule pressure was previously defined as:

$$Schedule\ Pressure = (TMDPSN - MDRM)\ /\ MDRM \qquad (7.2)$$

where

$TMDPSN = Total\ Man\ Days\ Perceived$
$to\ be\ Still\ Needed\ to\ complete\ the\ project$

$MDRM = Total\ Man\ Days\ Remaining\ in\ current\ plan$

Positive schedule pressures arise whenever the project is perceived to be behind schedule, that is, whenever the total effort still needed to complete the project is perceived to be greater than the total effort actually remaining (i.e., when the numerator in the schedule pressure equation is positive). Such a difference represents a perceived shortage in man-days on the project.

Software developers tend to work harder and allocate more man-hours to the project in an attempt to compensate for the perceived shortage and bring the project back on schedule [154, 131, 169] (9) (16) (18) (19) (20) (21). In one experiment Boehm finds that the number of man-hours increases by as much as 100% [49]. He asserts that most of the gains are achieved by "reallocating (i.e., compressing) people's slack time." In other words, under schedule pressure, people tend to spend less time on off-project activities such as personal business and non-project communication. This then decreases the man-hours lost per man-day while increasing the daily man-hours allocated to the project.

Recall that the value of the "Nominal Fraction of a Man-Day on Project" was set at 60%, which translates into 4.8 hours of project work per man-day. At most, another 3.2 hours per man-day can be gained under schedule pressure which, assuming an 8-hour day, is a 67% increase. Since it is unlikely that people would allocate every minute of their 8-hour working day to project work, the attainable increase will be even less than 67%. How then could we explain the 100% increase reported by Boehm?

A 100% increase is attainable because workers, in addition to partially compressing their slack time, may also work *overtime* hours. For example, by working 12 hours a day at 80% efficiency, a team member would be allocating 9.6 hours to the project, thereby doubling the nominal 4.8 hours.

By further compressing the slack time (say to 10 or 15%) and/or increasing the overtime hours, an increase of more than 100% could be achieved. But this would cause *actual* productivity to be larger than *potential* productivity. To some this may seem strange but it is explained by the fact that the definition of potential productivity is "the level of productivity that will be attained if the individual or group makes the best possible use of its resources *under regular working conditions*" where "regular" excludes overtime.

To recapitulate, when a project is perceived to be behind schedule, people tend to work harder to bring it back on schedule. They do that by compressing their slack time and/or working over-time, thus allocating more man-hours to the project.

7.5.2 Overwork Threshold and Exhaustion Factor If such a situation persisted, would workers be willing to work harder indefinitely? The answer, according to our interviewees, was overwhelmingly "no" [169] (9) (16) (18) (19) (20), and (21). There is a threshold beyond which employees would not be willing to work at an "above-normal" rate.

The findings are included in the model of Figure 7.3 as follows. When the project is perceived to be behind schedule, i.e., when the total effort still needed to complete the project is perceived to be greater than the total effort actually remaining in the project's plan, two factors determine the level to which the "Actual Fraction of Man-day on Project" is boosted. The first is the value of the "Perceived Shortage in Man-days," which is the difference between what is needed and what is remaining. If this difference is below a particular "threshold," then it will *all* be handled. That is, the employees will boost the hours they allocate to the project (e.g., by compressing their slack time) to what they perceive is necessary to handle *all* the "Perceived Shortage in Man-days." (How they determine this will be explained shortly.) The second factor is the "Maximum Shortage in Man-Days to be Handled," and it constitutes the "threshold" mentioned above. Thus, if the "Perceived Shortage in Man-Days" is greater than the maximum the employees are willing to handle, we assume that they could be motivated to work harder to accommodate that maximum value, while arranging with management to extend the schedule to handle what exceeds the "Maximum Shortage in Man-Days to be handled." (Such extension to the schedule will be explained in the Planning Section.)

As employees work harder to handle shortages in man-days, their tolerance for working harder decreases and the value of the "Maximum Shortage in Man-Days to be Handled" decreases. If this were not true and the maximum value were a constant parameter, then a persistent man-days shortage at moderate levels (i.e., at levels below the maximum value) would lead to an above normal work rate *throughout* the life of the project. This would contradict our finding that there is a threshold beyond which employees would not be willing to work above the normal rate.

At any point in the project the value of the "Maximum Shortage in Man-Days to be Handled" is determined by the product of three variables: the "Overwork Duration Threshold," the "Full-Time Equivalent Workforce," and the "Maximum Boost in Man-Hours." For example, if a work force of 10 full-time people is willing to work at an above normal rate for a maximum of 10 days and they could boost their work rate by as much as 100% (e.g., by allocating 9.6 hours per man-day to the project instead of the normal 4.8 hours), then they would conclude that during this ten-day period it is possible to handle $10 \times 10 \times 1 = 100$ Man-days' worth of backlogged work above the regular work planned for that period. In the model, the value of the "Maximum Boost in Man-Hours" is set, as in the example above, at a value of 100% (16) (27).

Estimates by the interviewees for the "Overwork Duration Threshold" ranged from 8 weeks (20) to 12 weeks (27). In the model we set the nominal value for the "Overwork Duration Threshold" at 50 working days (i.e., 10 weeks). Once people start working harder, their "Overwork Duration Threshold," which represents the maximum *remaining* duration for which they are willing to continue working harder, decreases below the nominal value. Thus the "Overwork Duration Threshold" is formulated as a nominal value (i.e., 10 weeks) adjusted downwards by a multiplier. One option for the multiplier was to have it be a function of the calendar time during which the project members have been working harder. This option was rejected, though, because it did not differentiate between, say, a ten-day period during which the staff were working 10% harder and another ten-day period in which they worked 100% harder. We wanted the multiplier to induce a cut in the "Overwork Duration Threshold" that would be greater at the end of the second ten-day period.

We formulated the "Multiplier to the Overwork Duration Threshold due to Exhaustion." "Exhaustion" is simply a level whose value reflects the level of exhaustion of the work force due to overwork. The rate at which this level increases needs to be a function of some measure of overwork, as shown in Figure 7.5.

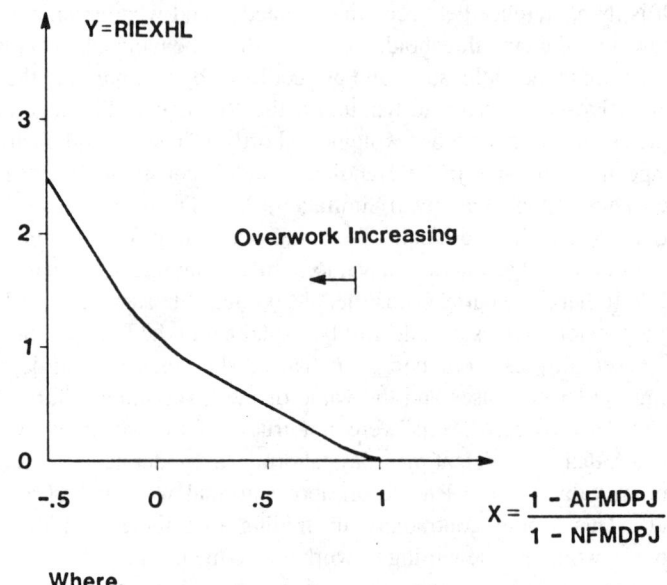

Where,

AFMDPJ = Actual Fraction of a Man-Day on Project

NFMDPJ = Nominal Fraction of a Man-Day on Project

RIEXHL = Rate of Increase in Exhaustion Level

Figure 7.5 Rate of increase in exhaustion level

Before interpreting Figure 7.5, let us review some assumptions made so far. First, we are assuming that a full time employee allocates, on the average, 60% of his or her time to the project (i.e., NFMDPJ = 0.6), which for an 8-hour day amounts to 4.8 hours. Under schedule pressure more time will be allocated to the project (i.e., AFMDPJ > 0.6). The increased allocation would be achieved by first compressing the slack time, and then if needed, by working overtime. Furthermore, we are also assuming that there is a "Maximum (Possible) Boost in Man-Hours" of 100%, i.e., AFMDPJ can attain a maximum value of $0.6 \times 2 = 1.2$.

The first thing to note about Figure 7.5 is that when AFMDPJ is less than or equal to NFMDPJ (i.e., X > 1) the value of RIEXHL is zero. That is, when people are working at their normal pace (or slower), there is no rise in their exhaustion level. This must be so by definition, since the "Exhaustion level" in the model is defined to be that of exhaustion due to *overwork*.

Second, note that the exhaustion rate is really a function of 1-AFMDPJ, since the denominator of X, 1-NFMDPJ, is a constant. Also note that the value of 1-AFMDPJ is a measure of the average "Slack Time." Therefore, the exhaustion rate of the work force is a function of the compression in the average slack time. The reason is that the exhaustion of working harder is mostly "psychological" rather than "physiological." That is, people enjoy their slack time (e.g., coffee breaks, social communications, personal business) and they would not tolerate prolonged deprivation of such "breathers." Thus a compressed slack time reduces their tolerance level for continued hard work since continued hard work means a continued "deprivation" of their slack time.

However, when the value of 1-AFDPRD approaches zero and moves into negative territory, people would be not only compressing their slack time but also working overtime. At those values, *in addition* to psychological exhaustion, there will also be "physiological" exhaustion. That is why the curve increases at a faster rate for negative values of X.

The effects of exhaustion on the "Overwork Duration Threshold" is formulated as the "Multiplier to the Overwork Duration Threshold due to Exhaustion." As we explained previously, the nominal value of the threshold is 50 days. As people start working at a rate above their normal rate, that threshold is cut down until possibly it reaches a value of zero. Notice that setting the nominal value of the "Overwork Duration Threshold" to 50 days is not enough; it is also necessary to specify the level of overwork, since people might be willing to work for 50 days at a rate 50% above their normal rate, but not be willing to work at a 100% increase. We thus amend our definition of the nominal value for the "Overwork Duration Threshold" to be 50 working days at a rate of 8 hours per man-day (i.e., when AFMDPJ is approximately 1). Notice that when AFMDPJ is approximately 1, RIEXML in Figure 7.5 is also 1. At such a work rate, each man-day contributes 1 to the Exhaustion level. After 50 such days, the Exhaustion level reaches a level of 50, which should be enough to drive the "Overwork Duration Threshold" to zero. That level of exhaustion is termed the "Maximum Tolerable Exhaustion" level. The "Maximum Tolerable Exhaustion" level could of course be reached in less than 50 days if people are working even harder (i.e., if AFMDPJ is greater than 1); conversely, if the work rate is less than 8-hours per man-day, it would be reached in more than 50 days. But once reached, it drives the "Overwork Duration Threshold" to zero. This is accomplished by the formulation of the "Multiplier to the Overwork Duration Threshold Due to Exhaustion" shown in Figure 7.6.

Once a period of overwork ends, either because the threshold has been reached and/or schedule pressures cease, and the work force returns to a normal work rate where AFMDPJ = NFMDPJ, the work force's "Exhaustion level" is depleted. The "Rate of Depletion of the Exhaustion level" is modeled as a first order exponential delay, with a time delay equal to 4 weeks. The 4-week delay was chosen based on discussion with the interviewees (23) and (25).

During the "de-exhausting" period, the work force remains unwilling to "re-overwork" (23) (25). This unwillingness is represented in the model through the formulation of the variable "Willingness to Overwork." This is a SWITCH variable that can attain one of two values, zero or one, and is multiplied into the formulation of the "Maximum Shortage in Man-Days to be Handled." Whenever the maximum exhaustion level is reached and the "Overwork Duration Threshold" is driven down to zero, the "Willingness to Overwork" variable switches to zero. The "Willingness to Overwork"

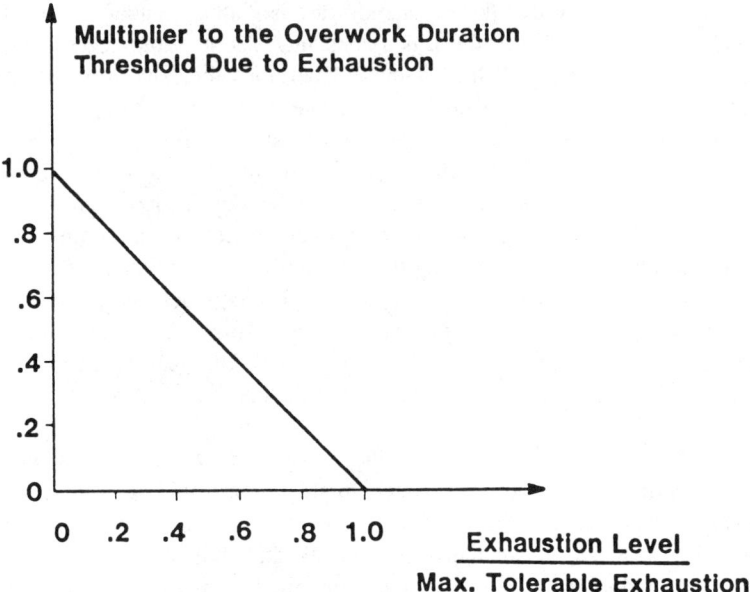

Figure 7.6   Multiplier to overwork due to exhaustion

variable remains at zero until the work force is "de-exhausted" i.e., until the "Exhaustion Level" is depleted. As long as the "Willingness to Overwork" is zero, the "Maximum Shortage in Man-Days to be Handled" is also zero. That is, the workforce remains unwilling to handle any (further) man-day shortages through overwork. When the "Exhaustion Level" is eventually depleted, the "Willingness to Overwork" switches back to a value of one, and the work force should again be willing to overwork (*if and when* the need arises).

7.5.3 Boost in Work Rate   Recall that determining the value of the "Overwork Duration Threshold" was necessary to determine the value of the "Maximum Shortage in Man-days to be Handled." The latter value, in turn, is necessary to determine the value to which the "Actual Fraction of Man-days on Project" is boosted. When the project is perceived to be behind schedule, indicating a shortage in man-days, the staff members seek to boost their work rate to what they perceive is necessary to handle either all the "Perceived Shortage in Man-Days" or the "Maximum Shortage in Man-Days to be Handled," whichever is smaller. The smaller of the two values constitutes the "Handled Man-Days." The "Percent Boost in Work Rate Sought" to handle these man-days equals the value of "Handled Man-Days" divided by the product of "Full-Time Equivalent Workforce" and "Overwork Duration Threshold." For example, if 100 man-days are to be handled by a 10 person team in 50 days, the percent Boost would be $100 / (10 \times 50) = 0.2$. That is, by increasing their work rate by 20%, the workers can handle the 100 man-days of backlogged work in addition to the regular work planned for the 50 day period. We assume that the backlogged work will always be stretched over the full period defined by the "Overwork Duration Threshold." The "Overwork Duration

Threshold'' should be a good approximation in cases when the value of "Handled Man-Days'' is close to the "Maximum Shortage in Man-Days to be Handled.'' When the "Handled Man-Days'' is much smaller, though, the team *might* decide on a shorter "spurt'' of overwork, e.g., "to get it over with.'' However, we use a single formulation for all cases, whereby the backlog is stretched over the "Overwork Duration Threshold'' period.

The "Percent Boost in Work Rate Sought'' defines a work rate goal in terms of man-hours allocated to the project. Such a goal is not achieved instantaneously, since workers take time to adjust their work habits. There is therefore a delay before the "*Actual* Fraction of Man-Days on Project'' attains the level sought. The average delay is set in the model at 2 weeks.

7.5.4 Excess Time   So far we have been discussing the effects of *positive* schedule pressures on productivity. We turn our attention next to those (probably rare) situations in which the project is perceived to be ahead of schedule, the case of negative schedule pressure.

Such a situation exists whenever the total man-days remaining in the project's plan exceed what the project members perceive to be needed to complete the project. This could happen, for example, if management over-estimates a project's scope. What effects would a perception of such "excess'' have on productivity?

For positive schedule pressures, the shortage in man-days was handled first by adjustments in productivity and then by adjustments in the schedule. Analogous behavior occurs in the negative schedule pressure situation. That is, when project members perceive some "excesses'' in the schedule, some excesses will be "absorbed'' by the workers as "under-work'' before downward adjustments are made in the project's schedule [49, 131] (6) (9) (16) (19). For example, Boehm comments:

> ... if the software cost or schedule estimate for meeting a milestone is higher than the ideal, Parkinson's Law indicates that people will use the extra time for ... personal activities, catching up on the mail, etc. [49].

As with positive schedule pressure, there are limits on how much "fat'' employees are willing or allowed to absorb. Beyond those limits, excesses are translated into cuts in the project's schedule.

The above ideas are captured in the table function of Figure 7.7. The dashed 45 degree line represents full disclosure of schedule excesses and thus the complete translation of any excesses into schedule cuts. A more realistic project behavior is the one depicted by the Solid Curve. In the upper right corner, excesses are small, and "Man-Days Perceived Still Needed'' is slightly less than "Man-Days Remaining.'' Under such conditions most of the slack will be absorbed; reports will show that the project is *on* (not ahead of) schedule, and "Man-Days Reported Still Needed'' will be equal to "Man-Days Remaining.'' As excesses become larger and larger, they will be only partially absorbed, and the balance translated into cuts in the project's schedule.

Absorbed excesses will mean a larger slack time, which in turn means a lower "Actual Fraction of a Man-Day on Project.'' The "Actual Fraction of a Man-Day on Project'' is determined here as it was for positive schedule pressure: through an adjustment to the value of the variable "Percent Boost in Work Rate Sought.'' In this case, however, the percent boost will be a negative value.

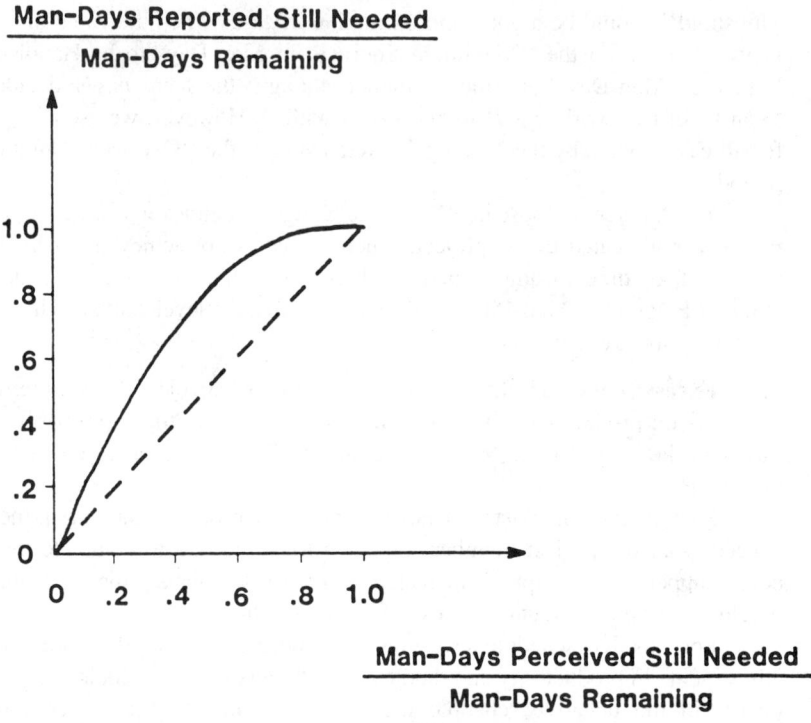

Figure 7.7 Reporting of excess time

There are two more differences. In calculating the percent boost, we will assume that the workers will stretch their absorption of the perceived excesses over the remaining life of the project. That is, instead of a short-lived and drastic drop in their work rate, workers are assumed to adjust to what they perceive as a stable, albeit comfortably lower, work rate.

The "Percent Drop in Work Rate Sought" defines a work rate goal in terms of man-hours allocated to the project. As with positive schedule pressure, such a goal is not achieved instantaneously, since workers take time to adjust their work habits. It is reasonable to expect, though, that the delay to adjust one's habits to a more comfortable state is shorter than that of adjusting to a less comfortable state. We therefore assume that the average delay in adjusting to a "Percent Drop" is 7.5 days, 25% lower than that of adjusting to a "Percent Boost" under positive schedule pressure.

7.6 Impact on Actual Productivity Due to Communication

The value of the "Actual Fraction of a Man-Day on Project" becomes an important determinant of *actual* software development productivity. It represents the losses in productivity due to motivational factors. But it is not the only determinant; additional losses in productivity are incurred due to communication overhead.

As shown in Figure 7.3, "Software Development Productivity" equals the product of "Potential Productivity" and the "Multiplier to Productivity Due to Communication and Motivation Losses." The multiplier represents the average *productive* fraction of a Man-Day: the fraction of the "Actual Fraction of a Man-Days on Project" that remains after accounting for communication overhead. For example, if the "Actual Fraction of a Man-Day on Project" is 0.6, then a full-time employee allocates on the average .6 × 8 = 4.8 hours to the project. If the *project* communication overhead consumes 25% of that allocation, then the average *productive* fraction of a Man-Day would be 0.75 × 0.6 = 0.45 or 3.6 hours.

What is communication overhead? There are those who might argue that human communication is an essential component of any software development effort and is actually part of the "job," not an overhead. Even though human communication is indeed an essential component of software development, it does constitute an overhead. To see why, let us examine what happens when a software system is developed not by a team but by one person.

Two things usually happen. First, time lost because of human communication is avoided. When a team is developing software,

> ... it is necessary that each individual spend part of his time communicating with each of the other team members. For example, the designer must confer with the coder to resolve any questions the coder may have about the design; both of these must talk to the individual testing the code to give him the benefit of their experience with the program; each of these must talk to the documentor to assure that the documentation is proper and complete; and so on [244].

Such human communication is unnecessary when software is developed by a single person.

Second, the amount of work itself usually increases when software is developed by a team. The increase takes two forms. The first and obvious one is that the amount of documentation increases, since in a one-person environment the developer usually needs no more than sketchy notes to augment his "mental documentation" [244]. The second is an increase in the size of the software product itself due to excessive modularization [69, 109]. For example, when a particular program is developed by two people instead of one, it might be designed as a two-module program instead of a single-module program, necessitating an inter-module *interface* that has to be agreed upon and developed.

So, what is communication overhead? The answer: It is the average team member's drop in productivity below his *nominal* productivity as a result of team communication, where communication includes verbal communication, documentation, and any *additional* work, such as that due to interfaces.

It is widely held that communication overhead increases in proportion to n^2, where n is the size of the team [57, 236, 180, 273, 231]. Such a relationship is shown in the table function of Figure 7.8. In the model, communication overhead is zero when the software is developed by one person; as the work force size (n) increases, communication overhead increases in proportion to n^2.

Consider the case where n=30; communication overhead is approximately 50%. If the "Actual Fraction of a Man-Day on Project" is 0.6, 4.8 hours are allocated daily on average by the full-time team member; 50% or 2.4 hours will effectively be lost due to

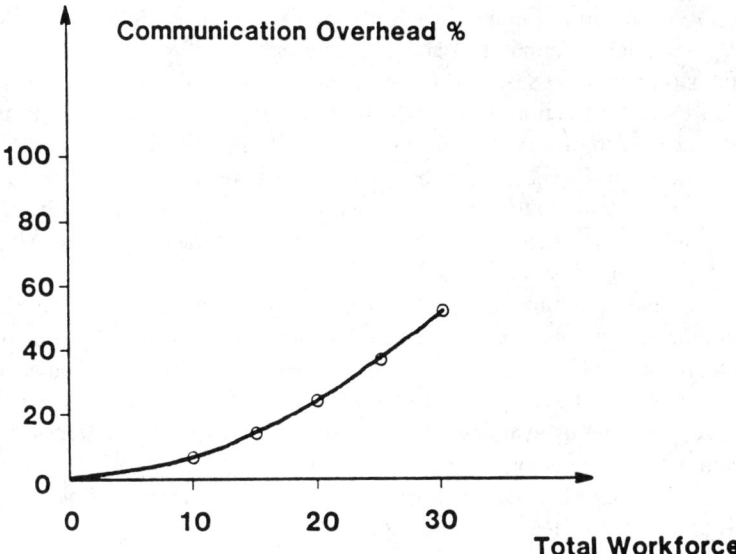

Figure 7.8 Communication Overhead

communication overhead. In other words, the "Multiplier to Productivity Due to Motivation and Communication Losses" is $0.6 \times 0.5 = 0.3$, which means that "Software Development Productivity" is 30% of the value of "Potential Productivity." For example, if "Potential Productivity" is 1 Task/Man-Day, then "Software Development Productivity" is 0.3 Tasks/Man-Day (after accounting for motivation and communication losses).

8

QUALITY ASSURANCE AND REWORK

8.1 Quality Assurance Sector

The development of software systems involves a series of production activities where the opportunities for interjection of human fallibilities are enormous. Errors may begin to occur at the inception of the process where the objectives of the software system may be erroneously or imperfectly specified, as well as during the later design and development stages where these objectives are mechanized. The basic quality factor for software is that it performs its functions in the manner that was intended by its architects. To achieve this quality, the final product must contain a minimum of mistakes in implementing their intentions as well as being void of misconception about the intentions themselves. Because of human inability to perform with perfection, software development is accompanied by a quality assurance activity [84].

Software quality assurance includes two distinct and complementary methodologies. The first is designing a coherent, complete, unambiguous, and nonconflicting set of requirements. The second is review and testing of the product [84].

In this section we will discuss the generation, detection, and correction of errors during the *development* phase, which includes the design, coding, reviewing, and testing but *excludes* requirements. We will assume that software design begins at the "successful completion" of a software requirement's review and that there would be no subsequent changes or modifications in the system's requirements (see section 2.4).

Errors come in many different "flavors."[147] Nelson delineated and described the most prominent software design and coding errors [197]:

1. Misinterpretation of specifications

2. Errors in developing the logic to solve the problem

3. Algorithm approximations that may provide insufficient accuracy or erroneous results for certain input variables

4. Data structure defects either in the data structure design specification or in the implementation of the specification

5. Singular or critical input values to a formula that may yield an unexpected result not accounted for in the program code

6. Misinterpretation of language constructions by the programmer

In a model such as ours it is feasible from a technical point of view to divide a variable such as errors into error types. However, it is *not* always necessary or useful.

There are two (and only two) considerations for reformulating a level (variable) as a sequence of two or more levels: policy analysis and model behavior. First, is the disaggregation required in order for the model to be able to address particular policy issues? ...

The second reason for disaggregating a level involves the dynamics of the system. Does the disaggregation of a level into two or more levels have the potential to change significantly the behavior of the model? ... The final arbiter should be model-based policy analysis. If the change in behavior has the potential to alter policy conclusions, then the disaggregation is essential [221].

Since our model focuses on the management of software development, rather than on technical issues of software reliability, an *explicit* division of errors into more than one type is unnecessary. On the other hand, there are significant behavioral differences among error types that have to be accounted for. For example, findings in the software engineering literature indicate that errors are generated at different rates at different points in the life cycle; for example, design errors in the early design phase are generated at a higher rate than are coding errors [165]. Such a factor is obviously of dynamic significance. For example, it could have a direct bearing on the allocation of the manpower resource.

Behavioral differences will be *implicitly* captured in the model. That is, while errors will be formulated as a single type, "Errors," the ways errors are generated, detected, and corrected will vary throughout the development life cycle. For example, "Errors" will be generated at a higher rate in the early portions of the life cycle (as design errors are) and they will, on the average, be "harder" to detect and correct (as design errors are).

Figure 8.1 depicts the quality assurance sector of the model encompassing the generation, detection, and correction of errors.

8.2 Error Generation Rates

Two sets of factors affect the "Error Generation Rate" in a software project. The first set includes organizational factors (e.g., the use of structured techniques [19], and the quality of the staff [42]) and project factors [236] (e.g., complexity, size of system, language). Even though such factors can differ from organization to organization and from project to project, they remain invariant during the life of a single project. The cumulative effect of all such factors is represented in the model as a single *nominal* variable, the "Nominal

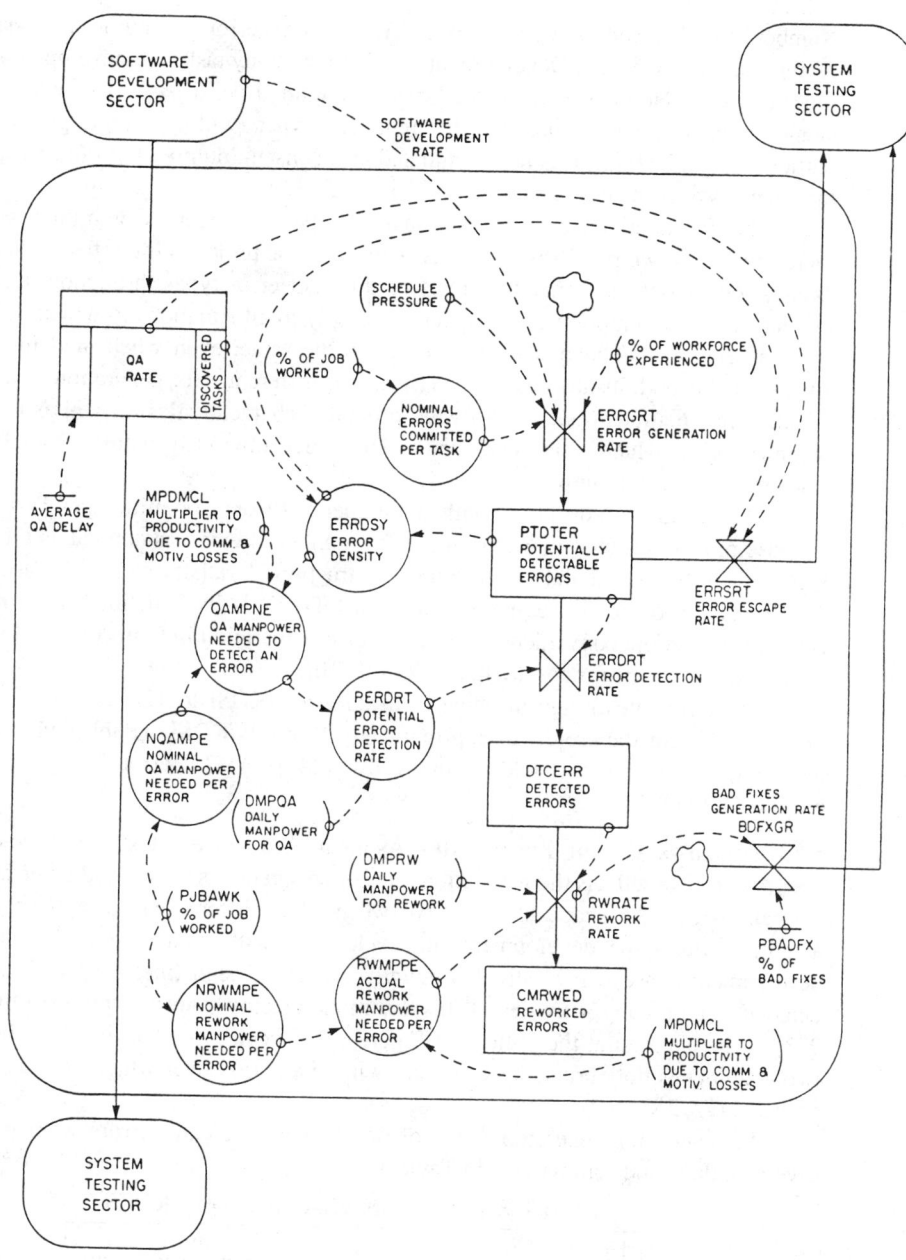

Figure 8.1   Quality assurance sector

Number of Errors Committed per Task." The nominal error generation rate is simply the product of the "Software Development Rate" (how many tasks are developed per unit of time) and the "Nominal Number of Errors Committed per Task." However, since this single nominal variable represents different error types (within a single project within a particular organization), it is not formulated as a constant number but rather as a variable that changes over the project's life.

The formulation of the "Nominal Number of Errors Committed per Task" therefore serves two purposes: First, its shape over the project's life reflects our modeling assumptions about the generation rates of different error types throughout the life of a project. These assumptions, are expected to apply to all situations to which the model is applied. Hence, its shape will always remain the same, even when modeling different situations. Second, its absolute value reflects the different error generation characteristics of different situations (i.e., the software product's characteristics as well as those of the organization in which it is developed). This value obviously would generally change when modeling different projects.

The formulation of the "Nominal Number of Errors Committed per Task" used in the base model is shown in Figure 8.2. The number of errors is defined as a function of KDSI, i.e., "thousand delivered source instructions" rather than of "Tasks." Both definitions are, of course, equivalent since a "Task" is itself defined in terms of DSI. However, it is more convenient to represent error generation in terms of KDSI since most published data on error rates are in terms of KDSI.

The error rates range in value from 25 errors/KDSI to 12.5 errors/KDSI with an average value for the project of approximately 19 errors/KDSI. (Published error rates in the literature include: 10-20 errors/KDSI [247], 15-25 errors/KDSI [49], 30-35 errors/KDSI [138].)

8.2.1 Design vs. Coding Error Rates As mentioned above, the shape of the curve over the project's life reflects the generation rates of design errors versus coding errors. Before we can specify the shape of the curve we need to differentiate design versus coding activities within the development life cycle. We will assume in the model that the development phase will be divided *equally* between design (including architectural and detailed) and coding activities. (This assumption stems from data reported by [49, 108, 273].) The diagram at the bottom of Figure 8.2 indicates that the transition between the two activities is not abrupt; instead there will be a period over which both activities will overlap [172, 252].

Estimates for generation rates of design versus coding errors were provided by several authors and summarized in Table 8.1.

TABLE 8.1. DESIGN VS. CODING ERRORS

Design : Coding Errors	Reference
3.8 : 1	Martin, 1982 [165]
2.0 : 1	Alberts, 1976 [19]
1.8 : 1	Jones, 1981 [140]
1.7 : 1	Boehm, 1981 [49]
1.6 : 1	Thayer et al., 1978 [247]

Figure 8.2 shows that the ratio assumed in the model achieves a maximum value of 2:1. That is, at the beginning of design the nominal number of errors committed is 25

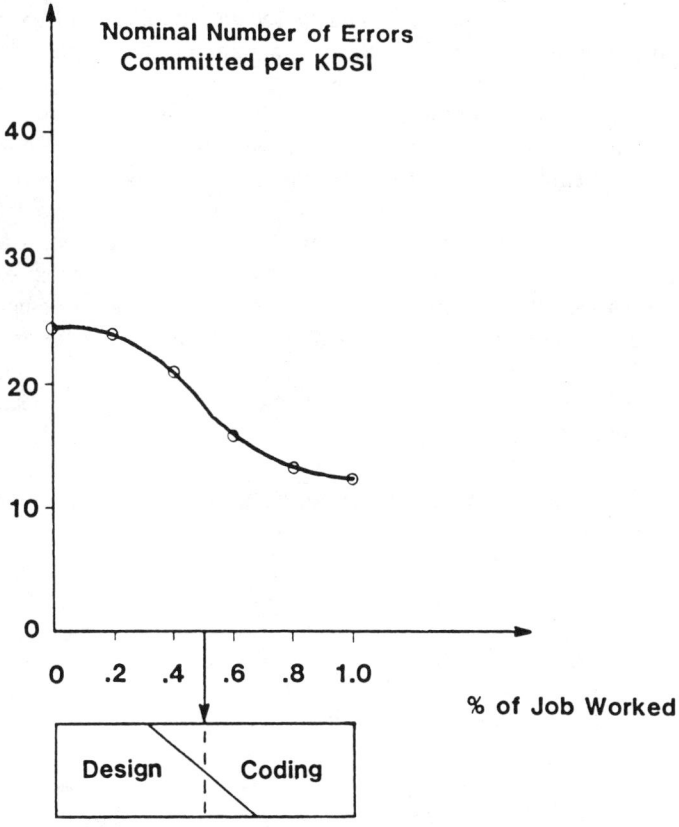

Figure 8.2   Nominal error generation rate

errors/KDSI, while towards the end of coding it drops to 12.5 errors/KDSI. The average rates for the design and coding phases are approximately 23 and 14.5 errors/KDSI respectively, a 1.6:1 ratio.

8.3 Workforce Mix and Schedule Pressure

The formulation of the nominal error generation rate represents the cumulative effect of *one* set of factors affecting error generation: the organizational and project factors. Such factors remain invariant during the life of a single project. There is a second set of factors that play a dynamic role during software development: the work force-mix and schedule pressures.

8.3.1 Impact of Workforce Mix As we saw, the work force comprises two types of employees, newly hired and experienced; newly hired employees pass through an "Orientation Phase" during which they are less than fully productive. The orientation process brings them up to speed through training that covers both the social and technical aspects of the project. For example, on the technical side, newly hired project members "often require considerable training to become familiar with an organization's unique mix of hardware, software packages, programming techniques, project methodologies, and so on" [269].

Newly hired employees are not only less productive on average but also more error-prone than their experienced counterparts [92, 189]. We assume in the model that a newly hired employee is twice as error-prone as an experienced employee (20) (25). To model this we formulate the "Multiplier to Error Generation Due to Workforce Mix" as a function of the "Percentage of Workforce that is Experienced." When the work force consists only of experienced staff, the value of the multiplier is set at 1, since it would have a neutral effect on the *nominal* error generation rate. In other words, what we are defining to be *nominal* is defined *with respect to* the average error generation rate of the *experienced* employee. As the fraction of newly hired employees increases, the multiplier increases linearly until it attains a maximum value of 2, which means that the work force consists of only new hires. See Figure 8.3.

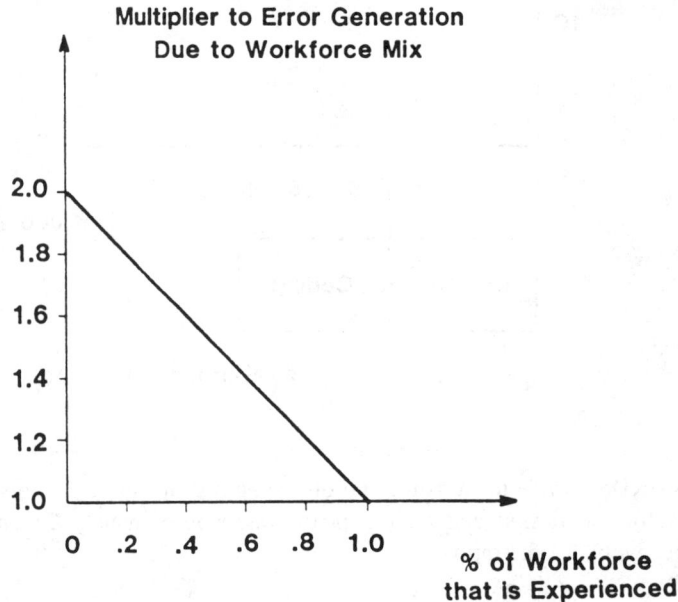

Figure 8.3 Multiplier to error generation due to workforce mix

8.3.2 Impact of Schedule Pressure Schedule pressure can also increase the number of errors [181, 213, 215] (1) (5) (7) (18) (19) (20).

People under time pressure don't work better, they just work faster... .

In the struggle to deliver any software at all, the first casualty has been consideration of the quality of the software delivered [81].

Shneiderman suggests that schedule pressures increase the "anxiety levels" of programmers [235]. A high anxiety level

... interferes (with performance), probably by reducing the size of the short-term memory available. When programmers become more anxious as deadlines approach, they (therefore) tend to make even more errors...

Thibodeau and Dodson suggest that schedule pressures often result in the "overlapping of activities that would have been accomplished better sequentially," and overlapping can significantly increase the chance of errors [252]. For example,

> When coding has begun before the completion of design, the designers are required to communicate their results to the programmers in a raw, unqualified state, hence significantly increasing the chance of design errors.... .
> This is not to suggest that systems cannot be developed with overlapping activities. Many systems have distinct parts that can be coded before the entire design is completed....   We are concerned here with the situation where the press of the development schedule or the slippage of preceding activities results in overlapping activities that would have been accomplished better sequentially [252].

The effect of schedule pressure on error generation in the model is shown in Figure 8.4. Under nominal conditions there are no schedule pressures, and the multiplier assumes a value of 1. As schedule pressures increase, the multiplier increases exponentially, indicating higher error-generation rates. As shown in the figure, error-generation can increase by as much as 50% under severe schedule pressures. We assume that errors will be generated below the nominal rate under the "relaxed" conditions of negative schedule pressures.

8.4 Error Detection

Errors are "Potentially Detectable Errors" until a task is reviewed and tested, at which point some of the errors get detected and reworked. Usually not all errors will be detected; some will pass undetected into the next phases of software development. In the next chapter we will see how those errors are eventually caught during system testing, albeit at a relatively high cost.

The detection of errors is the objective of the Quality Assurance (QA) activities. Pressman defines Quality Assurance as:

> (A set of activities) performed in conjunction with (the development of) a software product to guarantee the product meets the specified standards. These activities reduce doubts and risks about the performance of the product in the target environment [210].

The activities include walk-throughs , reviews, inspections, code reading (a process where code logic and code format are scrutinized by a programmer other than the original designer), and integration testing [141, 78]. Unit testing is not included; it is commonly considered to be part of the coding process [172].

The "QA Rate" of Figure 8.1 has a non-characteristic formulation: a third order delay. The characteristic way to formulate a rate is as a product of the effort allocated and its productivity. However, what we found (and what the third order delay formulation

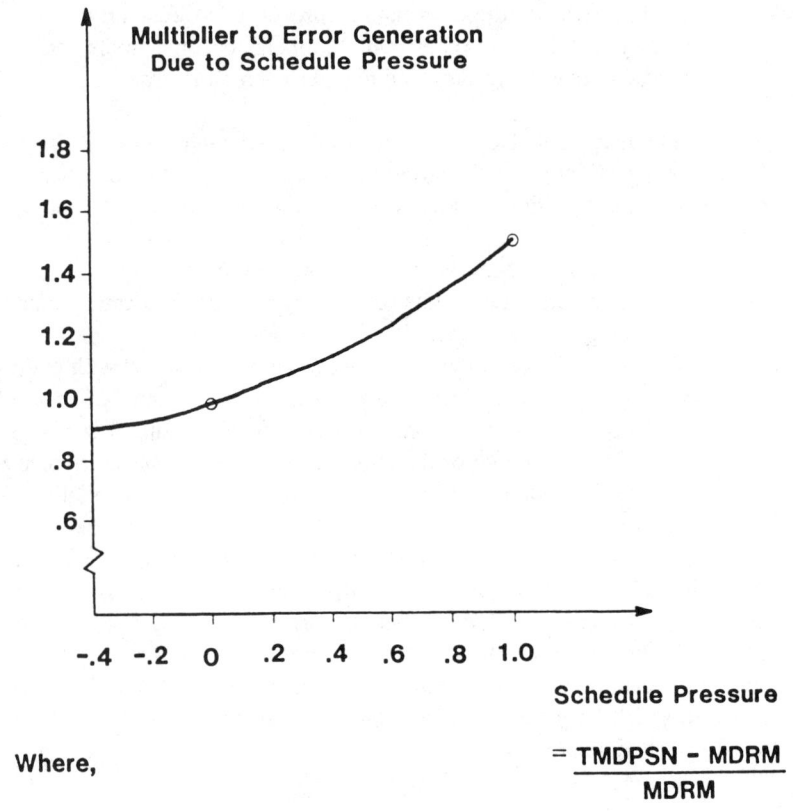

Figure 8.4 Multiplier to error generation due to schedule pressure

actualizes) is that the QA Rate is independent of the QA effort and its productivity. What we found [based on discussions with the interviewees (4) (13) (14) (16) (18)] is this: QA effort or "window" is planned and allocated, usually in a fixed schedule of group functions [183]. For example, a 2-hour walkthrough for the 5 members of a team is scheduled for every Friday. During the "QA Window," all tasks developed since the previous one are supposed to be processed. We were surprised to find that, in an almost perfect realization of Parkinson's Law, no matter how many tasks need to be processed within the "QA Window," they almost always are. Therefore no backlogs develop in the QA pipeline. Even when QA activities are relaxed or suspended because of schedule pressure (as discussed earlier), no backlogs develop. That is, when walkthroughs are suspended for a while on a project, the requirement for a "walk-through" is also suspended, *not* postponed [125].

Why does this happen? Since the objective of the QA activity is to detect errors, it becomes almost impossible to tell whether *all* those errors were in fact detected. By the same token, it is as difficult to tell that the job has not been completely done (except much later in the life cycle). Under such circumstances it becomes easy to rationalize that the QA job was sufficient. Furthermore, the QA effort that is possible to expend (i.e., in terms of available time and effort) is usually what is expended *and not more* because there seems to be no significant incentives to do otherwise. First, at the psychological level, there are actually dis-incentives for working harder at QA, since it only exposes more of one's mistakes [260]. Second, at the organizational level, there are seldom any rewards that promote quality or quality-related activities [72].

The formulation of the QA Rate as a third order delay provides a good approximation of Parkinsonian execution. (Figure 8.5 shows how a third-order delay looks schematically, how it is formulated mathematically, and how it behaves over time.) That is, software tasks will always be QAed or considered QAed after a delay that is assumed to be independent of the QA effort. In the model the "Average QA Delay" period is set at 2 weeks (i.e., 10 working days) (25).

However, while the rate at which tasks are QAed or considered QAed can proceed under QA policies and procedures independently of the actual QA effort, the *effectiveness* of QA will, obviously, depend on that effort. That is, the number of errors detected will be a function of how much QA effort is allocated for error detection.

8.4.1 Potential Error Detection Rate   In the model (see Figure 8.1) the variable "Potential Error Detection Rate" represents the maximum number of errors that can be detected at one time and is determined by dividing the value of the QA effort allocated by the value of the QA effort that is needed on average to detect an error. For example, if 5 man-days are allocated per week to QA and the "QA Manpower Needed to Detect an Error" is on average 1 man-day, then the "Potential Error Detection Rate" would be 5 errors per week.

What are the determinants of the "QA Manpower Needed to Detect an Error"? The first is whether an error is a design or a coding error. Thus, even if a project proceeds under some invariant set of nominal conditions, the QA manpower that would be needed on average to detect an error would change simply because the errors to be detected change from design errors to coding errors.

Design errors are not only generated at a higher rate but, as Figure 8.6 indicates, they are also more costly to detect [19, 54, 189]. Alberts estimates that design errors are 2.5 times more costly to detect *and* correct [19]. The formulation of Figure 8.6 assumes that on average a design error is 1.6 as costly *to detect* as a coding error. Furthermore, in terms of absolute values, the average detection effort per error is 0.3 man-days. Thus, on the average it would take approximately 2.4 man-hours (30% of an 8-hour man-day) to detect an error. In walk-throughs and inspections, the detection effort would include the effort expended during the walk-through/inspection and the effort expended in preparation for it such as reviewing documentation and gaining familiarity with the product. Estimates in the literature for the error detection effort per error include: 3 man-hours [183], 2.36 man-hours [236], and 0.5-1.25 man-hours [235].

8.4.2 Actual Error Detection Rate   The *actual* QA manpower needed to detect an error is a function of error-type, and how efficiently people work. In our discussion on productivity we indicated that a full-time employee's work day does not translate into an 8 man-hour input to the project. Man-hours are lost on communication and other non-project activities. The "Multiplier to Productivity Due to Communication and

(A) Schematic

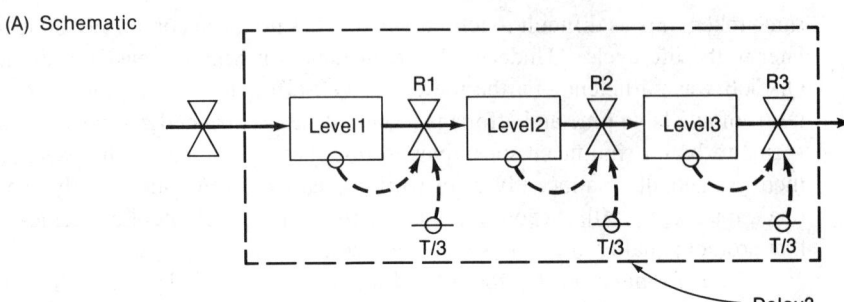

(B) Mathematical
    Formulation

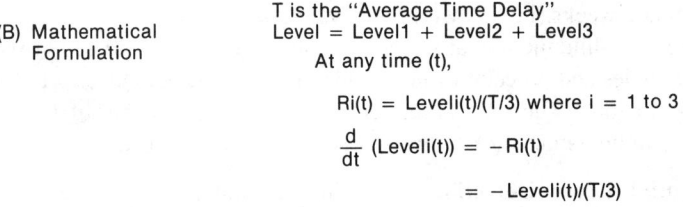

(C) Behavior

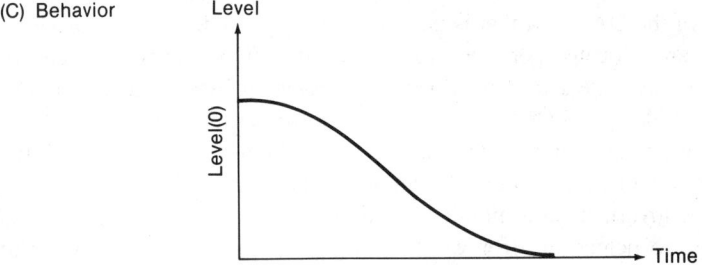

Figure 8.5 Third-order delay

Motivation Losses" represents the average productive fraction of a man-day. For example, if the communication and motivation losses amount to a 4 man-hour loss per day (for the average employee), half of the nominal 8 man-hour value, then the value of the multiplier would be 0.5. Under such a circumstance, the *actual* QA manpower needed to detect an error becomes twice what is *nominally* needed. If a design error normally requires 0.4 man-days to be detected, it would actually require twice as long, or $0.4 \times 2 = 0.8$ man-days, in the above example.

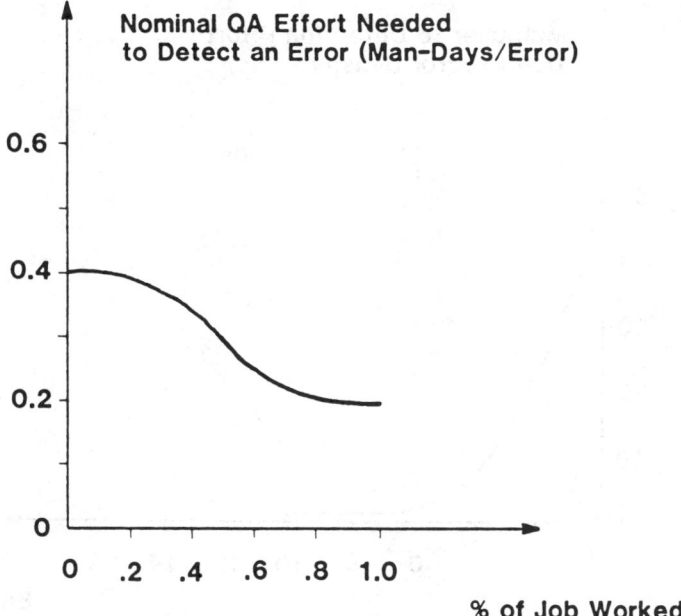

Figure 8.6   QA effort needed to detect an error

8.4.3 Hierarchy of Errors Evidence suggests that "In any sizable program, it is impossible to remove all errors" [236]. Thus, even when generous effort allocations are made to QA, it is still unlikely that all errors will be detected [49]. One reason is that "... some errors manifest themselves, and can be exhibited only after system integration" [236]. At any time one could therefore view the collection of "Potentially Detectable Errors" as a hierarchy of errors in which some are more subtle and therefore more expensive to detect than are others. Empirical results reported by Basili and Weiss suggest that the distribution is pyramidal, with the majority of errors requiring a few hours to detect, a few errors requiring approximately a day to detect, and still fewer errors requiring more than a day to detect. The results show that a few subtle errors can be of an order of magnitude more expensive to detect [38].

We assume in the model that as QA activities are performed, the more obvious errors will be detected first. It becomes more and more expensive to uncover the remaining more subtle (although less predominant) errors. This is represented in the model through the "Multiplier to Detection Effort Due to Error Density," shown in Figure 8.7. At moderate-to-large error densities the multiplier assumes a neutral value of 1. But as those "obvious" errors are all detected and a few "subtle" errors remain, the multiplier increases exponentially such that at a density level of 2-4 (subtle) errors per KDSI it becomes much more expensive to detect an error.

8.4.4 Summary of Error Detection Factors To recapitulate: the "QA Manpower Needed to Detect an Error" is a function of error type, work efficiency and error density. As the value of this needed effort increases, because of a decrease in error density, the number of errors that can be detected at some level of QA effort decreases. At any time

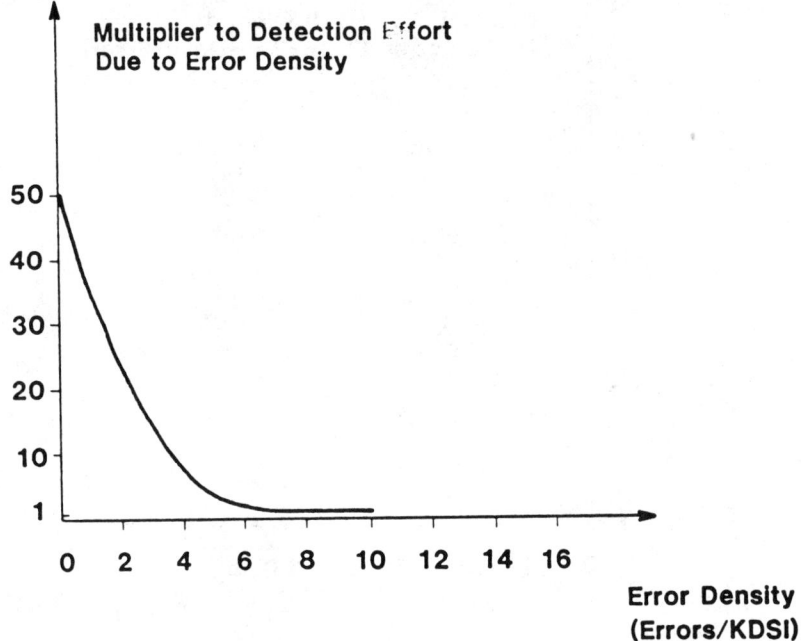

Figure 8.7   Multiplier to detection effort due to error density

the "Potential Error Detection Rate" (determined by dividing the value of the QA effort allocated by the value of the "QA Manpower Needed to Detect an Error") represents the maximum number of errors that can be detected. Because manpower allocations to QA are often "modest," this maximum value is seldom large enough to secure the detection of all errors. Even when effort is allocated generously to QA, a few subtle errors will be so prohibitively expensive to detect that, whatever the effort allocated, it will not be enough to detect all errors. As a result, as shown in Figure 8.1, some errors will "escape" QA and pass undetected into the subsequent phases of software development.

8.5 Rework

Errors that are detected through QA are reworked. The rework rate is a function of how much effort is allocated to rework activities and the rework manpower needed per error. For example, if the project members commit 10 man-days per week to rework detected errors and the "Actual Rework Manpower Needed per Error" is on average 1 man-day, then errors will be reworked at the rate of 10 per week.

8.5.1 Nominal Rework   The "Actual Rework Manpower Needed per Error" has two components. The first is the "*Nominal* Rework Manpower Needed per Error." As in the case of error detection, this nominal component is a function of error-type: design or coding.

The values of the nominal rework effort needed per error are shown in Figure 8.8 as a function of the project's phase and hence of error-type. Design errors, generated at a

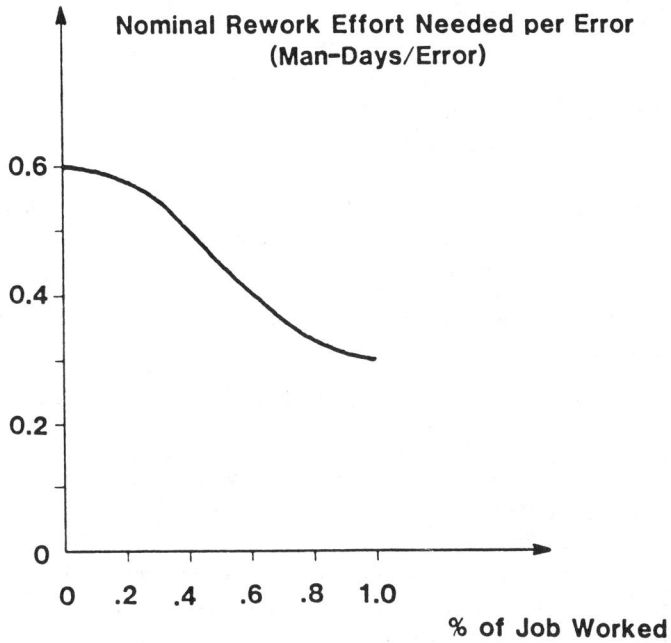

Figure 8.8   Nominal rework effort needed

higher rate and more costly to detect, are also more costly to rework [19, 54, 189]. As Figure 8.8 indicates, we assume that on average a design error is approximately 1.5 times more costly to correct than a coding error. Under nominal conditions a design error would require on average 0.54 man-days to be corrected while the average correction effort for a coding error is assumed to be 0.36 man-days. For the nominal 8-hour working day these averages translate into 4.3 man-hours/design error and 2.9 man-hours/coding error. The values were chosen based on the empirical results reported in [37] and [265], which suggest that the average rework effort (for all errors) is in the range of 0.25 to 1.0 man-days per error.

8.5.2 Actual Rework   The *actual* rework man-power that would be needed to correct an error, in addition to being a function of error-type, must also depend on how efficiently people work. That is, we need to account for communication and motivation losses. For example, if the "Multiplier to Productivity Due to Communication and Motivation Losses," which represents the average productive fraction of a man-day, is 0.5, then the *actual* rework manpower needed to correct an error becomes twice what is *nominally* needed. A design error that requires under nominal conditions (i.e., under conditions of *no* losses) 0.5 man-days to be corrected would actually require $0.5 \times 2 = 1$ man-day.

To recapitulate: as errors are detected through QA, they are reworked. The rate at which errors are reworked is a function of the manpower committed to the rework activity and the rework effort needed per error. The "Actual Rework Manpower Needed per Error" is, in turn, a function of error-type (i.e., design versus coding errors) and work efficiency.

8.5.3 Bad Fixes The reworking of software errors is not itself an errorless activity:

> Human tendency is to consider the "fix," or correction, to a problem to be error-free itself. Unfortunately, this is all too frequently untrue for fixes to errors found by inspections and by testing [94].

The problem of "bad fixes" is widely documented in the literature (e.g., [92, 94, 138, 189, 236] and [247]). Shooman and Natarajan suggest some of the ways in which bad fixes may be generated:

1. The correction is based upon faulty analysis; thus complete bug removal is not accomplished.

2. The corrections of a bug may work locally only (i.e., the global aspects of the error remain).

3. The correction is accomplished; however, it is accomplished by the creation of a new error [237].

Thus, as detected errors are reworked, some fraction of the corrections will be bad fixes. Unfortunately, there are no published data on how large that fraction is. However, some results indicate that bad fixes constitute 6.5 - 10% of all errors caught at the system testing stage [106, 140]. The balance of the errors consists of those errors that escape detection by QA during development. If we assume that 50-60% of errors are detected and reworked during development and that most of the remaining errors and bad fixes are later detected at the system testing phase, then the above findings on bad fixes imply that between 4.5-11% of corrections will be bad fixes. The "Percent Bad Fixes" has been set in the model at 7.5%.

The detection and correction of bad fixes as well as those errors that escape QA detection is the topic of the next chapter.

9

SYSTEM TESTING

9.1 System Testing Sector

Errors that QA fails to detect *while* the software is being designed and coded and bad fixes resulting from faulty rework remain undetected until the system testing phase. We will assume that *all* such errors will get detected and corrected at the system testing phase. Thus, even though in practice some errors often remain in a software product after system testing is completed, those errors will be excluded from our formulation. The generation, detection, and correction of those errors are issues of maintenance of the operational system and so lie beyond the scope of our model.

Furthermore, errors that escape detection at the system testing phase are generally a "small" fraction of all the errors handled at that phase [84]. This assertion might sound surprising, since it is common to assume that maintenance is as costly as it is *primarily* because of the costs incurred in handling such "lingering" errors. Empirical results have shown, however, that corrections of such errors consumes only a small portion of software maintenance [160]. The major portion is devoted to software updates (e.g., enhancements for users and adaptations to new data or hardware) [202].

The System Testing Sector of our model is shown in Figure 9.1. This sector models two sets of processes: the growth of the undetected error populations and the system testing that results in the detection and correction of those errors.

9.2 Growth of Undetected Errors

Undetected errors consist of errors that escape detection of QA and bad fixes resulting from faulty rework. Undetected errors do *not* remain dormant until detected and corrected at the system testing phase. They lead an "active existence," producing more and more errors in the system. For example, a design error that remains undetected until the system testing phase often causes additional errors in the code, user and maintenance manuals, training material, and so on [49].

Shooman determines that detecting and correcting a design error during the design phase (i.e., through QA) is one-tenth the effort ("cost-to-fix escalation") that would be needed to detect and correct it later during the system testing phase because of an additional inventory of specifications, code, user and maintenance manuals, and so on

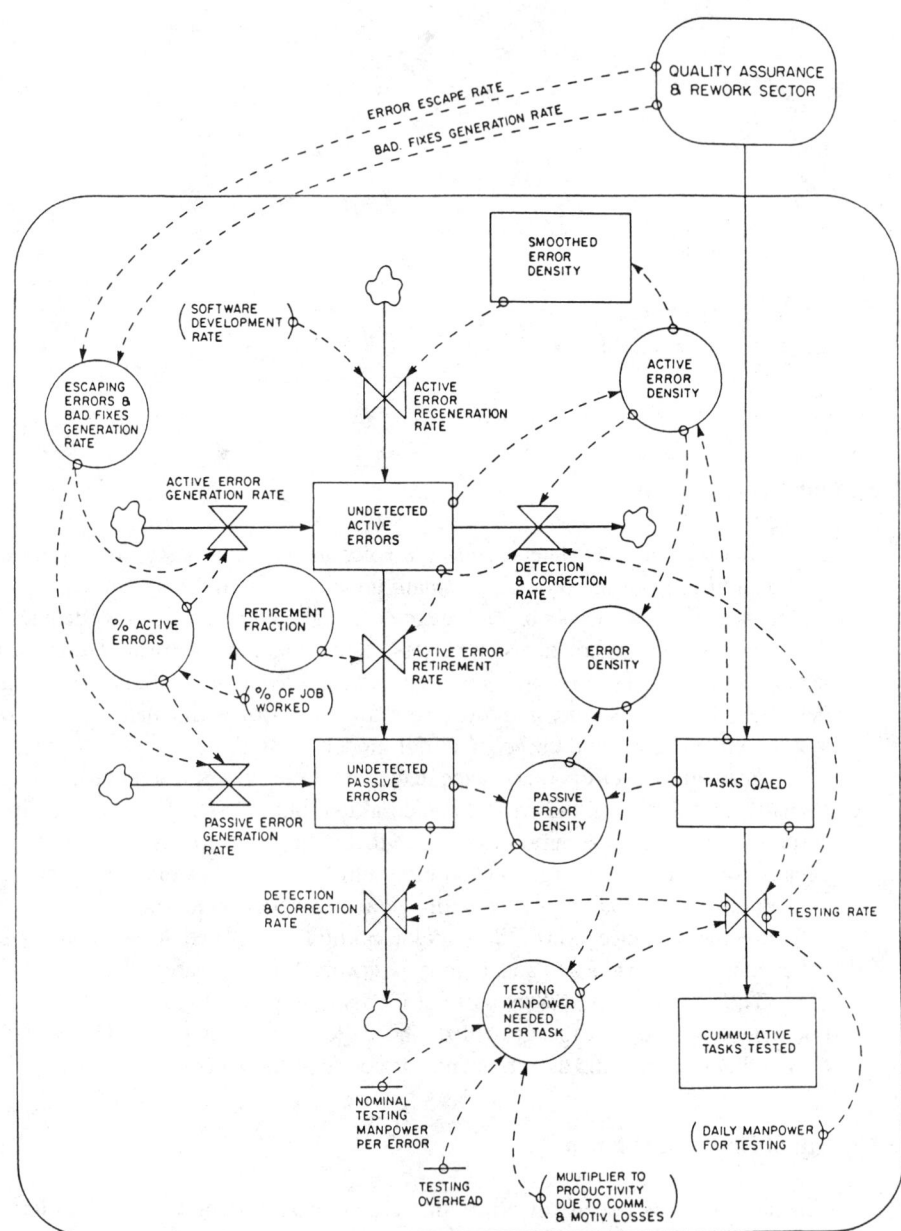

Figure 9.1 System testing sector

would also have to be corrected [166]. Shooman's 10:1 ratio was supported by data in Boehm, but only for larger projects [49]. For smaller projects, the ratio was around 4:1 because, Boehm argued, ''The smaller size meant that there was a relatively smaller inventory of items to fix in later phases.''

Although we do have *static* estimates on cost-to-fix escalations at different points in the software life cycle, no data are available in the literature to describe the *dynamics* of the "error-reproduction" processes. That is, we know that an undetected design error reproduces enough errors in code, documentation, and so on, to become four to ten times more expensive to fix at the system testing phase, but we do not have data that explain exactly how and when these reproduction processes occur.

When the dynamic relationships are not well understood and theory is not well developed, as it is in this case, then "the best one can do is attempt to imitate the change process itself in the hope of learning more about such relationships. Thus the model becomes an aid to theory development" [229]. Our "proposed theory" of the error reproduction process is incorporated in Figure 9.1.

9.2.1 Dynamics of Error Reproduction In Figure 9.1, we assume that undetected errors will become either "Active Errors" (errors that reproduce more errors) or "Passive Errors." Because design specs are the blueprints of the system's code, any errors in design will get translated into coding errors. Thus, all undetected design errors should be active. As development moves into the coding stage, a mixture of active and passive errors can be expected. If we assume, for example, that the system is coded top-down, then in the early parts of coding, most of the errors committed are in the high-level modules and will be active. As development proceeds to lower level modules, the reverse should be true, since the errors become more and more localized. These assumptions on how the mixture of active and passive errors changes over the project's life are represented in the model by the variable "Percent Active Errors" shown in Figure 9.2.

"Undetected Passive Errors," as Figure 9.1 illustrates, remain dormant until they become detected and corrected in the system testing phase. "Undetected Active Errors," on the other hand, are a greater cause for concern, since they introduce more and more errors into the system. The error production process is a continuous one that keeps feeding on itself. It is represented in the model by the positive feedback loop, in which an increase in the "Undetected Active Errors" level leads to an increase in the "Active Error Regeneration Rate," which leads to further increases in the level, and so on.

9.2.2 Active Error Regeneration Rate The "Active Error Regeneration Rate" is a function of the "Software Development Rate," since errors can be generated only as *new* tasks are developed. If development stops, no errors can be generated. The regeneration rate is a function of "Active Error Density," which is simply the number of existing active errors divided by the tasks developed so far. More precisely, the generation rate is a smoothed function of the "Active Error Density" because when errors are committed in one part of the system, they would not, in general, affect other parts that are being developed in *parallel*. Errors tend to propagate through succeeding tasks that build on one another, such as through coding tasks built on incorrect design specs. Thus there is a delay before one error reproduces additional errors. The average delay is set in the model at three months.

In the model, we do not separate errors into different explicit types such as errors in data structures, syntax, and logic. There is only one explicit type of error, namely, "Error." As a result, the escalation in the cost-to-fix of an undetected "Error" is realized in the model only through the *number* of "Errors" that the "Error" reproduces. For example, if an "Error" at the early phases of the project reproduces over several generations a total of 9 more "Errors," then at testing time instead of dealing with one

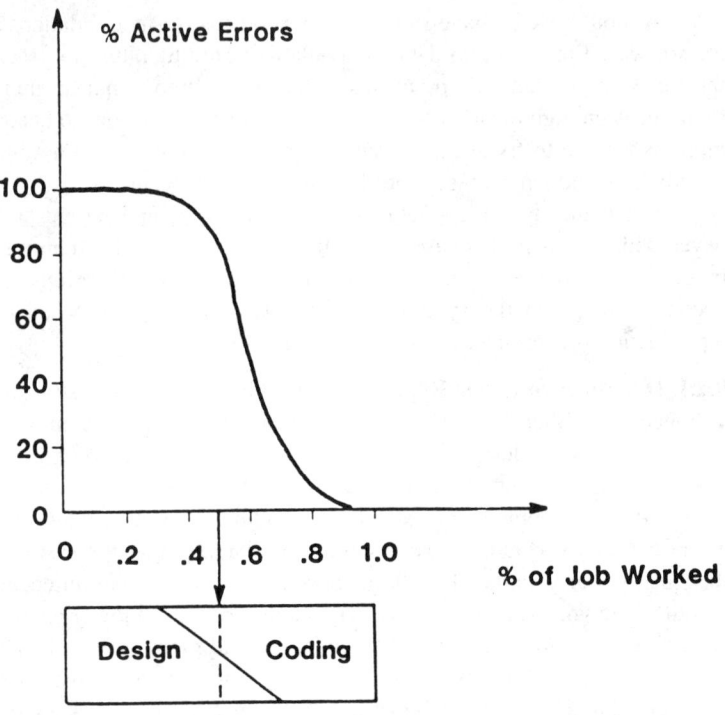

Figure 9.2 Percent active errors

original ''Error,'' we must now deal with 10 ''Errors,'' a ten-fold escalation in cost.

9.2.3 Impact of Error Density on Active Error Regeneration The escalation in the *number* of active errors in the model comes in two ways. The first is through ''feeding on itself,'' which the reproduction positive feedback depicts. The earlier the undetected-error is, the more ''generations'' of errors it will produce, and thus the more costly it will end up being. The second is through the ''Multiplier to Active Error Regeneration due to Error Density.'' The interpretation of this multiplier is simple: it represents the average number of new errors that a single active error reproduces in *one* generation. It is a measure of ''Error Fertility!'' The multiplier is a table function, and is shown in Figure 9.3.

   The multiplier's value will always be greater than one: an undetected error will always generate more than one additional error in a single generation. Also, the value of the multiplier increases as the density of active errors increases. Studies have shown that errors are *not* homogeneously distributed throughout the modules of a software system [92, 189]; instead, systems were ''characterized by the presence of 'error-prone modules' that show a high frequency of the system's total error content'' [140]. For example, if there are 5 undetected errors in a system consisting of 5 modules, it is possible that all 5 errors will be clustered in one error-prone module, as opposed to being evenly distributed among the 5 modules. If there is many more undetected errors (e.g., 100), though, it would be unlikely that all the errors would still be clustered in a single *extremely*-error-

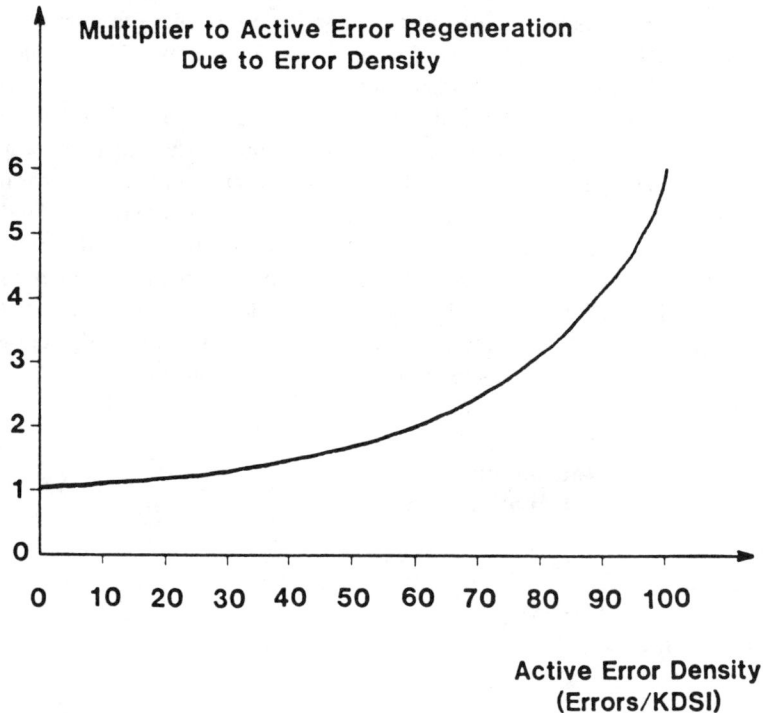

Figure 9.3   Multiplier to active error regeneration

prone module. Such a situation is unlikely because we are dealing here with modules that have already "passed" some QA testing.

Thus, as the error density increases, the distribution of errors among the system's modules generally also increase; errors become less localized. They also become more expensive to detect and correct. For example, because of the set-up cost of testing any single module, it is generally less expensive to fix 10 errors that all reside within a single module, than to fix an equivalent set of 10 errors that are distributed among two or more modules. Thus, higher densities of undetected errors mean a wider (but not necessarily an even) distribution of errors among the system modules, which leads to an escalation in the cost to fix those errors. Since the cost-to-fix escalation of an undetected error is represented in the model through an increase in the *number* of errors that the error produces, higher error densities lead to a higher error production rate (per error). Thus there are higher values of the "Multiplier to Active Error Regeneration due to Error Density," at higher error densities.

9.2.4 Active Error Retirement As was stated above, "Undetected Active Errors" can continue to produce new errors as long as new tasks are being developed. Not all the active errors will do so, however. For some errors the production activity will *not* continue up until the end of the development phase; rather, it might cease after producing one or two "generations" of errors. For example, an error in a high-level module might produce interface errors at a lower level without necessarily leading to any further errors in the user manuals. When undetected active errors cease to reproduce, they effectively become "Undetected *Passive* Errors." The rate at which this occurs is termed the "Active Error Retirement Rate," shown in Figure 9.1.

This rate is regulated through the "Retirement Fraction," the fraction of active errors that become passive every unit of time. The fraction is a function of the development phase, as shown in Figure 9.4. Because any design error must translate into coding error(s), the "Retirement Fraction" remains at zero during the design phase since no active *design* errors will retire and become passive; instead, every design error will produce at least one generation of coding errors. As the project progresses toward the last stages of development — the coding of the lower level functional modules — error propagation quickly decreases, and the "Retirement Fraction" consequently increases sharply and reaches a value of 1 at the end of development.

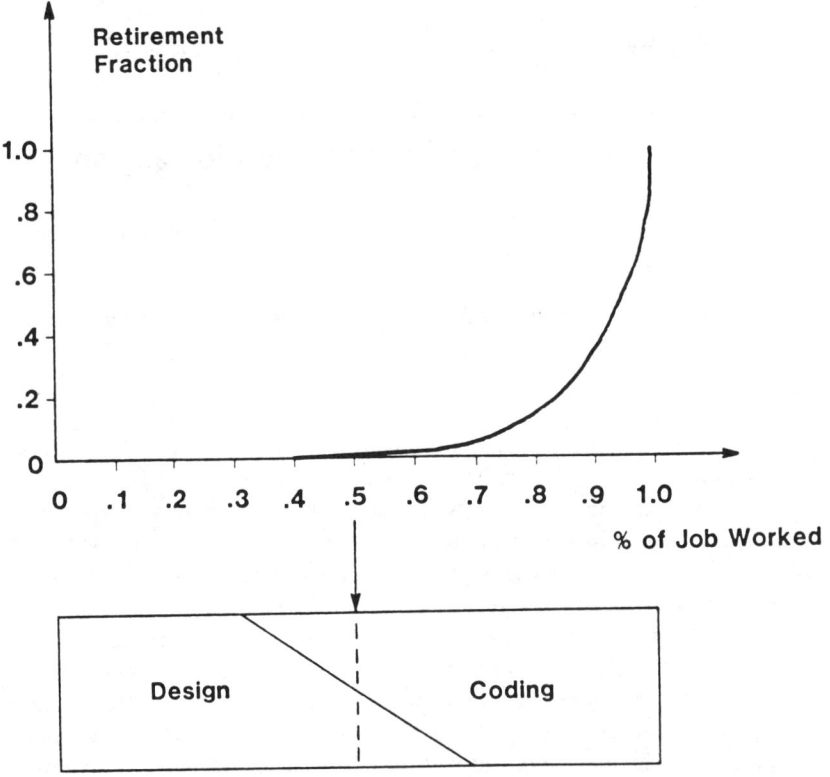

Figure 9.4 Active error retirement fraction

9.3 System Testing Activities

As the project approaches the last stages of development, something else happens: System Testing activities are initiated. The objective of System Testing is to verify "that all elements (of the system) mesh properly and that overall system function and performance are achieved'' [210]. The System Testing activities are also depicted in Figure 9.1.

As explained in chapter 7, the switch in manpower allocation from development to testing is represented in the model by the variable ''Fraction of Effort for System Testing.'' The value of this variable is initially set to zero since no effort is initially allocated for System Testing. When development (the coding and design) is perceived to be completed, the value of the ''Fraction of Effort for System Testing'' becomes 1, since 100% of the manpower effort available for development or testing is allocated to the testing function. The switch is not abrupt, however. There is usually some overlap between the development and testing phases [78, 126, 252]. The overlap is represented in Figure 7.2, which shows the gradual increase in the value of the ''Fraction of Effort for System Testing'' as a function of the fraction of development tasks perceived to be remaining.

The objective of System Testing is operationalized in the model as follows: Test all tasks that have been developed to detect and correct any remaining (active and/or passive) errors.

The rate at which developed tasks are tested is determined by dividing the ''Daily Manpower for Testing'' by the ''Testing Manpower Needed per Task.'' For example, if 5 man-days are allocated daily to System Testing, and it takes on average 1 man-day to test a task, then 5 tasks will be tested a day.

The ''Normal Testing Manpower Needed *per Task*'' has a fixed and a variable component [19, 128]. The variable component is a function of the number of errors in a task, and it represents the testing effort that would be expended in the actual detection and correction of errors. The fixed component is independent of the number of errors. It involves overhead activities such as developing test plans, installing test tools, and designing test cases.

9.3.1 Testing Overhead ''Nominal Testing Overhead,'' the fixed component, is defined in the model in terms of *nominal* man-days/KDSI. Boehm [49] estimates that this overhead effort is about 2 man-days/KDSI. For example, for a 32 KDSI project, Boehm's estimate for the above overhead functions, which he labelled ''Test Planning,'' amounted to 64.41 man-days. If we assume that motivation and communication losses will result in a 50% loss in productivity, then Boehm's estimate translates into an overhead of 1 *nominal* man-day/KDSI.

This constant parameter could then be transformed into an equivalent value of nominal man-days/*task*. For example, if a ''task'' is defined to be, say 100 DSI, the nominal testing overhead would be 0.1 man-day/*task*.

9.3.2 Detect and Correct Errors In addition to the overhead incurred in testing a task, effort is needed to detect and correct any remaining errors. The effort is the product of the ''Error Density'' and the ''Nominal Testing Manpower Needed per Error.'' The value of the former is obtained by dividing the sum of both the active and passive errors remaining by the number of tasks yet to be tested. It represents the average number of errors per task. The value of the ''Nominal Testing Manpower Needed per Error'' is set at 0.15 Man-Days/Error. For the nominal 8-hour working day, the value is 1.2 Man-Hours/Error. This value was chosen based on empirical results reported in [128] and [236].

9.3.3 Efficiency of Testing The *actual* testing effort needed per task is a function not only of testing overhead and error density, but also of how efficiently people work. We need to account for the Communication and Motivation losses incurred. For example, if the ''Multiplier to productivity due to Communication and Motivation losses,'' which represents the average productive fraction of a man-day, is 0.5, then the *actual* manpower needed to test a task becomes twice what is nominally needed.

9.4 Conclusion of Software Production Analysis

The testing activity continues until all the tasks that have been developed are all tested. When testing is accomplished, the project is declared completed since our analysis extends only until the end of the testing phase.

   With the completion of the testing activities, we also complete our presentation of the software production processes in the model. We have discussed the allocation of the manpower resource, the development activities (i.e., coding and design), quality assurance and rework, and finally, system testing. In the next two chapters, we turn our attention to two managerial functions of software development: controlling and planning.

10

CONTROLLING

10.1 Controlling Subsystem

Any control function has at least three elements [22]:

1. Measurement — detection of what is happening in the activity being controlled.

2. Evaluation — assessment of its significance, usually by comparing information on what is *actually happening* with some standard or expectation of what *should be happening*.

3. Communication — report of what has been measured and assessed, so that behavior can be altered if the need for doing so is indicated.

These three elements are included in the control function of software project management (see Figures 10.1 and 10.3). Progress in a software project is measured by the number of resources consumed, tasks completed, or both. The "Total Man-Days Perceived to be Still Needed" to complete the project are determined from the measurements. Total man-days include those perceived to be still needed to develop QA tasks, to rework any detected errors, and to complete system testing. The effort perceived to be still needed is compared to the actual "Man-Days Remaining" in the project's plan. For example, if 100 man-days are perceived to be still needed to complete the project but only 50 man-days are remaining, the project is perceived to be behind schedule. Conversely, if only 25 man-days are perceived to be still needed but 50 man-days remain, then the project is perceived to be ahead of schedule.

Once an assessment is made of any man-day shortages or excesses, behavior on the project could be altered if the need for doing so is indicated. For example, if the project is perceived to be behind schedule, then project members can be motivated to work harder or the project's schedule could be extended or both. In this chapter we explain in detail how control processes are formulated in the model.

At any point the amount of work that will be perceived as remaining will in general be a combination of three things: (1) work needed to develop and QA new tasks, (2) work needed to rework any detected errors, and (3) work needed to conduct the system testing activities. Thus the "Total Man-Days Perceived to be Still Needed" to complete the project is the sum of "Man-Days Perceived Still Needed for New Tasks," "Man-

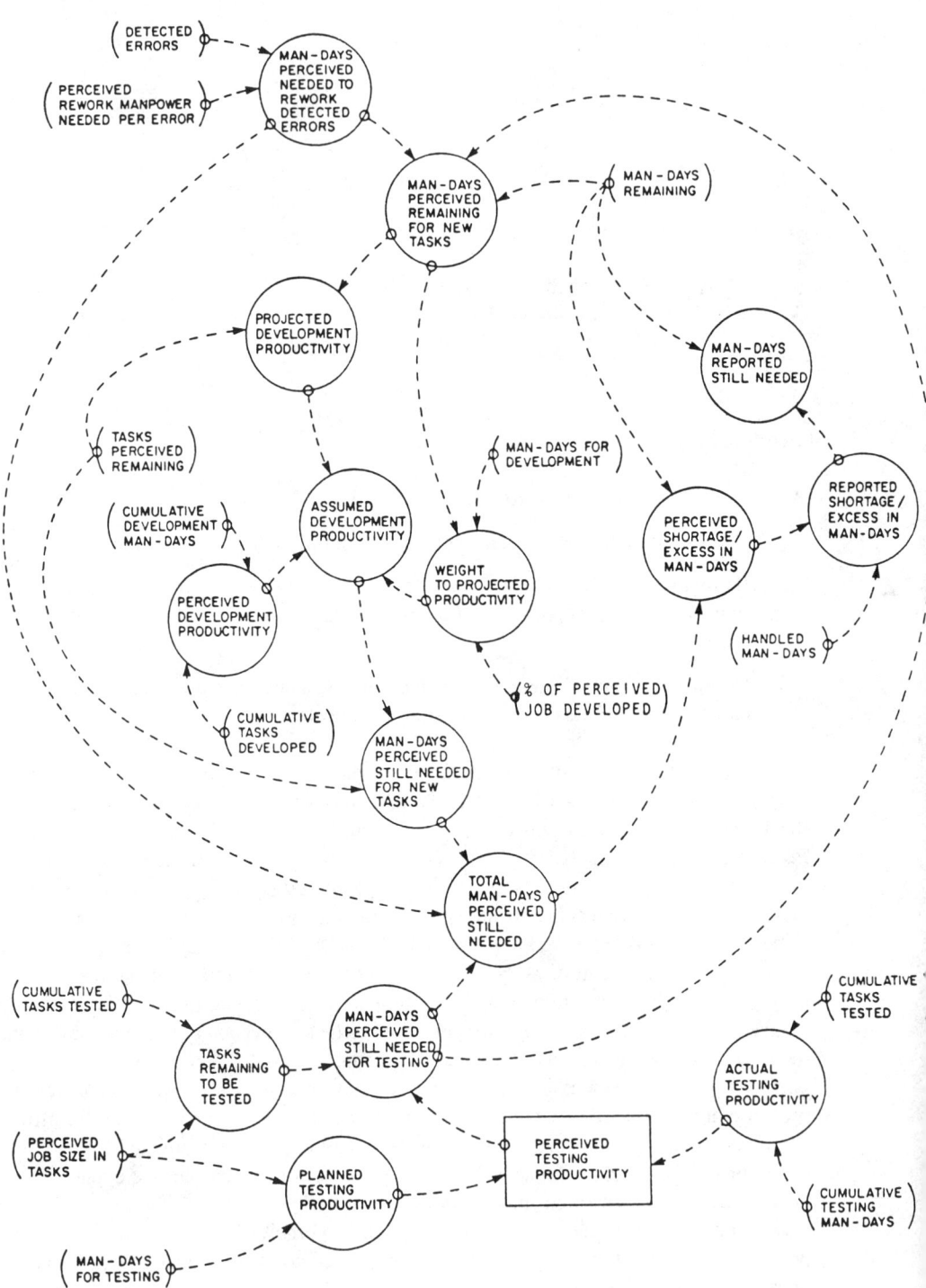

Figure 10.1 Controlling subsystem

Days Perceived Needed to Rework Detected Errors,'' and ''Man-Days Perceived Still Needed for Testing.''

10.2 Measuring Progress on New Tasks

Because software is an intangible product during most of the development process and because there are no visible milestones to measure progress as there is with a physical product, ''it is difficult to measure performance in programming. ...   It is difficult to evaluate the status of intermediate work such as underdebugged programs or design specification and their potential value to the complete project'' [181]. How then is progress in a software project measured? Our own interview findings corroborate those reported in the literature, namely, that progress, especially in the earlier phases of software development, is measured by the rate of expenditure of resources rather than by some count of accomplishments [81] (6), (8), (10), (16), (20). For example, a project for which 100 man-days have been estimated is 10% complete when 10 man-days have been expended; when 50 man-days have been expended, it is 50% complete. Baber writes:

It is impossible for the programmers to estimate the fraction of the program completed. What is 45% of a program? Worse yet, what is 45% of three programs? How is he to guess whether a program is 40% or 50% complete? The easiest way for the programmer to estimate such a figure is to divide the amount of time actually spent on the task to date by the time budgeted for that task. Only when the program is almost finished or when the allocated time budget is almost used up will he be able to recognize that the calculated figure is wrong [28].

As progress is measured during the early phases of development by the rate at which resources are expended, status reporting ends up being nothing more than an echo of the original plan. In other words, ''Man-Days Perceived Still *Needed* for New Tasks'' will be equal to the ''Man-Days Perceived *Remaining* for New Tasks.''

As the project develops, though, and the work becomes more visible, discrepancies between percent of tasks accomplished (remaining) and percent of resources expended (remaining) become increasingly apparent. For example, while it might not be too apparent that a project that has consumed 50% of its estimated resources is only 25%, rather than 50%, complete, any such discrepancy becomes obvious when the allocated resources are almost used up. At the same time, as the project advances towards its final stages, project members become increasingly able to perceive how productive the work force has actually been (3), (18). As a result the value of the ''Man-Days Perceived Still Needed for New Tasks'' ceases to be a function of ''Man-Days Perceived Remaining for New Tasks,'' and instead becomes a function of what the project members perceive to be the amount of work that is remaining.

These *differing* modes of measuring progress are captured in the model through a *single* formulation of ''Man-Days Perceived Still Needed for New Tasks.'' As shown in Figure 10.1, ''Man-Days Perceived Still Needed for New Tasks,'' MDPNNT, is determined by dividing the value of ''Tasks Perceived Remaining,'' TSKPRM, by the ''Assumed Development Productivity,'' ASSPRD. That is,

$$MDPNNT = TSKPRM/ASSPRD \qquad (10.1)$$

where "Assumed Development Productivity," ASSPRD, is a weighted average of "Perceived Development Productivity," PRDPRD, and a variable we are calling "Projected Development Productivity," PJDPRD. That is,

$$ASSPRD = PJDPRD \times WTPJDP + PRDPRD \times (1 - WTPJDP) \qquad (10.2)$$

where the weighting factor, WTPJDP, moves from 1 at the beginning of the project to zero at the end of the development phase.

The conception behind this formulation is somewhat subtle and will, therefore, require some explanation.

10.2.1 Early Phases of Software Development In the early phases of software development, progress tends to be measured by the rate at which resources are expended. As a result status reporting ends up being nothing more than an echo of the original plan. "Man-Days Perceived Still *Needed* for New Tasks,' MDP*N*NT, becomes, under such conditions, simply equal to the "Man-Days Perceived *Remaining* for New Tasks," MDP*R*NT. That is,

$$MDPRNT = MDPNNT \qquad (10.3)$$

Substituting for MDPNNT, we get

$$MDPRNT = TSKPRM / ASSPRD \qquad (10.4)$$

which leads to

$$ASSPRD = TSKPRM / MDPRNT \qquad (10.5)$$

This is an interesting result. For, it suggests that as project members measure and report progress by the rate of expenditure of resources, they, by so doing, would be *implicitly* assuming that their productivity equals "Tasks Perceived Remaining," TSKPRM, divided by the "Man-Days Perceived Remaining for New Tasks," MDPRNT. This is interesting because such an assumed value for productivity is solely a function of future projections (i.e., of *remaining* tasks and man-days) as opposed to being a reflection of accomplishments (i.e., of *completed* tasks and expended resources). This implicit notion of productivity is represented in the model by the variable "*Projected* Development Productivity," PJDPRD, defined, as the above equation suggests, to be equal to "Tasks Perceived Remaining," TSKPRM, divided by "Man-Days Perceived Remaining for New Tasks," MDPRNT.

Thus, in the early phases of software development, equation (10.1) becomes

$$MDPNNT = TSKPRM / PJDPRD \qquad (10.6)$$

where

$$PJDPRD = TSKPRM / MDPRNT \qquad (10.7)$$

which is achieved by setting the weighting factor WTPJDP in equation (10.2) at 1 and substituting it into equation (10.1).

10.2.2 Final Phases of Software Development As the project advances towards its final stages, accomplishments become more visible and project members become increasingly more able to perceive how productive the work force has actually been. As a result, what the project members assume their productivity to be, the value of "Assumed Development Productivity," ceases to be a function of future projections (i.e., of *remaining* tasks and man-days) and instead becomes a function of perceived accomplishments. This explicit notion of productivity is represented in the model by the variable "Perceived Development Productivity," PRDPRD. Discussions with interviewees (3), (18), and (23) suggest that, towards the final stages of development, the value of the team's overall productivity is determined by dividing the value of "Cumulative Tasks Developed," CUMTKD, by "Cumulative Development Man-Days," CUMDMD. In other words, if 100 man-days have been expended to develop the project's 100 tasks, then "Perceived Development Productivity" would be 1 task/man-day.

Thus, in the final stages of software development, we would like to reduce equation (10.1) to

$$MDPNNT = TSKPRM \: / \: PRDPRD \qquad (10.8)$$

where

$$PRDPRD = CUMTKD \: / \: CUMDMD \qquad (10.9)$$

which is achieved by setting the weighting factor (WTPJDP) in equation (10.2) at zero and substituting it into equation (10.1).

10.2.3 Transition from Early to Final Phases People's assumptions about their productivity change as the project develops. The change is often gradual and not abrupt (3), (18), (23). For example, the transition of "Assumed Development Productivity" from determination solely on future projections early in the project to determination entirely on perceived accomplishments, towards the end of development, is a smooth rather than instantaneous transition.

The transition in people's assumption about their productivity is represented in the model by the weighting factor WTPJDP of equation (10.2). The rate at which WTPJDP moves from a value of 1 to a value of 0 is the *product* of two factors: the rate of expenditure of resources and the rate of development of tasks. Recall Baber's quote: "Only when the program is almost finished or when the allocated time budget is almost used up will the programmer be able to recognize the discrepancy between the percent of tasks accomplished and the percent of resources expended" [28]. In the model, the weighting factor, WTPJDP, is the *product* of two multipliers, the "Multiplier to Productivity Weight Due to Resource Expenditures" and the "Multiplier to Productivity Weight Due to Development." In Figure 10.2, both multipliers are assumed to have the same shape, moving from a value of 1 at the beginning of the project to a value of zero when all estimated development resources are expended or all tasks are developed.

10.3 Measured Progress on Rework and Testing

Thus far we have been only discussing how "Man-Days Perceived Needed for *New Tasks*" is determined. At any point in the project the amount of work perceived as remaining will in general consist not only of work needed to develop and QA new tasks, but also of work needed to rework any detected errors and to conduct system testing. Thus, the "Total Man-Days Perceived to be Still Needed" to complete the project is the sum of "Man-Days Perceived Still Needed for New Tasks," "Man-Days Perceived Needed to Rework Detected Errors," and "Man-Days Perceived Still Needed for Testing."

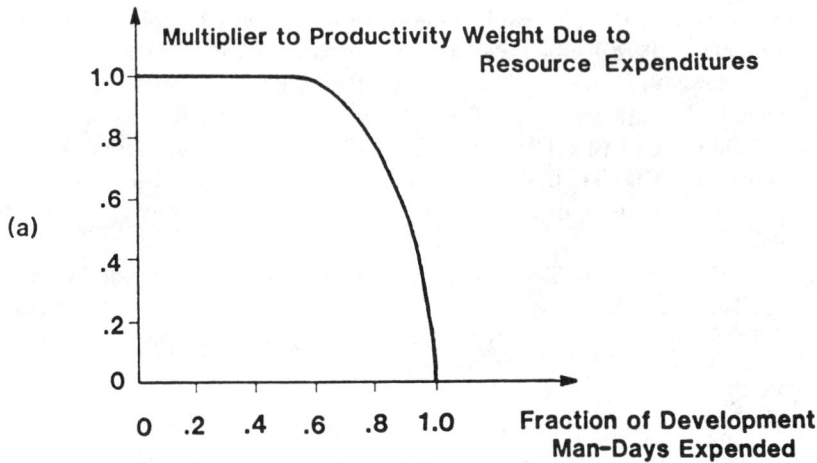

(a)

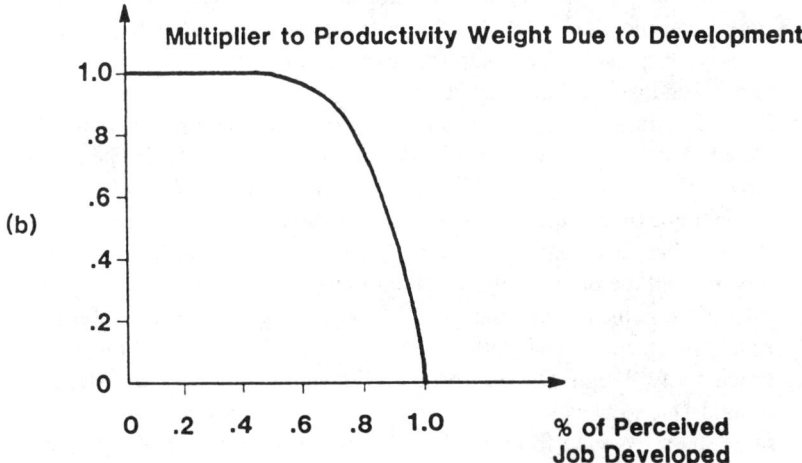

(b)

Figure 10.2   Multipliers to productivity weight

10.3.1 Rework The "Man-Days Perceived Needed to Rework Detected Errors" is the product of "Detected Errors" and "Perceived Rework Manpower Needed per Error." The latter is a smoothed function of the "*Actual* Rework Manpower Needed per Error" (See chapter 6). For example, if at some point 50 errors detected through QA are still uncorrected and if it is perceived that an error requires 0.2 Man-Days to correct, then the "Man-Days Perceived Needed to Rework Detected Errors" would be $50 \times 0.2 = 10$ Man-Days.

10.3.2 Testing The "Man-Days Perceived Still Needed for Testing" is determined by dividing the value of "Tasks Remaining to be Tested" by the "Perceived Testing Productivity." The "Tasks Remaining to be Tested" is simply the "Perceived Job Size in Tasks" minus "Cumulative Tasks Tested." For example, if the perceived job is 100 tasks and 60 have already been tested, then "Tasks Remaining to be Tested" amount to $100 - 60 = 40$ tasks.

Throughout most of the development phase, and *before* the commencement of the System Testing phase, the value of "Perceived Testing Productivity" is set equal to "Planned Testing Productivity," the value of testing productivity that is implicit in the project's plan. For example, if the 100 task project's plan allocates 20 Man-Days for system testing, then the "Planned Testing Productivity" would be 5 tasks/man-days. However, as system testing gets underway, people's perceptions of their productivity become a function of how productive the testing activity *actually* is as opposed to how productive it was *planned* to be. The "Actual Testing Productivity" is determined by dividing the "Cumulative Tasks Tested" by "Cumulative Testing Man-Days." Because "full and immediate action is seldom taken on a change of incoming information (e.g., on the sudden drop in yesterday's testing productivity) ... (and because there is a) tendency to delay action until the change is insistent. ... " [99], "Perceived Testing Productivity" is formulated as a smoothed function. The smooth delay is set at 50 working days.

10.4 Adjustment of Job Size

Once "Man-Days Perceived Still Needed for New Tasks," "Man-Days Perceived Needed to Rework Detected Errors," and "Man-Days Perceived Still Needed for Testing" are determined, they are added together to determine the "*Total* Man-Days Perceived Still Needed" to complete the project. The total is then compared to the actual "Man-Days Remaining" in the project's plan. So, if 100 man-days are perceived to be still needed to complete the project but only 50 man-days remain, the project is perceived to be behind schedule. Conversely, if only 25 man-days are perceived to be still needed while 50 man-days remain, the project is perceived to be ahead of schedule.

After an assessment is made of man-day shortages or excesses, behavior on the project can then be altered. The mechanisms that determine how much of any perceived man-day shortage (excess) is absorbed by the project members as increased (decreased) work rate were explained in our discussion of software development productivity. Any shortages (excesses) that are not absorbed will be reported and lead to adjustments to the project's scope. Such adjustments are then translated into adjustments to the schedule or adjustments to the work force level or both.

Let us consider an example: the case of 100 man-day project. If, after 60 man-days have been expended, the values of "Man-Days Remaining" and "Total Man-Days Perceived Still Needed" were 40 man-days and 65 man-days respectively, then the "Perceived Shortage in Man-Days" would be 25. If the project members (based on the many factors discussed in the productivity section) decide to absorb only 10 of the 25 man-days, then the "Reported Shortage in Man-Days" would be 15 man-days. If these are added to the 40 "Man-Days Remaining" in the project's plan, we come up with a value of 55 man-days for the "Man-Days Reported Still Needed" to complete the project.

Any time the "Man-Days Reported Still Needed" are greater (less) than the "Man-Days Remaining" in the project's plan, it in effect constitutes a *revision* of what the project's scope is perceived to be. For example, in the case above, reporting that 55 (rather than 40) man-days are still needed after having had 60 man-days already expended constitutes a revision in what the project's size is perceived to be, from the original estimate of 100 man-days to a revised value of $60 + 55 = 115$ man-days — a 15% increase. When such a "revelation" occurs in a project, project management reacts to transform those revised *perceptions* about the "Total Job Size in Man-Days" into *actual* adjustments.

10.4.1 Rate of Adjustment The adjustment process is represented by the "Rate of Adjusting the Job's Size in Man-Days" (See Figure 10.3). It is the rate at which the "Total Job Size in Man-Days" is adjusted upward or downward to what is perceived as its new value. The "Rate of Adjusting the Job's Size in Man-Days" is computed as

$$(GOAL - LEVEL) / (ADJUSTMENT\text{-}TIME) \tag{10.10}$$

where

$$GOAL = Revised\ value\ of\ job\ size\ in\ Man\text{-}Days$$
$$= Man\text{-}Days\ Reported\ Still\ Needed\ +$$
$$Cumulative\ Man\text{-}Days\ Expended$$
$$LEVEL = Total\ Job\ Size\ in\ Man\text{-}Days$$
$$ADJUSTMENT\text{-}TIME = Delay\ in\ Adjusting\ the$$
$$Job's\ Size\ in\ Man\text{-}Days$$

Thus, the adjustment process is not an instantaneous one; instead it takes place over a time defined as the "Delay in Adjusting the Job's Size in Man-Days."

The above formulation of the "Rate of Adjusting the Job's Size in Man-Days" produces the behavior pattern shown in Figure 10.4. Up until time t_1, LEVEL = GOAL. Then, at time t_1 there is a sudden permanent increase H in the GOAL; for example, the "Revised Value of the Job's Size" jumps from 100 man-days to 115 man-days. In response to such a steep rise in the value of the GOAL, the value of LEVEL (the value of "Total Job Size in Man-Days") rises exponentially to achieve the goal. The rate at which LEVEL rises is such that it would close 63% of the gap after one "Adjustment time" and 95% of the gap after three "Adjustment-times."

The "Delay in Adjusting the Job's Size in Man-Days" ranged in the organizations we interviewed from 2 days (22), (23) to 5 days (20). In the model the "Delay in Adjusting the Job's Size in Man-Days" is set at 3 working days. This value and those of our interviewees might strike some readers as somewhat lower than expected. But remember, this adjustment process is really the project's final, not first, reaction to man-day shortage/excess. When the project is perceived to be behind (ahead) of schedule, people react *first* by absorbing the shortage (excess). Only when this is not enough are adjustments to the project's size made. If the decision to adjust the project's size is ever made, people in the project are already "geared-up" for it.

10.4.2 Adjustment Due to Underestimation Falling behind schedule is not the only reason a project's size in *man-days* might be adjusted upwards. It could also happen, as Figure 10.3 indicates, as a result of an upward adjustment in the project's size in *tasks*.

As a software project develops, project members often realize that they have under-estimated the number of tasks (e.g., modules) that constitutes the software system being developed [61]. Boehm provides an explanation for this tendency to underestimate software size:

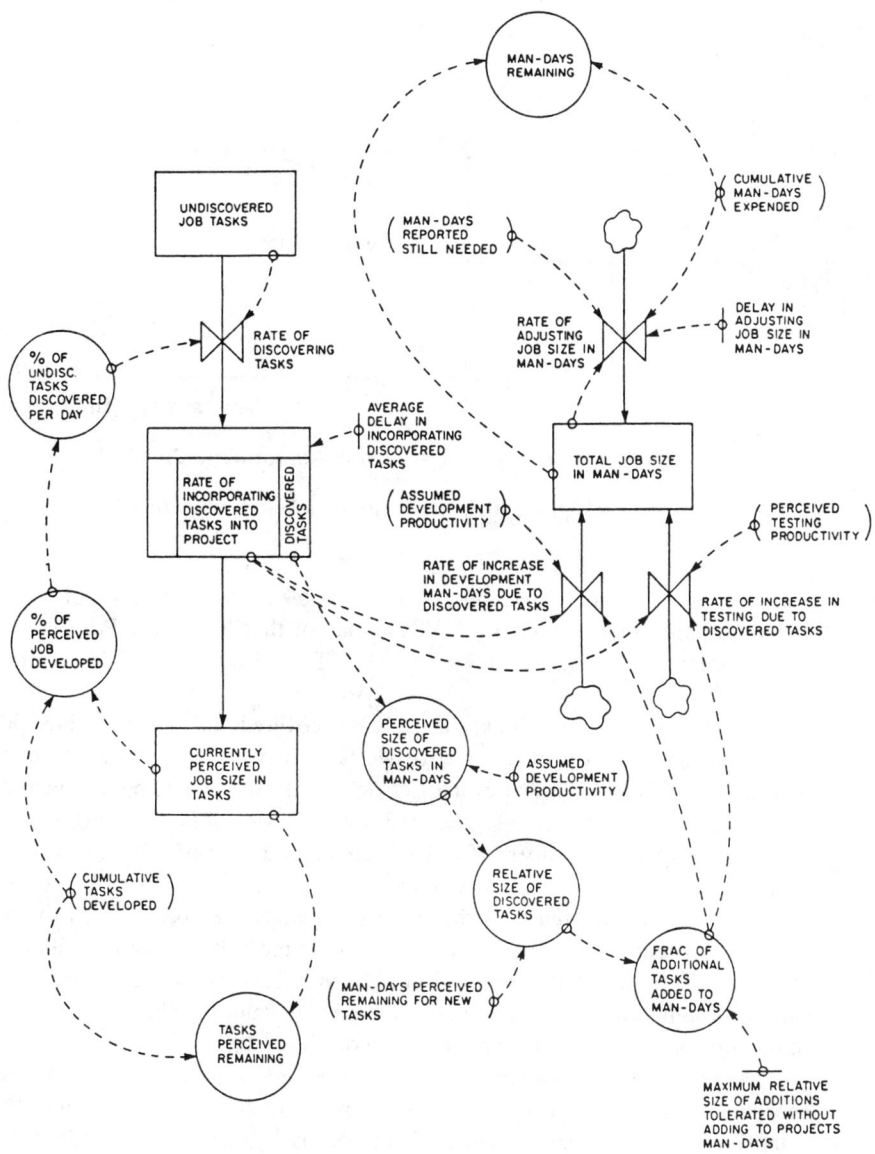

Figure 10.3 Adjustment of job size

There is a powerful tendency to focus on the highly visible mainline components of the software, and to underestimate or completely miss the unobtrusive components (e.g., help message processing, error processing, and moving data around) [49].

In the model we define an initializing parameter called ''Tasks Underestimation Fraction.'' This parameter simulates any software under-sizing situation we wish to investigate. For example, if the *actual* size of the software product to be developed is 100

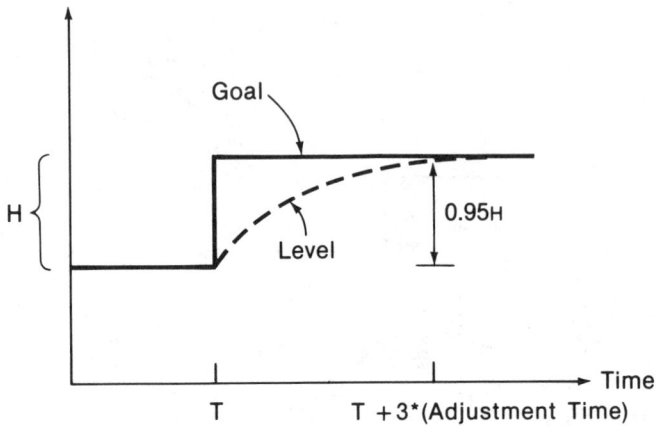

$$\text{Rate} = (\text{Goal} - \text{Level})/(\text{Adjustment Time})$$

Figure 10.4 Behavior of job size adjustment

tasks, then to simulate a 25% under-sizing "problem" we would simply set the "Tasks Underestimation Fraction" to 0.25. The value of the "Currently Perceived Job Size in Tasks" becomes $(1 - 0.25) \times 100 = 75$ tasks. The "Undiscovered Job Tasks" becomes $0.25 \times 100 = 25$ tasks.

As the project develops, the "Undiscovered Job Tasks" are progressively discovered as "the level of knowledge we have of what the software is intended to do (increases)" [49]. The number of undiscovered tasks that would be discovered per unit of time is regulated, as shown in Figure 10.3, by the "Rate of Discovering Tasks," which is the product of the number of "Undiscovered Job Tasks" and the "Percent of Undiscovered Tasks Discovered per Day." The rate at which undiscovered-tasks are discovered tends to increase as the project develops [78] because, as the above quote indicates, the team's level of knowledge of what the software product is intended to do increases. Thus, the "Percent of Undiscovered Tasks Discovered per Day" is not a constant but instead a variable that increases in value as the project progresses. Its formulation is depicted in the table function of Figure 10.5.

As the additional tasks are discovered, they are then incorporated into the project — incorporated into the project's Work Breakdown Structure, the Gantt and/or PERT charts, or the Earned value system. This, of course, takes time. In the model this process is modeled as a third-order delay with the "Average Delay in Incorporating Discovered Tasks" set at 10 working days (22).

10.5 Adjustment to Man-Day Allocation

The final piece of structure we would like to discuss is the one that models the process by which the discovery of additional tasks is translated into additions to the project's allocation of man-days. This structure occupies the lower portion of Figure 10.3.

When additional tasks are discovered in a project, they do *not* necessarily trigger an adjustment to the project's man-days estimate [49]. Only if the additional tasks are

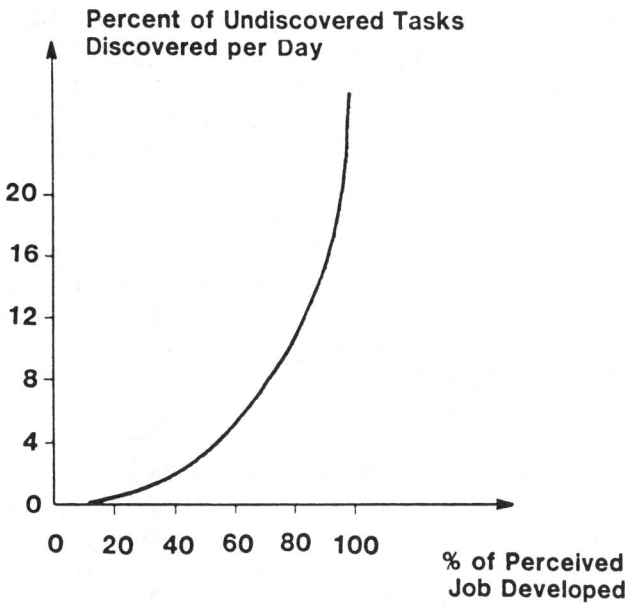

Figure 10.5   Percent of undiscovered tasks discovered per day

perceived as requiring a *relatively* "significant" amount of effort to handle would project members "bother" to go through the trouble of formally developing cost estimates and incorporating them in the project's work plan (20), (23), (26) and (27).

As Figure 10.3 indicates, the number of discovered tasks are first sized-up "mentally" by dividing them by the "Assumed Development Productivity." For example, if 10 tasks are discovered and if, at that point in the project, the value of the "Assumed Development Productivity" is 1 task/man-day, then the "Perceived Size of Discovered Tasks in Man-Days" is 10 man-days. This absolute number by itself is not enough to decide whether the new tasks do or do not deserve a "formal treatment." That decision is based not on the perceived *absolute* size of the discovered tasks but instead on the perceived size *relative* to the amount of effort that is perceived remaining. For example, while it would be possible that a 100 man-day task discovered at the beginning of 100,000 man-day project would not trigger any adjustments in the project's man-days estimate, it would be unlikely for this to happen if the 100 man-day task is discovered at the end of the development phase when only 50 man-days remain in the project's plan. Thus, the value of the "Perceived Size of Discovered Tasks in Man-Days" is divided by the "Man-Day Perceived Remaining for New Tasks" to determine the "*Relative* Size of Discovered Tasks."

Once this relative size is determined, it is then compared to the threshold value: the "Maximum Relative Size of Additions Tolerated Without Adding to the Project's Man-Days." If the relative size is lower than that threshold, the newly discovered tasks are totally absorbed without triggering any adjustments to the project's man-days estimate. If, however, the relative size exceeds the threshold value, part or all of the additional tasks are translated into additional man-days in the project's plan. This behavior is represented in the table function of Figure 10.6. Based on discussions with interviewees (26) and (27), we set the "Maximum Relative Size of Additions Tolerated Without Adding to Schedule to the Project's Man-Days" at 1%. For example, for a 1000 man-day development phase (10 people working for 100 working days) the threshold is 10 man-days.

A decision might be made to incorporate either part or all of those tasks discovered, at some point in the project, into the project's man-days estimate. Such an adjustment involves producing two estimates, one for the effort to develop and QA the new tasks and the other for system testing. Both estimates are determined in a similar manner, the former by dividing the number of discovered tasks that are to be incorporated by the "Assumed Development Productivity," and the latter by dividing by the "Perceived Testing Productivity."

Any such adjustments to the project's total man-days estimate will trigger further adjustments in either the project's scheduled completion date, the work force level, or both. These reactions are explained next in the chapter on planning.

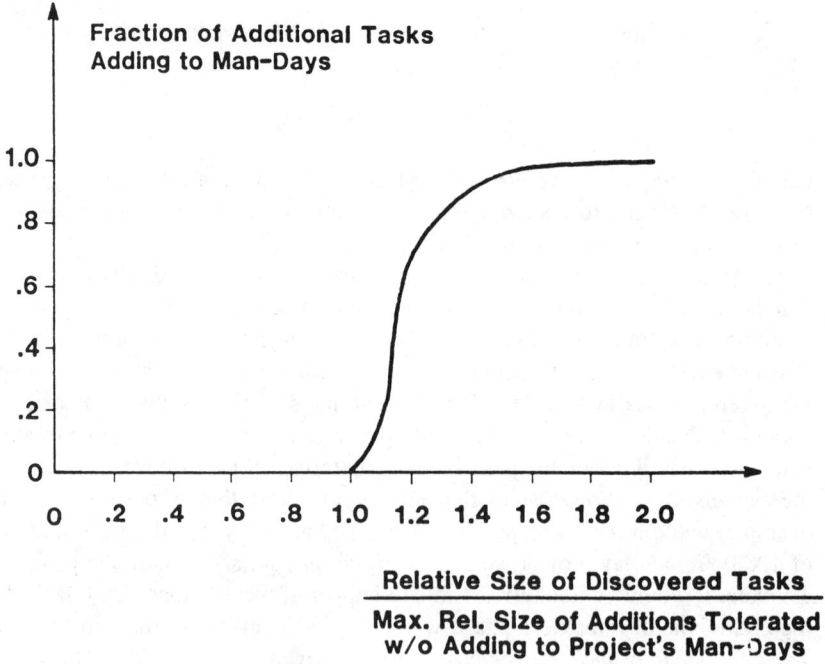

Figure 10.6 Adjustment to Man-Day Allocation

11

PLANNING

11.1 Planning Subsystem

In the planning subsystem initial project estimates are made to start the project, and then those estimates are revised as necessary throughout the project's life. The planning subsystem is depicted in Figure 11.1.

The "Schedule Completion Date" represents not an actual date but the number of working days from the beginning of the project (e.g., 200 days). Thus, by simply subtracting the current value of "Time" (which represents the number of working days elapsed in a simulation run), we can determine the scheduled "Time Remaining." By dividing the value of "Man-Days Remaining" by "Time Remaining," we can determine the "Indicated Work Force Level" at any point in the project. The "Indicated Work Force Level" represents the number of full-time employees believed to be necessary and sufficient to complete the project on time according to the current "Scheduled Completion Date."

For example, suppose the "Scheduled Completion Date" is 100 days. If at time = 40 days, the value of "Man-Days Remaining" is 600 man-days, the "Indicated Work Force Level" would be determined as follows: First, the value of "Time Remaining" would be 100 - 40 = 60 days. Dividing 60 into 600 man-days, we determine the value for the "Indicated Work Force Level" as 10 men. This value is in terms of full-time employees. If actual employees are *not* assigned full-time to the project, adjustments should be made. The model adjusts by dividing the value of the "Indicated Work Force Level" by the value of the "Average Daily Manpower per Employee." For example, if employees are assigned only 50% of their time to the project, "Average Daily Manpower per Employee" equals 0.5; the "Indicated Work Force Level" obtained above would be adjusted to become 10 / 0.5 = 20 actual employees.

If the "Indicated Work Force Level" turns out to be lower than the "Total Work Force," excessive employees could be transferred out of the project. The transfer operation was explained in detail in "Human Resource Management Subsystem." If the "Indicated Work Force Level" is larger, then more people need to be hired. However, as also explained in "Human Resource Management Subsystem," hiring decisions are *not* determined only because of scheduling considerations. Consideration is also given to the stability of the work force. That is, before hiring new project members, management tries to estimate how long new members will be needed. In general, the relative

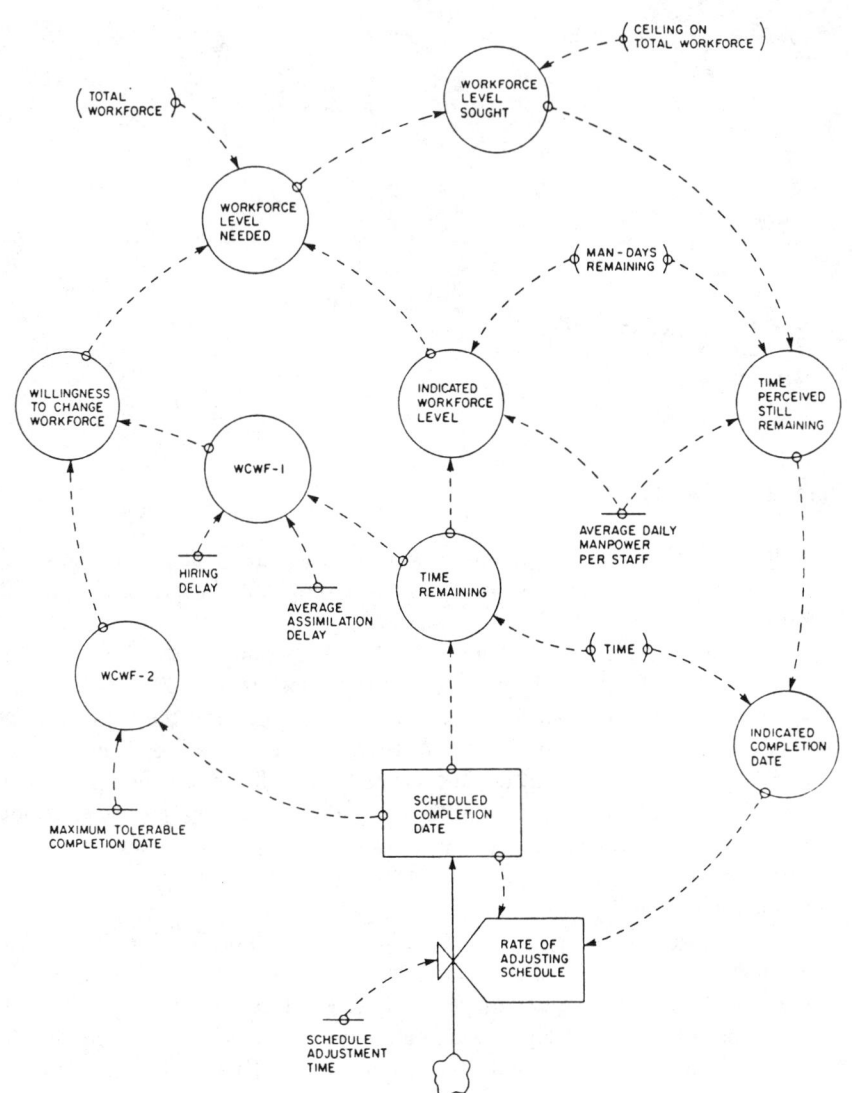

Figure 11.1 Planning subsystem

weighting of the desire to have a stable work force and the desire to complete the project on time changes from stage to stage of the project.

11.2 Work Force Level Adjustments

The "Work Force Level Needed" is a weighted average of the current "Total Work

Force Level'' and the ''Indicated Work Force Level.'' It accounts for the stable work force level and the number of employees that would be required to complete the project on time:

$$WF\text{-}Level\ Needed = Indicated\ WF\text{-}Level \times WCWF +$$
$$Total\ WF\text{-}Level \times (1 - WCWF)$$

This formulation applies only when the value of the ''Indicated Work Force Level'' is larger than ''Total Work Force,'' indicating a need for hiring more people. When the opposite is true, ''Work Force Level Needed'' would simply be set to the lower value, and any excessive employees transferred out of the project.

11.2.1 Willingness to Change Work Force Level The weighting factor WCWF is termed the ''Willingness to Change Work Force Level.'' It is a variable that assumes values between 0 and 1, inclusive. When WCWF = 1, the weighting considers only the ''Indicated Work Force Level''; management is adjusting its work force level to the number perceived required to finish on schedule. As WCWF moves towards 0, more and more weighting is given to the stability of the work force. When WCWF equals 0, the weighted number of employees desired is wholly dependent on work force stability.

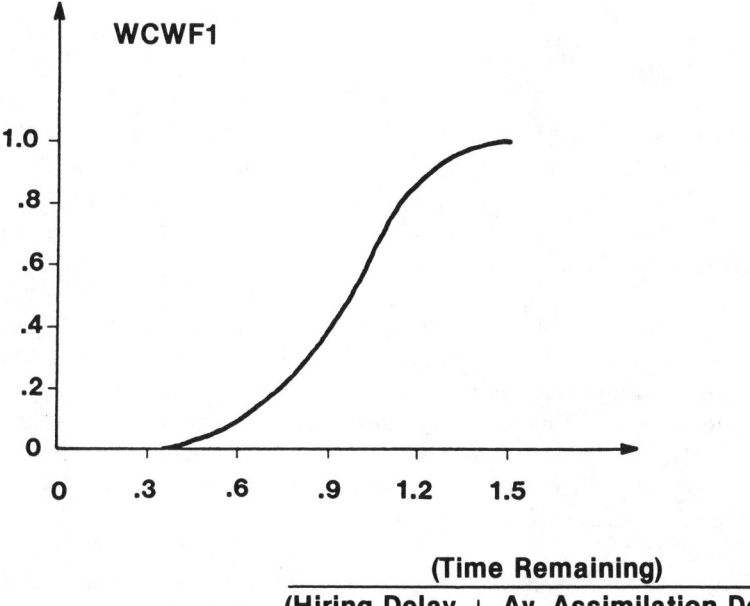

Figure 11.2   General form of WCWF1

11.2.2 Work Force Stability The ''Willingness to Change Work Force Level'' consists of two components. The first, WCWF1, represents the pressures that develop for work force stability as the project proceeds toward its final stages. The general form of WCWF1 depicted in Figure 11.2 is based on discussions with interviewees (23), (24), and

(25). To understand what Figure 11.2 represents, assume for the moment that "Willingness to Change Work Force Level" consists only of WCWF1. In the early stages of the project when "Time Remaining" is usually much larger than the sum of the "Hiring Delay" and the "Average Assimilation Delay," WCWF would be equal to 1, and there would be total willingness to adjust the size of the work force to whatever level is necessary to suit the project's scheduled completion date. As the number of days perceived remaining drops below $1.5 \times$ (Hiring Delay + Average Assimilation Delay), the figure illustrates the reluctance to increase the work force level.

For example, if the "Hiring Delay" is 40 working days and the "Average Assimilation Delay" is 80 days, then as "Time Remaining" drops below 180 days, management starts becoming reluctant to hire new people, even though the time and effort perceived remaining imply that more people are needed. The reluctance stems from the realization that most of those remaining 180 days would be "wasted" in hiring new people, acquainting them with the mechanics of the project, integrating them into the project team, and training them in the necessary technical areas. When the "Time Remaining" drops below $0.3 \times$ (Hiring Delay + Average Assimilation Delay), the table function of Figure 11.2 suggests that no more additions will be made to the project's work force and the hiring rate will fall to zero. If the project is behind schedule, project management would be coping *only* by pushing back the scheduled completion date.

11.3 Schedule Stability

In our discussions at MITRE, we learned that in projects involving embedded software for weapon systems, serious schedule slippages can not be tolerated. In such projects, software development is often on the critical path of overall system development; as a result, any serious slippages in the software schedule become very costly slippages in the overall delivery schedule of the system (10).

> Let's see what this meant in a recent software development for a large defense system. It was planned to have an operational lifetime of seven years and a total cost of about $1.4 billion — or about $200 million a year worth of capability. However, a six-month delay caused a six-month delay in making the system available to the user, who thus lost about $100 million worth of needed capability — about 50 times the direct cost of $2 million for the additional software effort [45].

Because of the software industry's less than impressive track record in delivering projects on schedule, such embedded software projects are often scheduled with a "safety factor" incorporated (10). For example, if the "Maximum Tolerable Completion Date" is 100 days, and a 20% safety factor is used, then the project would be initially scheduled to complete in $0.8 \times 100 = 80$ days. If such a project starts to fall behind schedule, what would happen? We will assume the following scenario (10): As long as the "Scheduled Completion Date" is comfortably below the "Maximum Tolerable Completion Date," then decisions to adjust the schedule, add more people, or do a combination of both will continue to be based on the balancing of scheduling and work force stability, as represented by WCWF1. However, as the "Scheduled Completion Date" starts approaching the "Maximum Tolerable Completion Date," pressures develop that override the work force stability considerations. That is, management becomes increasingly willing to "pay any price" necessary to avoid overshooting the "Maximum Tolerable Completion Date." In such cases, management is often willing to hire more people.

11.3.1 Willingness to Change Work Force Level The development of such overriding schedule pressures are represented by the "Willingness to Change Work Force Level," WCWF,

$$WCWF = MAXIMUM\,(WCWF\,1,\ WCWF\,2)$$

where WCWF2 is the table function depicted in Figure 11.3.

As long as "Scheduled Completion Date" is comfortably below the "Maximum Tolerable Completion Date," the value of WCWF2 is zero; that is, it has no bearing on the determination of WCWF and consequently no bearing on the hiring decisions. When "Scheduled Completion Date" starts approaching the "Maximum Tolerable Completion Date," the value of WCWF2 starts to rise gradually. Because such a situation develops toward the end of the project, the value of WCWF1 is probably close to zero and decreasing. As WCWF2 exceeds the value of WCWF1, the "Willingness to Change Work Force Level" becomes totally dominated by scheduling with a goal not to overshoot the "Maximum Tolerable Completion Date."

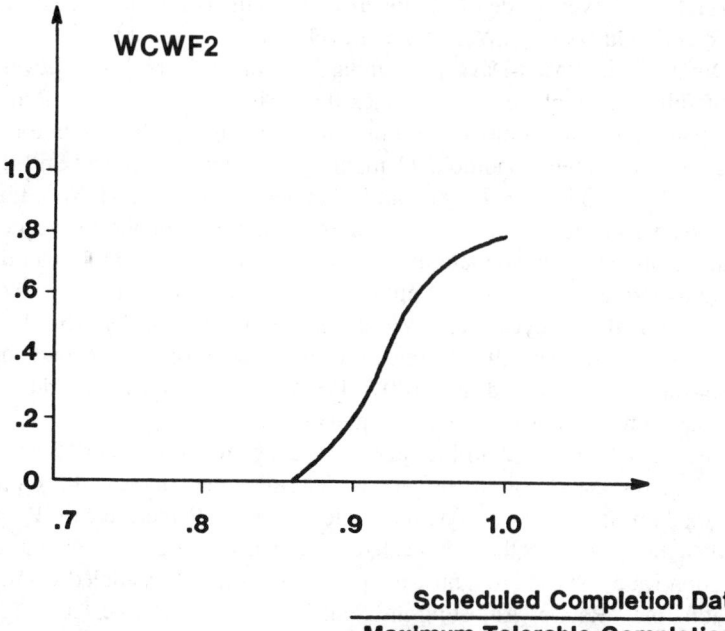

Figure 11.3 General form of WCWF2

WCWF allows us to represent projects in which there are no tight time commitments. We need only to set the value of "Maximum Tolerable Completion Date" at some high value, which would keep WCWF2 always at the zero level. WCWF would become solely a function of WCWF1.

11.3.2 Policy Implications It is important to realize that the variable WCWF is an expression of a *policy* for managing projects. A range of functions is possible here (e.g., different forms of the table functions WCWF1 and WCWF2), representing different strategies on how to balance work force and schedule adjustments throughout the project to minimize overruns and costs. In the later chapters, we will take the opportunity to explore a range of other alternate policies.

11.4 Completion Date Determination

The ''Work Force Level Needed'' determines whether management hires employees or transfers them out of the project. The adjusted number becomes the ''Work Force Level Sought.'' The ''Work Force Level Sought'' is *almost* always identical to the ''Work Force Level Needed.'' They can, however, differ. When they do, it is usually in the early stages of the project, when the project's manpower build-up rate tends to be at its highest level. In our model, we allow for the project's ability to absorb new people into its organization. The ''Work Force Level Sought'' in effect defines a ceiling on the number of employees to be hired. That is, ''Work Force Level Sought'' would be set at the value of ''Work Force Level Needed'' as long as it is less than or equal to the ''Ceiling on Total Work Force.'' Otherwise, ''Work Force Level Sought'' is set at the value of the latter.

Dividing the ''Man-Days Remaining'' by the ''Work Force Level Sought'' (in terms of full-time employees) determines the ''Time Perceived Still Required,'' which represents the remaining time, in working days, perceived to be required to complete the project, given its current condition. Computing the ''Time Perceived Still Required'' as a function of the ''Work Force Level *Sought*'' rather than the ''Total Work Force'' assumes that schedule adjustments are made with full awareness of the hiring decisions being made in the project. For example, if at some point as many as 1100 man-days remain to complete the project, 10 full-time employees are working on it, and it has been decided to hire an additional employee (i.e., ''Work Force Level Sought'' is $10 + 1 = 11$), then we assume that management (often through a back-of-the-envelope computation) determines that the time still required is $1100 / 11 = 100$ days. (Our procedure is based on discussions with interviewees (11), (14), and (16).)

The ''Time Perceived Still Required'' is added to the value of ''Time,'' the number of working days elapsed on the project, to determine the ''Indicated Completion Date.'' For example, if at time = 40 days, the value of ''Time Perceived Still Required'' is 100 days, then the value of the ''Indicated Completion Date'' is 140 days. ''Indicated Completion Date'' is used to adjust the project's formal ''Scheduled Completion Date.'' Calculating the ''Rate of Adjusting the Schedule'' is similar to calculating the ''Rate of Adjusting the Job's Size'' presented in the previous chapter:

$$(GOAL - LEVEL) / ADJUSTMENT\text{-}TIME$$

where

GOAL = Indicated Completion Date
LEVEL = Scheduled Completion Date
ADJUSTMENT-TIME = Schedule Adjustment Time

The ''Schedule Adjustment Time'' is set in the model at 5 working days (22), (20).

11.5 Summary of Model Development Activities

In Part II of the book (chapters 3 and 4) we identified the sources of information used in developing the model. The model was developed based on an extensive review of the literature, supplemented by 27 focused field interviews of software project managers in 5 organizations. The model focuses on the development phases of software production, extending from the beginning of the design phase of the software life cycle, to the end of the system testing phase.

In Part III (chapters 5 through 11), we detailed the four sectors of the model's structure. At the heart of the model is the Software Production Sector, comprising software production activities such as coding and testing. The project management activities comprise the remaining three sectors: Human Resource Management, Controlling, and Planning.

In Part IV (chapters 12 through 20), which follows, we will present a case study and a series of experiments to test the model and examine the implications of various management policies.

PART FOUR

CRITICAL

LESSONS

LEARNED

12

A CASE STUDY

12.1 The NASA DE-A Software Project

In this chapter we report the results of a case study conducted to test the model. The objective of the case study is to examine the model's ability to reproduce the dynamic patterns of a completed software project. We tracked a set of variables pertaining to project management, including completion date estimates, man-day estimates, cost (in man-days), and work force loading.

The case study was conducted at the Systems Development Section of NASA's Goddard Space Flight Center (GSFC) at Greenbelt, Maryland. This organization is engaged in the development of application software that supports ground-based spacecraft attitude determination and control. The subsystems included in a typical attitude system are telemetry processing, sensor calibration, attitude computation, and maneuver planning. First, we provide a detailed description of one such project, namely, the DE-A project. Then we discuss model parameterization: the set of model parameters that are set to simulate the particular DE-A project environment (e.g., project size). Finally, we simulate the DE-A project, observe the simulation's behavior, and compare it to DE-A's actual behavior.

12.2 The DE-A Project

The requirements for the DE-A project were to design, implement, and test a software system that would process telemetry data and provide definitive attitude determination as well as real-time attitude determination and control support for NASA's DE-A satellite. The DE-A satellite was designed to study the earth's upper atmosphere, ionosphere, and magnetosphere. The overall requirements were similar to those of previous space missions at the GSFC System Development Section [193].

The DE-A project was selected for the case study by NASA to satisfy three criteria we furnished: it had to be (1) medium in size (i.e., 16-64 KDSI), (2) recent, and (3) "typical," i.e., developed in a familiar in-house software development environment.

The data presented were extracted from two primary sources:

1. Interviews with the Head of the Systems Development Section of the Goddard Space Flight Center, who managed the project [168]. Two lengthy personal

interviews were conducted at the Goddard Center. These were then followed by four 15-minute telephone interviews.

2. Project documentation, including:

   a. "Software Development History for Dynamics Explorer (DE) Attitude Ground Support System (AGSS)." [193]

   b. "DE-A Resource Summary" [194]

The life cycle phases covered in the case study include the design, coding, and system testing phases. Excluded from the study are the requirements definition phase and the acceptance testing phase because they both lie outside the boundary of our model, and the requirements phase had not been included in the group's project responsibility. Requirements were instead the responsibility of the user organization, the Attitude Determination and Control Section (ADCS) of the Goddard Space Flight Center. The ADCS thus developed the functional requirements of the system, including system input and output, algorithms, timing and accuracy requirements. The responsibility for the acceptance testing phase, on the other hand, was shared by both the development team and an independent testing group. Excluding the acceptance testing phase posed no complications for our analysis simply because it was the last phase in the life cycle; hence its exclusion had no impact on any of the other life cycle phases studied.

The development and target operations machines were the IBM S/360-95 and -75. The programming language was mostly Fortran (85%); assembler language and assembler language macros constituted the remaining 15%. The size of the system in Delivered Source Instructions (DSI) is 24,400 DSI.

The size of the project in DSI is determined by NASA as follows [193]:

$$Size\ in\ DSI = New\ Statements\ +$$
$$extensively\ modified\ statements\ +$$
$$0.2 \times (Slightly\ Modified\ Statements) \qquad (12.1)$$

where a "Statement" is a non-comment source instruction.

The project's actual key development dates were:

TABLE 12.1. ACTUAL DEVELOPMENT DATES

Phase	Start	End
Design	Oct. 1, 1979	May 9, 1980
Coding	May 10, 1980	March 27, 1981
Sys. Test	Nov. 15, 1980	April 24, 1981

Thus, the project was completed in 19 calendar months. The project consumed 2,222 man-days of effort. (2,784 man-days were expended to complete the total project, of which 562 man-days were consumed in the acceptance testing activity.)

12.3 Model Parameterization

Four sets of parameters need to be set in the model to simulate this particular project situation. These are:

Human Resource Management

1. Average daily manpower per staff member

2. Hiring delay

3. Average employment time

4. Training overhead

5. Average assimilation delay

Software Development Environment

1. Nominal Potential Productivity

2. Error rate

3. Distribution between Development and Testing

4. QA Effort Allocation

Planning Environment

1. Maximum Tolerable Completion Date

Initial Project Estimates

1. Project size in DSI

2. Man-day expenditures

3. Project duration

4. Staffing level

12.4 Human Resource Management

The parameters needed for Human Resource Management were obtained directly from the DE-A Resource Summary report and interviews with the managers.

12.4.1 Average Daily Manpower per Staff (ADMPPS) On project DE-A the "Average Daily Manpower per Staff" was set at 0.5. On average, DE-A project personnel were assigned half-time to the project.

12.4.2 Hiring Delay (HIREDY) The "Hiring Delay" was set at 30 working days — six calendar weeks. This is somewhat lower than the industry average (40 days). The reason is that prompt hirings are often made from the Computer Science Corporation (CSC) under a task order contract between CSC and the Goddard Center.

12.4.3 Average Employment Time (AVEMPT) The average employment time at the Systems Development Section of the GSFC is 1000 working days (i.e., 50 calendar months). This translates into a turnover rate of approximately 20%.

12.4.4 Training Overhead (TRPNHR) The amount of effort committed to the training of new employees is determined by managerial intuition and organizational custom. At the System Development Section 25% of an experienced employee's time is committed per new employee.

12.4.5 Average Assimilation Delay (ASIMDY) The "Average Assimilation Delay" was set for the DE-A project at 20 working days (4 calendar weeks). This value is much lower than values reported in the literature. The reason has again to do with the special arrangement this group has with the Computer Sciences Corporation. On many occasions, software professionals are recruited from CSC to work on Goddard projects. This pool of software professionals is one that over the years has gained experience with the NASA project environment. As a result, when recruited on a new project, such a CSC professional is assimilated at a faster rate.

12.5 Software Development Environment

The parameters needed to characterize the Software Development Environment, such as Nominal Potential Productivity, are not directly measurable. A certain degree of deduction must be used to estimate them.

12.5.1 Nominal Potential Productivity (DSIPTK) This parameter represents the set of productivity determinants that distinguish different software development environments, such as availability of software tools, computer hardware characteristics, and product complexity. DSIPTK is the set of factors that affect productivity that tend to remain invariant during the life cycle of a single project.

One way to determine the nominal *potential* productivity for the DE-A project environment is to work backwards from the *actual* development productivity. As stated above, the total effort expended to develop the 24.4 KDSI project amounted to 2,222 man-days. Of these, 228 man-days were expended on system testing and approximately 914 man-days on QA and rework [193]. Thus 1,080 man-days were expended on the *development* (design and coding) of the system. The average development productivity was $24,400/1,080 = 22.59$ DSI/man-day. This, however, is still not the value we are looking for. We are looking for the "Nominal *Potential* Productivity" and what we have is the *actual* productivity. Potential productivity is

> ... the level of productivity that will be attained if the individual or group makes the best possible use of its resources (that is, if there is no loss of productivity due to faulty process) [240].

As explained earlier, actual productivity rarely equals potential productivity because of losses from communication and motivation problems. These losses are represented in the model by the "Multiplier to Productivity due to Communication and Motivation Losses." Actual productivity in the model is the product of potential productivity and the "Multiplier to Productivity due to Communication and Motivation Losses." Thus, if we can estimate the value of this multiplier, we can then divide it into the value of *actual* productivity calculated above, to come up with an estimate for DE-A's "Nominal Potential Productivity."

The multiplier is itself a product of two variables: the "Actual Fraction of a Man-Day on Project" and "Communication Overhead." The nominal value of the former was set at 0.6 (i.e., a full-time employee allocates, on the average, 60% of his or her time to productive work on the project). The "Communication Overhead" was a function of team size. The DE-A team size was approximately 10 people during most of the development period. From Figure 7.8, we can determine that the loss due to "Communication Overhead" is 60%. Thus, the value of the "Multiplier to Productivity Due to Communication and Motivation Losses" becomes: $0.6 \times (1 - 0.06) = 0.564$. By dividing this into the value of actual productivity (22.59 DSI/Man-Day), we come up with the estimate for the "Nominal Potential Productivity," namely 22.59/0.564 = 40 DSI Man-Day.

12.5.2 Error Rate (TNERPT) Earlier we explained that the formulation of the table function "Nominal Number of Errors Committed per Task" serves two purposes. First, its shape over the project's life reflects the relative generation rates of different error types (e.g., design versus coding errors) throughout the life of the project. These assumptions, as all others in the model, are expected to apply to all project situations modeled. Hence, this shape would remain the same even for different project situations. The second purpose of the formulation, its absolute value, reflects the different error generation characteristics of different project environments. This, obviously, would generally change when modeling different project environments.

In the DE-A project the actual number of errors committed was somewhere between 495 and 510. (The exact figure is not known because of "errors" in counting errors.) We formulated the "Nominal Number of Errors Committed per Task" for the DE-A project environment as shown in Figure 12.1. The shape of the curve is exactly similar to that of the base case (shown in Figure 8.2), however, for DE-A the absolute values are slightly lower, ranging from 24 errors/KDSI at the beginning of design to 12 errors/KDSI towards the end of coding with an average value for the project of 18 errors/KDSI.

Notice that an average nominal error rate of 18 error/KDSI would generate $18 \times 24.4 = 439$ errors only, not 495-510. The reason is that this error rate is the *nominal* rate. The nominal error rate was defined to be that generated by the average *experienced* employee. Such a rate is therefore a lower bound, attained only when the work force contains only experienced personnel. Otherwise, the error rate would be adjusted upwards through the "Multiplier to Error Generation Due to Work Force Mix." By setting the *nominal* average error rate to 18, we are assuming that 15% more errors (i.e., above the nominal level) will be produced because of new hirees on the DE-A project ($18 \times 24.4 \times 1.15 = 505$ errors).

12.5.3 Development vs. Testing (DEVPRT) The total man-day estimate is distributed among the project's life cycle phases. In the DE-A project the distribution used was 85% for development (design and coding) and 15% for system testing.

12.5.4 QA Effort Allocation (TPFMQA) Finally, effort is also allocated to the QA activity. The "Planned Fraction of Manpower for QA" for project DE-A is shown in Figure 12.2.

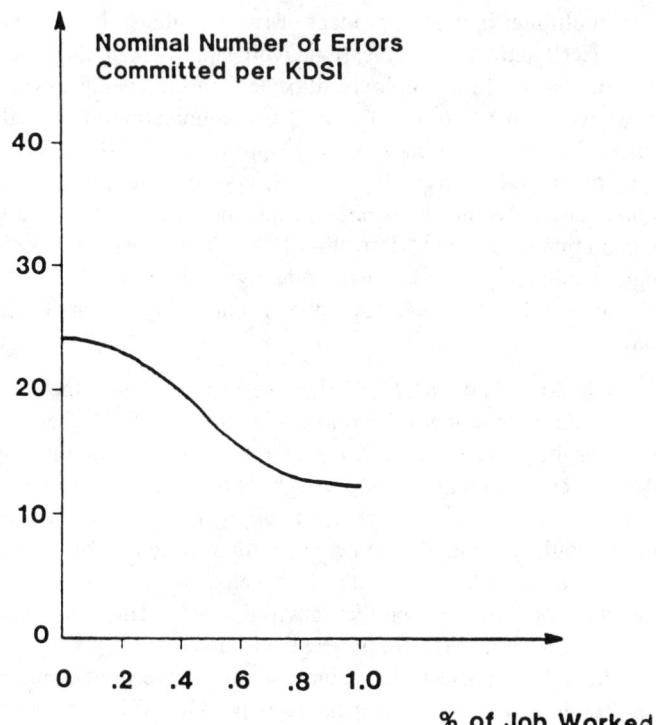

Figure 12.1 Nominal number of errors committed

12.6 Planning Environment

Because NASA's launch of the DE-A satellite was tied to the completion of the DE-A software, serious schedule slippages were not tolerated. Specifically, "all software was required to be accepted and frozen 90 days before launch" [193].

12.6.1 Maximum Tolerable Completion Date (MXSCDX) The DE-A Software Project was initiated on October 1, 1979 and the DE-A satellite's launch date was August 3, 1981. All software had to be accepted and frozen by May 3, 1981. Because the acceptance testing phase was scheduled for 2 months, the "Maximum Tolerable Completion Date" for the system testing phase was March 3, 1981. That is, the DE-A project was initially scheduled for 16 months with the realization that it should not slip by more than 2 more months. (Note: the project was completed on April 24. It overshot the 18-month ceiling by approximately 20 calendar days. As a result the acceptance testing phase was "compressed.")

12.7 Initial Project Estimates

12.7.1 Initial Estimate of Project Size (UNDEST) The *actual* DE-A project size was 24.4 KDSI. At the initiation of the design phase, the project's size was under-estimated by 35%: the project was perceived to be only $24.4 \times (1 - 0.35) = 16$ KDSI [193]. (Note:

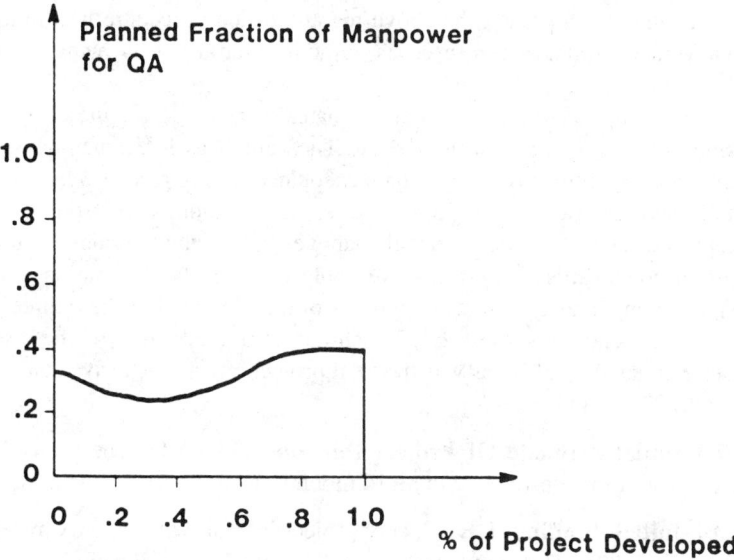

Figure 12.2   Planned Fraction of Manpower for QA

Initial estimates were made in terms of source instructions *with comments*. The actual size of the project in source instructions with comments was 49,500; the initial estimate was 32,600, a 35% underestimation.)

12.7.2 Initial Estimates of Man-Day Expenditures (TODMD1) The NASA document *Recommended Approach to Software Development* [192] provides the following guidelines for estimations:

> It is important for the manager to use a model that is tuned to the specific environment and corresponds well with the resources expended for similar past projects. The Meta-Model has been developed using SEL data. However, managers must never completely rely on any formal resource estimation model. Rather, they must use the results of the model, together with historical knowledge of similar systems, to update resource and cost estimates. The new estimates are more accurate because they are based on additional information and model support.

The Meta-Model is a software estimation model developed by the Software Engineering Laboratory (SEL). The SEL is a research organization established in 1977 at the NASA Goddard Space Flight Center (Systems Development and Analysis Branch) in cooperation with the University of Maryland (Computer Science Department) and the Computer Sciences Corporation (Flight Systems Operation). The Meta-Model is discussed in [31].

In the DE-A project the above recommended procedure was followed [193]. The Meta-Model estimates were used as guidelines, adjusted by managerial experience and judgment.

For Project DE-A the initial estimates were made for the design, coding, system testing, *and acceptance testing phases*. The value was 1,380 man-days. Since the actual man-day expenditures (including the acceptance testing phase) were 2,784 man-days, the initial estimate was 50% off the actual. Recall, though, that our model excludes the acceptance testing phase. Thus, the above 1,380 value cannot be used and must be adjusted downwards. To do this, we apply the man-day estimation error of 50% to the design, coding, and system testing phases of the project. For these three phases the *actual* man-day expenditures were 2,222 man-days. If the effort for these three phases was under-estimated by 50% (as was the total project effort), we arrive at an initial estimate of $0.5 \times 2,222 = 1,111$ man-days.

12.7.3 Initial Estimate Of Project Duration (TDEV1) The project's duration (until system testing) was estimated to be 16 months or $16 \times 20 = 320$ working days [193].

12.7.4 Initial Staffing Level The project began with approximately 1.5 full-time employees [193]. The initial staffing level is calculated in the model as the product of the average staffing level (TOTMD1/TDEV1) and the initial understaffing factor (INUDST).

12.8 Summary of DE-A Model Parameters

The DE-A model parameters are summarized in Table 12.2. They are referred to by their DYNAMO names used in the model presented in the Appendix.

TABLE 12.2. SUMMARY OF DE-A MODEL PARAMETERS

Parameter Name	Units	Value
H1. ADMPPS	Dimensionless	0.5
H2. HIREDY	Days	30.0
H3. AVEMPT	Days	1,000.0
H4. HTRPNHR	Dimensionless	0.25
H5. ASIMDY	Days	20.0
S1. DSIPTK	DSI/TASK	40.0
S2. TNERPT	Errors/KDSI	24/22.9/20.75/15.25/13.1/12
S3. DEVPRT	Dimensionless	0.85
S4. TPFMQA	%	.325/.29/.275/.255/.25/.275/.325/.375/.4/.4/0
P1. MXSCDX	Dimensionless	1.16
I1. UNDEST	Dimensionless	35.0
I2. TOTMD1	Man-Days	1,111.0
I3. TDEV1	Days	320.0
I4. INUDST	Dimensionless	0.4

The parameterization process did not involve any of the model's policy formulations. By "policy" we mean the criteria for decision-making. The set of parameters defines the particular environment within which the policies are exercised. For example, by setting parameters such as "Hiring Delay" and "Turnover," we do not alter in any way the rationale that determines how hiring and firing decisions will be modulated throughout the project's life cycle. Thus while we can determine that the DE-A project began with 1.5 full-time-equivalent employees, we *cannot* ascertain the project's work force loading pattern. The dynamic behavior of management systems tends to be largely a function of the interaction of policies that govern such systems [101]. For example, we will see in the next section how the work force loading pattern of the DE-A software project is a function not only of human resource policies but also of the interaction between those policies and other policies such as those for project scheduling.

12.9 Actual and Simulated Project Behavior

Once the model was parameterized, it was run to simulate the DE-A project. In this section we discuss the model's output and compare it to DE-A's actual behavior. We examine the dynamic behavior of the following four project variables: (1) estimated completion date, (2) estimated project man-day expenditures, (3) cumulative man-day expenditures, and (4) work force level.

12.9.1 Completion Date and Man-Day Expenditures Figure 12.3 depicts how DE-A's estimated completion date, measured in terms of number of elapsed days until completion, and estimated total workforce expenditures, measured in man-days, charged during the project. The actual project values are shown as circles with a dot inside. The time axis is in terms of working days (a calendar month is 20 working days).

The model accurately portrays management's inclination not to adjust the project's scheduled completion date during most of the development phase. Adjustments are instead made in the project's work force level. This behavior pattern arises, according to DeMarco, for political reasons:

> Once an original estimate is made, it's all too tempting to pass up subsequent opportunities to estimate by simply sticking with your previous numbers. This often happens even when you know your old estimates are substantially off. There are a few different possible explanations for this effect: ''It's too early to show slip. ... If I re-estimate now, I risk having to do it again later (and looking bad twice).'' ... As you can see, all such reasons are political in nature. [81]

Adjustments in the project's man-days budget start toward the end of the design phase. The adjustments are triggered as ''Undiscovered Job Tasks'' are discovered [168]. Initially, the project was incorrectly perceived to be (only) 16 KDSI. The adjustments made in DE-A are, however, somewhat larger than those estimated by the model. This indicates that the visibility in the DE-A project is somewhat higher than that assumed in the model. That is, DE-A management detected more of the discrepancies between the project's actual scope, and it detected them faster. Indeed, in a post-project evaluation the project was rated as ''above average'' in project visibility [193] because of the use of a number of project management tools including librarians who maintained a central repository of the project's records, configuration analysis tools (CATs), and Unit Development Folders (UDF).

However, while visibility in the DE-A project is somewhat better than the industry's norm (according to our model), it is by no means total. Significant adjustments

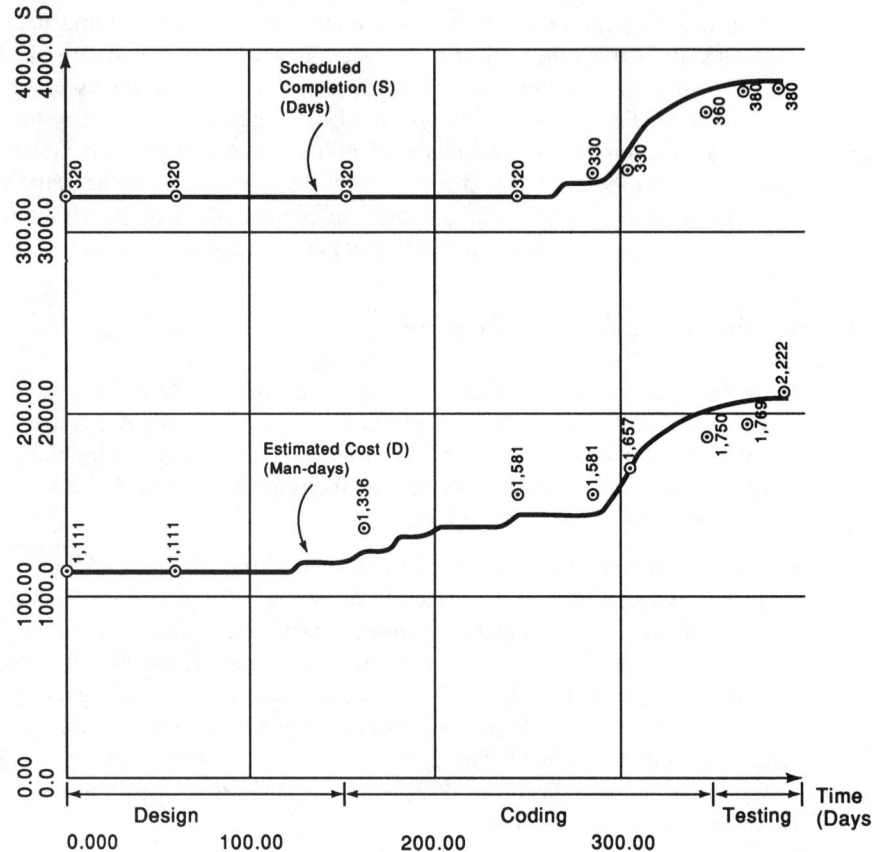

Figure 12.3 Scheduled completion and estimated cost (simulated and actual)

in both the project's man-days and the schedule continue to be made until the final stages of development, an outcome that the model successfully reproduces.

The model's values for the project's final man-day expenditures (2,092) are slightly lower than the actual (2,222). The reason is that while the model successfully reproduces the project's manpower loading *pattern* (as we shall see later), it slightly underestimates the values of the manpower *level*. Lower manpower levels mean lower communication and training overheads, which mean a slight over-estimation of productivity.

Also, the model's project duration (387.5 days) is slightly longer than DE-A's actual (380 days). The DE-A management behaved slightly more aggressively than is assumed in the model in acquiring manpower, especially during the final stages of the project; the work force level at the end of the system testing phase was approximately 16 full-time people while the model's value was 14.8. With more people at hand in the actual project a smaller schedule overshoot was achieved.

12.9.2 Manpower Loading We turn next to Figure 12.4, which depicts the simulated and actual manpower loading patterns. For the reader's convenience we plotted a number of actual values alongside the simulation output.

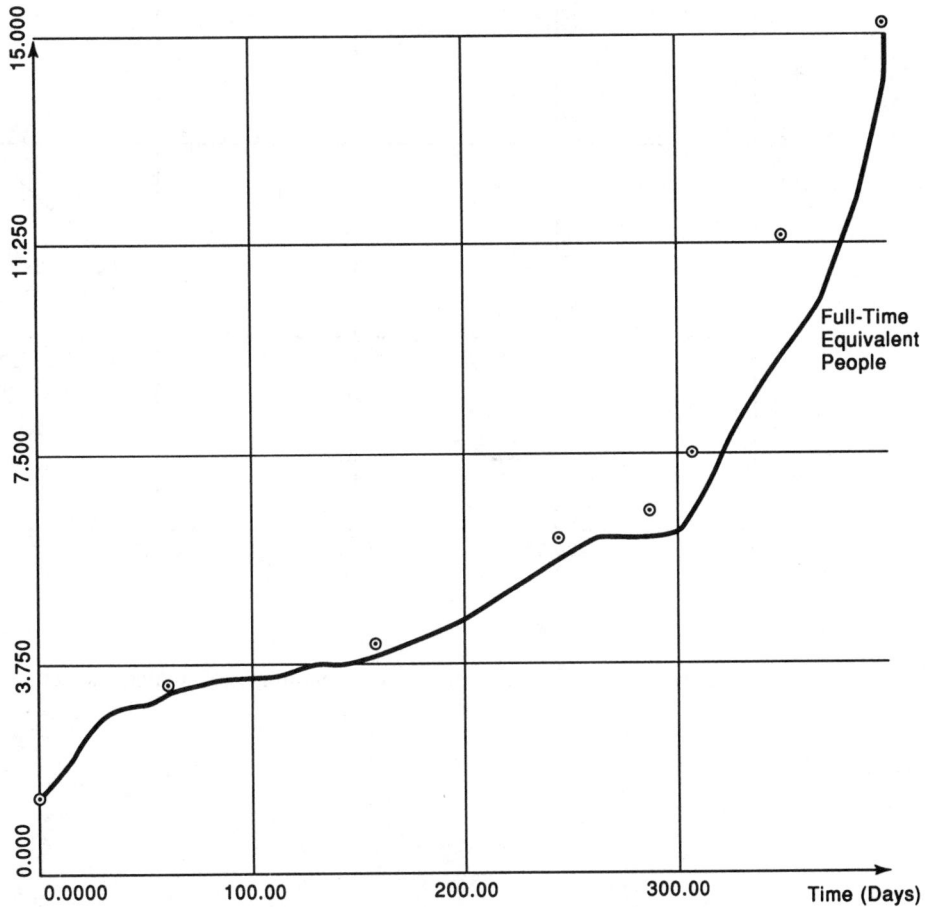

Figure 12.4   Manpower loading (simulated and actual)

The model accurately replicates the actual DE-A pattern. It reproduced the "atypical" work force loading pattern. The "typical" software project work force pattern discussed in the literature is a concave curve that rises, peaks, and then drops to lower

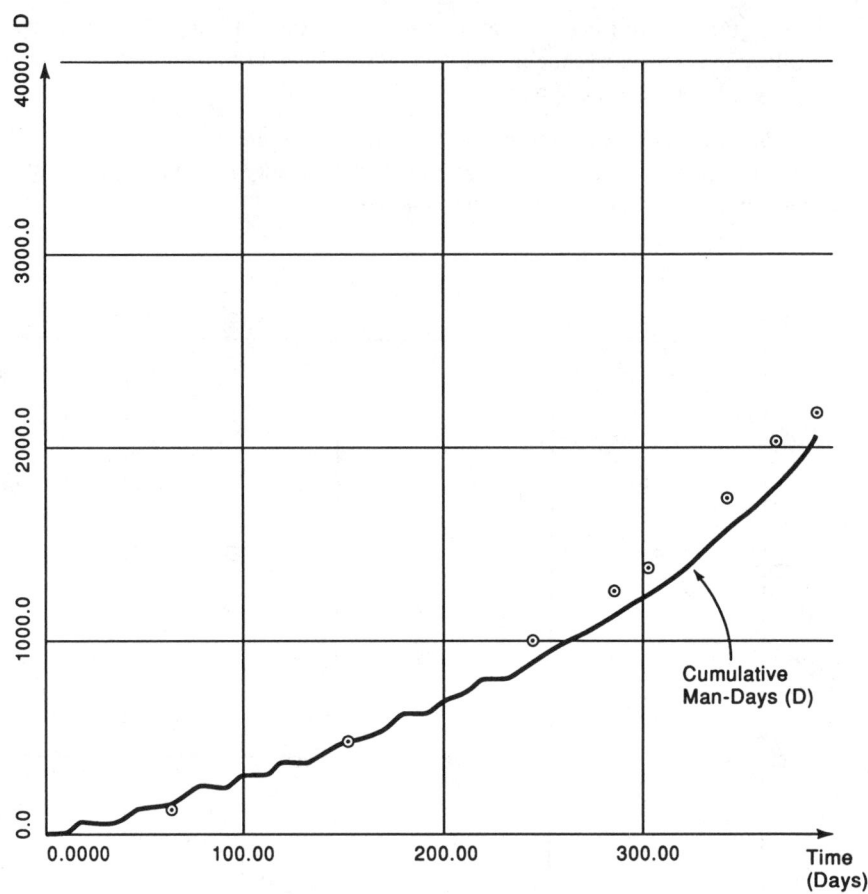

Figure 12.5 Cumulative man-day expenditures (simulated and actual)

levels as the project proceeds towards the end of the system testing phase [20, 49, 81].

The work force level shot upward toward the end of the project because of NASA's tight scheduling constraints. As explained earlier, serious schedule slippages were not tolerated. The "Maximum Tolerable Completion Date" or DE-A was day 380 from the start. As the date approached, pressures developed that overrode the work force stability: management became increasingly willing to "pay any price" necessary to avoid overshooting the "Maximum Tolerable Completion Date." As the figures indicate, management was increasingly willing to add more people.

12.9.3 Cumulative Man-Day Expenditures Finally in Figure 12.5 we plot the model's cumulative man-day expenditures together with actual project results. The model captures the exponentially increasing pattern. The actual figures are slightly higher, however, because, as explained earlier, the model slightly under-estimates the work force level, especially toward the second half of the project; DE-A management's "Willingness to Change Work Force" did not decrease as the project proceeded toward its final stages as much as the model assumed.

12.10 Summary of NASA DE-A Case Study

The objective of the case study was to test the model's ability to reproduce the dynamic behavior of a completed software project: the NASA DE-A software project. We first parameterized the model by setting model parameters that reflected the particular DE-A project environment. The parameters were obtained from two sources: interviews at NASA and project documentation. The model parameters (e.g., "Hiring Delay" and "Turnover Rate") did *not* involve any changes in the formulation of the model's policy structures. The parameter set merely defines the (DE-A) environment within which the policies were exercised. This is significant since the dynamic behavior is largely a result of the interaction of the model's policy structures, which were unchanged.

Four DE-A project variables were examined: completion date estimates, man-day estimates, cost in man-days, and work force loading. While the model was quite accurate in reproducing the project's patterns of dynamic behavior, it slightly underestimated the absolute value of DE-A's work force level. DE-A's management was more aggressive in its manpower acquisition policy than the model assumed. The underestimate caused the model to underestimate by 6% the project's cost in man-days and to overestimate by 2% the project's duration.

12.10.1 What-If Questions One advantage of system dynamics modeling is that it allows us not only to generate the dynamic implications of a given set of policies but to explore the implications of new and different sets of managerial policies and procedures. Let us ask some of the "what-if" questions that DE-A's management might ask:

1. What if a different estimation tool was used? In the DE-A project, estimation by NASA's Meta-Model was used and adjusted by management's experience and judgment. Like NASA, other software development organizations have developed quantitative software estimation tools, e.g., TRW's COCOMO model. How can the applicability of such new tools to the NASA environment be evaluated? To what extent are such models portable to the NASA environment? If not, why not? How can the relevancy of new estimation models be improved?

2. What if more or less quality assurance (QA) effort was expended? In the DE-A project 30-40% of the development effort was allocated to QA, a level that is significantly higher than the industry average. Is this an "optimal" allocation? How can we determine what an "optimal" allocation is? What project/organizational factors affect such a determination?

3. What if more people had *not* been added at the final stages of the project? Brooks' Law suggests that adding more people to a late project makes its completion date later. When would the DE-A project have been completed had management resisted

adding more people at DE-A's final stages?

In the following chapters we explore an array of such managerial policies on the management of software projects.

13

MODEL BEHAVIOR

13.1 Controlled Experimentation

A system dynamics model is a tool that allows repeated experimentation with the system, testing assumptions or altering management policies. The purpose is to gain an understanding of and make predictions about the implications of managerial actions, policies, and procedures.

> The most important advantage of a simulation model is its ability to 'play out' the dynamic consequences of a given set of assumptions in a way the human mind can do neither well nor consistently; a useful model produces scenarios that are both realistic and explainable in the policymaker's own terminology. In addition, a simulation model provides an experimental arena for discovering the sources of real-life problems and evaluating alternative policy options in relatively little time and with little cost [129]).

Using the system dynamics model as an experimentation vehicle can provide many benefits to the software engineering community. Weiss commented:

> ... in software engineering it is remarkably easy to propose hypotheses and remarkably difficult to test them. Accordingly, it is useful to seek methods for testing software engineering hypotheses [265].

Unfortunately, controlled experiments in the area of software development tend to be costly and time-consuming [190]. Furthermore, the isolation of the effect and the evaluation of impact of any given practice within a large, complex, and dynamic project environment can be exceedingly difficult.

In addition to permitting less costly and less time consuming experimentation, simulation models make perfectly controlled experiments possible.

> The effects of different assumptions and environmental factors can be tested. In the model system, unlike real systems, the effect of changing one factor can be observed while all other factors are held unchanged. Such experimentation will yield new insights into the characteristics of the system that the model represents.

By using a model of a complex system, more can be learned about internal interactions than would ever be possible through manipulation of the real system. Internally, the model provides complete control of the system organizational structure, its policies, and its sensitivities to various events. Externally, a wider range of circumstances can be generated than are apt to be observable in real life [99].

In the following chapters our model will be used to predict and study the implications of an array of managerial actions, policies, and procedures pertaining to the development of software. Four areas will be studied: (1) scheduling; (2) controlling; (3) quality assurance; and (4) staffing. We start by analyzing a software project called EXAMPLE.

13.2 The EXAMPLE Software Project

EXAMPLE is the prototype project for the experiments. We run the model to simulate the EXAMPLE project and observe and analyze the behavior of several significant project variables (work force level, schedule completion time, errors, and productivity). Our goal is to demonstrate that the model's behavior replicate those reported in the literature. The EXAMPLE project parameters will be used in chapters 14 through 19 to study the implications of an array of managerial actions, policies, and procedures about software development.

EXAMPLE is 64,000 DSI, where DSI stands for "Delivered Source Instructions" as defined previously in section 7.3.

13.3 Setting Nominal Potential Productivity

In chapter 7 productivity was defined, not in terms of *DSI*/Man-Day, but in terms of *Tasks*/Man-Day. The notion of a "Task" is tied to that of "Nominal Potential Productivity." A "Task" is defined in terms of a number of DSI, and its value, for a particular simulation, is set to the numerical value of "Nominal Potential Productivity," expressed in terms of *DSI*/Man-Days. For example, if "Nominal Potential Productivity," for a particular project situation, is 50 DSI/Man-Day, then the value of "Task" is 50 DSI. The value of "Nominal Potential Productivity" is then 1 *Task*/Man-Day for *all* project situations (See section 7.3).

To determine the value of "Task" in EXAMPLE we need to: select a project environment, determine the value of "Nominal Potential Productivity" in terms of DSI/Man-Day for that environment, and set the value of "Task" at the numerical value of "Nominal Potential Productivity."

13.3.1 Determining Actual Productivity Few project environments are adequately characterized in the literature. One exception is Barry Boehm's excellent book, *Software Engineering Economics*, which provides a wealth of data on the software production environment at TRW. To maintain consistency, EXAMPLE will be characterized totally on these TRW data. We draw on projects Boehm described as "the most common type of software project: the small-to-medium size (project) developed in a familiar, in-house, organic software development environment" [49].

For a 64,000 DSI project, Boehm's data indicate that overall productivity is 338.4 DSI/Man-Month. This value is arrived at by dividing the project's size in DSI by the *total* effort expended to develop, QA, rework, and test the software. Boehm's data also indicate that system testing consumes approximately 22% of the total effort, while the effort expended on QA activities range from 15 to 20% of the total effort. No explicit estimates are given, however, for the effort to rework errors during development. If we assume that rework will be approximately 10% of total effort, then QA, rework, and testing activities together constitute approximately 50% of the project's man-months. (Note: Boehm's data cover the design, coding, and system testing stages of software production, as does our model.) The amount of effort expended on designing and coding the product is half the total man-days expended on the project; the *development* productivity is $2 \times 338.4 = 676.8$ DSI/Man-Month. To translate this into DSI/Man-*Day* we divide by 20 and get 33.84 DSI/Man-Day. This is not the value we are looking for. We are looking for the "Nominal *Potential* Productivity" and what we have is an estimate for the *actual* productivity.

13.3.2 Determining Nominal Potential Productivity   Actual productivity rarely equals potential productivity because of losses from communication and motivation problems. In the model, actual productivity is the product of potential productivity and the "Multiplier to Productivity due to Communication and Motivation Losses." If we can estimate the value of the "Multiplier," we can divide it into the value of *actual* productivity to come up with an estimate for EXAMPLE's "Nominal Potential Productivity."

The multiplier is itself a product of two variables: the "Actual Fraction of a Man-Day on Project" and "Communication Overhead." The nominal value of the former was set at 0.6 (a full-time employee allocates, on the average, 60% of his or her time to productive work on the project). The "Communication Overhead" was shown to be a function of team size. Referring to Boehm's results, we find his estimate for the average staffing level for the 64,000 DSI project, to be 10 people. From Figure 7.8 we can determine that the loss due to "Communication Overhead" will be 6%. The value of the "Multiplier to Productivity due to Communication and Motivation Losses" becomes $0.6 \times (1 - 0.06) = 0.564$. By dividing this into the value of actual productivity (33.84 DSI/Man-Day) calculated above, we estimate "Nominal Potential Productivity" to be 33.84 / 0.564 = 60 DSI Man-Day.

There were three steps to determine the value of "Task" in the EXAMPLE project. The third step is to set the value of "Task" at the numerical value of "Nominal Potential Productivity" when the latter is expressed in terms of DSI/Man-Day. For EXAMPLE, "Task" is 60 DSI and "Nominal Potential Productivity" is 1 *Task*/Man-Day.

13.4 Initializing Schedule and Manpower

For EXAMPLE we initialize its manpower and schedule allocation variables by using Boehm's COCOMO model. COCOMO stands for the COnstructive COst MOdel, and is a software project estimation model developed and used by TRW. COCOMO exists in a hierarchy of increasingly detailed forms. In our analysis we use the version called "Basic COCOMO" which, according to Boehm, is the most appropriate version for this type of project [49].

The development period covered by COCOMO estimates begins at the beginning of the product design phase (successful completion of a software requirements review) and ends up at the end of the system testing phase, as does our model. The primary input to COCOMO is the *perceived* size of the project in KDSI (thousand delivered source instructions). It is the perceived and not the real size of the project that is input to COCOMO, since at the beginning of development the *real* size of the project is often not known.

Boehm notes that "The software undersizing problem is our most critical road block to accurate software cost estimation." This is substantiated by the experiences of several other authors [61, 78, 81, 85]. A major cause for this undersizing problem is

> ... (the) powerful tendency to focus on the highly visible mainline components of the software, and to underestimate or completely miss the unobtrusive components (e.g., help message processing, error processing, and moving data around) [49].

But how much undersizing? There is, obviously, a wide range of reasonable possibilities. For EXAMPLE we assume that management underestimates the project's size by a factor of 1.5. This value conforms to Boehm's estimates [49]. A project of size N KDSI would be incorrectly perceived as being only 0.67N KDSI in size. In terms of our EXAMPLE software project, this means that the project would be perceived as being only $0.67 \times 64 = 42.88$ KDSI in size.

In other words, we assume that at the beginning of EXAMPLE management's perception of its size will (incorrectly) be 42.88 KDSI. This value then becomes the input that management uses in COCOMO's effort and schedule estimation equations.

The COCOMO equation for the number of man-days (MD) to develop and test the project is:

$$MD = 2.4 \times 19 \times KDSI^{1.05} \tag{13.1}$$

For EXAMPLE we get,

$$MD = 2.4 \times 19 \times (42.88)^{1.05} = 2,359 \; man-days$$

This represents the *total* man-days to develop and test the software product. For planning purposes, this effort is then distributed among the project's life cycle phases. How much would management allocate to development versus testing in EXAMPLE? Boehm provides several phase distribution guidelines. For a 42 KDSI project (which is what EXAMPLE is *perceived* as being) a development to testing distribution of 80% to 20% is suggested [49]:

$$MD \; \text{for} \; Development = 0.8 \times 2,359$$
$$= 1,887 \; man-days$$

$$MD \; \text{for} \; Testing = 0.2 \times 2,359$$
$$= 471 \; man-days$$

In addition to estimating the project's man-day requirements, management also estimates the project's development time and the staffing level.

The COCOMO equation for the development time (TDEV) is:

$$TDEV = 47.5 \times (MD/19)^{0.38} \; days \tag{13.2}$$

Substituting for the value of man-days (MD), we get

$$TDEV = 47.5 \times (2,359/19)^{0.38}$$
$$= 296 \ days$$

Finally, the average staffing level (ASL) is determined by dividing the estimated value of the total man-days (MD) by the estimated value of the development time (TDEV). For EXAMPLE we get

$$ASL = MD \ / \ TDEV$$
$$= 2,359 \ / \ 296$$
$$= 8 \ full-time-equivalent \ software \ personnel$$

We assume that project members will be working full-time on EXAMPLE; the model's parameter "Average Daily Manpower per Staff" would be set to 1 man-day. The average staffing level calculated above would be 8 *actual* software personnel. Not all 8 personnel will be on-board at the *beginning* of the project. Most software projects start with a smaller core of designers, and as the project develops, the work force slowly builds up to higher levels. For EXAMPLE, we assume that the project starts with a work force equal to half the "Average Staffing Level," i.e., with $0.5 \times 8 = 4$ software personnel on board, based on the results reported in *Software Engineering Economics* [49].

Now we can run the model to simulate project EXAMPLE and observe its behavior. The remainder of this chapter is devoted to a discussion of the model's results. The following will be discussed:

- Project progress

- Manpower distribution

- Work intensity

13.5 Project Progress

The dynamic behavior of six key measures of progress are depicted in Figure 13.1, namely, cumulative tasks developed, cumulative tasks tested, cumulative man-days, the perceived job size in tasks, the perceived job size in man-days, and the scheduled completion date in days. In Table 13.1, the project's key statistics are summarized.

13.5.1 Discovery of Additional Job Tasks EXAMPLE was initially perceived not as a 64,000 DSI project but as a 42,880 DSI project comprising only 714.6 tasks rather than 1,067 tasks — its true size. As the project develops, "Undiscovered Job Tasks" are progressively discovered as the "level of knowledge we have of what the software is intended to do (increases)" [49]. The rate at which the "Perceived Job Size" rises remains low for a significant portion of the development phase, before it starts to accelerate rapidly. (Such behavior was also observed in the NASA case study.) The early phase of development constitutes the architectural design phase; the emphasis is on determining the overall structure of the system, decomposing the system into its major components, and specifying the interfaces between the components [109]. Many implementation details such as help message processing or error processing would still not be visible. The rate of discovering such necessary job tasks remains low. The rate, however, starts to accelerate rapidly as the project work moves into the detailed design phase.

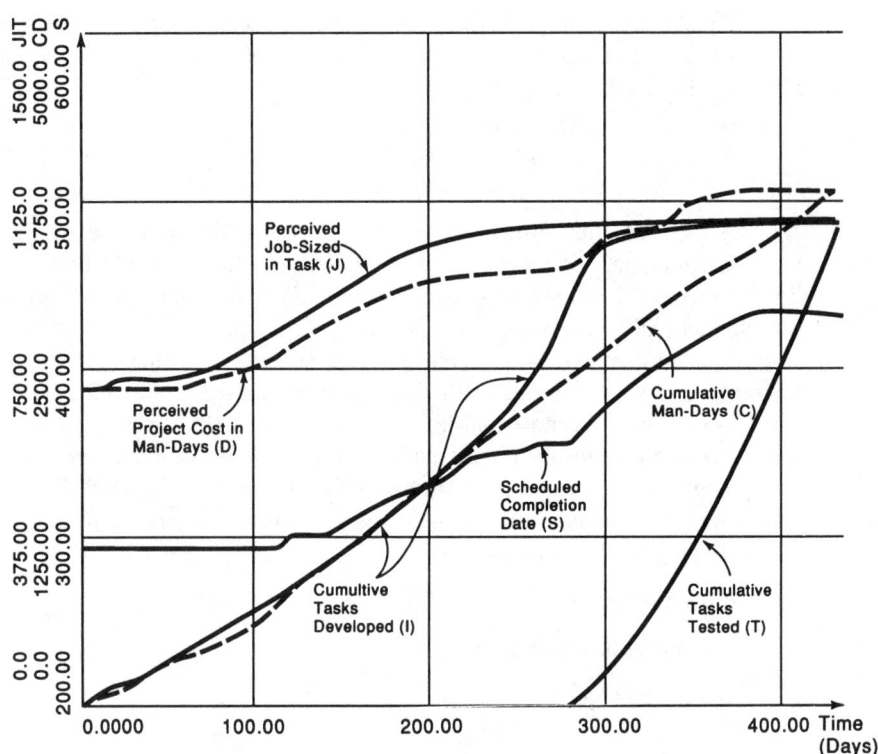

Figure 13.1 Progress on Project Example

As the additional tasks are discovered and project members start realizing that the project's scope is larger than what has been expected, adjustments are made in the project's plan to accommodate the additional work load. As Figure 13.1 indicates, both the "Job Size" and the "Scheduled Completion Date" are adjusted upwards. Two interesting observations may be made about these adjustments. First, the adjustments prove to be inadequate to fully accommodate the additional work load, and second, the first adjustment to the schedule lags considerably behind the first adjustment to man-days.

TABLE 13.1 KEY STATISTICS OF PROJECT EXAMPLE

1. Project Size			=	64,000	man-days
2. Man-Days					
	Total		=	3,795	man-days
	Development		=	2,681	man-days
		Coding + Design	=	1,782	man-days
		QA	=	380	man-days
		Rework	=	519	man-days
	Testing		=	1,114	man-days
3. Completion Time			=	430	working-days
4. Errors					
	Total Error Generated		=	1,494	→ 23 Error/KDSI
	Total Error Caught				
	During Development		=	728	→ 49% of Error Generated

13.5.2 Adjustments to Man-Day Estimates The additions to the project's man-days and schedule that are triggered *explicitly* by the discovery of new tasks level off at approximately day 200 when almost all the "Undiscovered Job Tasks" have been discovered. As shown in Figure 13.1, at approximately day 200 the value of perceived job size levels off at 1,067 tasks: the true size of the project. At that point, the project's size in man-days plateaus at a value of 3,200 man-days. However, notice that while the perceived job size remains unchanged after day 200, further significant additions are made to the project's man-days and its schedule. These further adjustments are *not* triggered by the discovery of further "additional tasks." Their direct cause (as will be explained in more detail later) is the realization at approximately day 300 that the project is behind schedule: the "Total Man-Days Reported Still Needed" to complete the project is *more* than "Man-Days Remaining" in the project's plan. (Such a shortage in man-days can arise, of course, even if the project's size had not been underestimated. For example, if management overestimates its staff's productivity, it does not allocate enough man-days to the project.) In this case, however, the man-day shortage problem is largely the result of the project's undersizing problem. When additional tasks are discovered in a software project, the additions made in the project'-days to accommodate those additional tasks are often not sufficient. The reason is that some of the discovered tasks are absorbed by project members without any formal adjustments to the project's plans. Only if the additional tasks are perceived as requiring a significant amount of effort would project members go through the trouble of formally developing cost estimates and incorporating them in the project's work plan.

Thus, by day 200 when almost all the "Undiscovered Job Tasks" have been discovered and the perceived job size attains the job's true size of 1,067 tasks, the value to which the "Job's Size in Man-Days" would be raised — 3,200 man-days — would not be high enough to accommodate all the additional tasks. Compare the 3,200 man-day value (which is supposedly enough to develop a 1,067 task product) to the number of man-days that would be allocated to a project perceived *from the start* as being 1,067 tasks (i.e., 64 KDSI) in size. To do this we use COCOMO's man-days (MD) equation.

$$MD = 2.4 \times 19 \times KDSI^{1.05}$$
$$= 2.4 \times 19 \times (64)^{1.05}$$
$$= 3,593 \; man-days$$

Increasing the number of man-days from 2,359 to only 3,200 falls approximately 400 man-days short of the above 3,593 man-days benchmark. This would constitute a significant deficit in the project's man-days budget.

When and how is the man-days deficit handled? It is handled when it becomes visible. This usually happens towards the later stages of development when the development work is almost finished and/or when the allocated man-days budget is almost used up. Once visible, the man-days deficit would be handled by working overtime and/or adjusting the project's man-days budget upwards. Both of these responses take place in EXAMPLE. The adjustment in the man-days budget is evident in Figure 13.1 as the "Job's Size in Man-Days" makes a significant upward adjustment around day 300.

13.5.3 Adjustments to Scheduled Completion Date
The second adjustment for Figure 13.1 concerns the schedule completion date. The first adjustment to the schedule lags considerably behind the first adjustment to the man-days. (Such behavior was also observed in the NASA case study.) The first adjustment to the "Job's Size in Man-Days" is made around day 80, whereas the first adjustment to the schedule is made 60 days later, around day 140. Why?

When the "Job's Size in Man-Days" is adjusted upwards, it is done by adjusting the project's work force level, the project's schedule completion date or both. The choice is really an expression of management's policy on how to balance work force and schedule adjustments throughout the project. In general, though, the decision is a function of the project's stage of completion. In the early stages of a project, project managers are generally willing to adjust the work force level to maintain the project on its scheduled course. However, as the project proceeds, management becomes increasingly reluctant to add new people out of an increasing desire that the work force stabilize. Additions to the project's man-days get absorbed by adjustments not only to the project's work force level, but also to the schedule. The shift away from work force adjustments to schedule adjustments continues as the project progresses.

We can now refer to Figure 13.1 and explain why the first adjustment to EXAMPLE's completion date lags considerably behind the first adjustment to the man-days level. The first adjustment to man-days is made at day 80. At that relatively early point, the additional man-days are absorbed totally by adding more people to the project, rather than by changing the schedule. Figure 13.2 clearly shows this. The figure depicts EXAMPLE's manpower level for the project's full life cycle. It also shows curve (*), which depicts what the manpower level of EXAMPLE would have been for the first 150 days *if* none of the "Undiscovered Job Tasks" was ever discovered. The two curves coincide up until day 100, approximately 40 days after "Undiscovered Job Tasks" are first discovered in EXAMPLE.

As EXAMPLE's man-days level escalates, the schedule starts absorbing part of the newly added man-days load around day 140. The rate at which the schedule is adjusted upwards remains low, as most of emphasis is still on adjusting the work force level. However, as the project proceeds, emphasis shifts away from work force adjustments and toward schedule adjustments. The project's schedule completion date is adjusted upwards

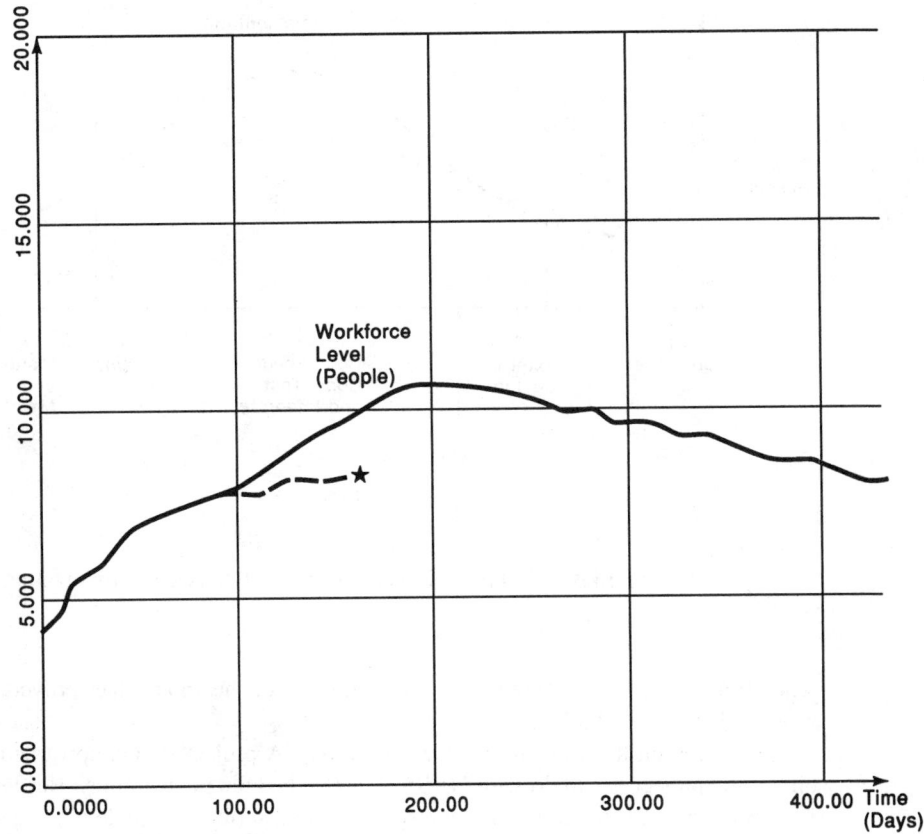

Figure 13.2 Workforce Level

at a much faster rate during the *second* set of adjustments in the project's man-days, starting around day 300. During this second adjustment process, adjustments in the project's scheduled completion date do *not* lag behind the adjustments in man-days: they both start around day 300.

13.6 Manpower Distribution

In Figure 13.2, the shape of EXAMPLE's manpower distribution curve conforms to manpower distributions reported in the literature (e.g., see [39, 49, 81]). Figure 13.3 represents the manpower distribution at IBM's DP Services organization [20].

Consider the simulated and the actual NASA work force distributions in Figure 13.4. Interestingly, the NASA work force distribution does not conform to the "typical"

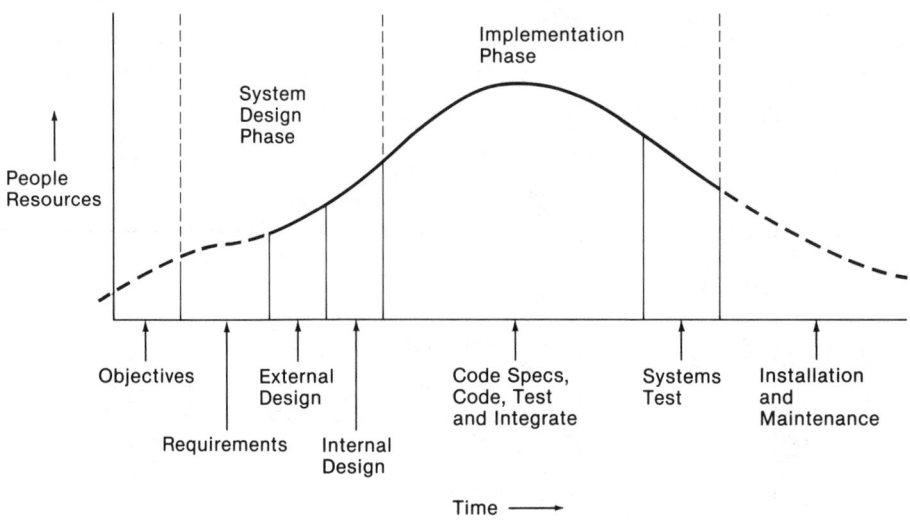

Figure 13.3 Workforce Level at IBM's DP Services Organization

work force patterns discussed in the literature. Yet the model has proved capable of reproducing its distribution.

The reason the work force level in the NASA project shoots upwards towards the end of the project has to do with NASA's tight scheduling constraints. Because software is embedded in a large and expensive space system, serious schedule slippages cannot be tolerated. When software projects are planned, they are provided with not only a "Scheduled Completion Date," but a "Maximum Tolerable Completion Date." As long as the "Scheduled Completion Date" is below the "Maximum Tolerable Completion Date" then decisions to adjust the schedule, add more people, or do a combination of both are based on the balancing of scheduling and work force stability. However, as the "Scheduled Completion Date" starts approaching the "Maximum Tolerable Completion Date," as it does in the NASA project, pressures develop that override work force stability; management becomes increasingly willing to "pay any price" to avoid overshooting the "Maximum Tolerable Completion Date" even if they must hire more people.

13.7 Work Intensity

The typical eight-hour day of a full-time staff member on a software project is not devoted entirely to productive project-related work. Time is lost on personal matters, coffee-breaks, non-project communication, and other non-project related activities. Non-productive time accounts for about 40% of the software person's time on the job.

The loss in productivity does not, of course, remain constant at the 40% level throughout the life of the project. The motivational effects of schedule pressures can push the "Actual Fraction of a Man-Day on Project" to higher (under positive schedule pressure) or lower (under negative schedule pressure) values.

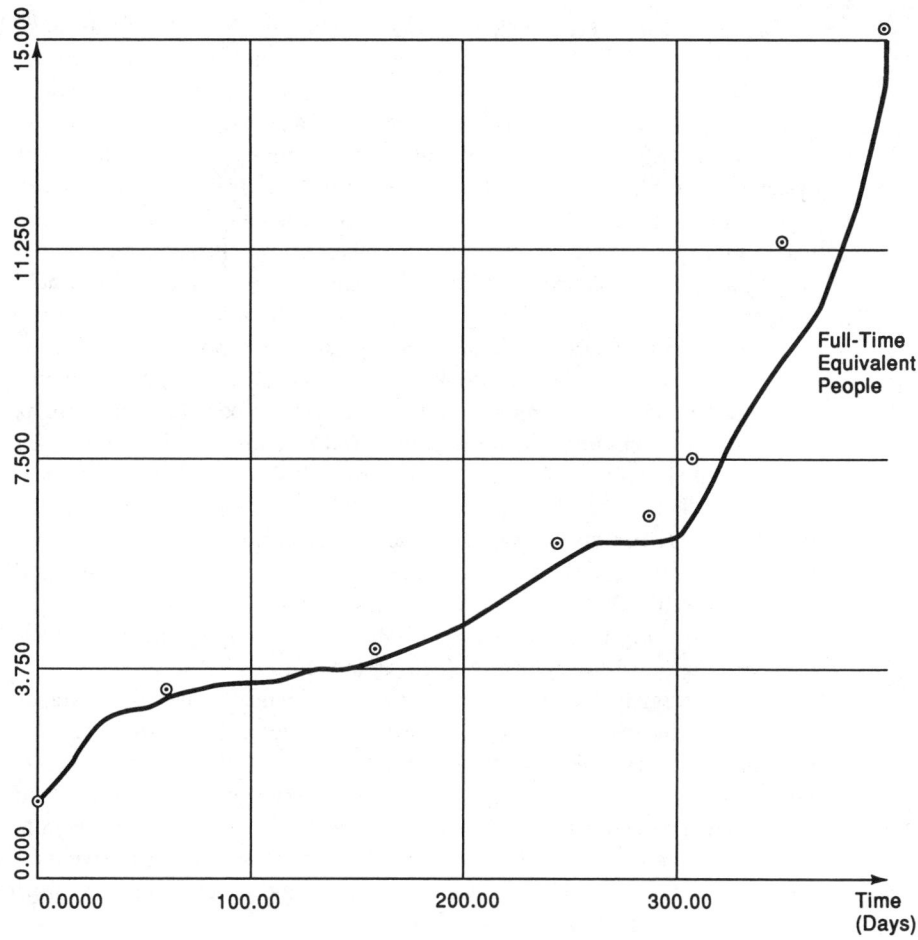

Figure 13.4 Workforce Level of NASA Case Study

For example, positive schedule pressures arise whenever the project is perceived to be behind schedule. When confronted with such a situation, software developers tend to work harder by allocating more man-hours to the project in an attempt to compensate for the perceived shortage and bring the project back on schedule. They compress their slack time, and then, if necessary, work overtime. The man-hours lost per-day decreases, while the "Actual Fraction of a Man-Day on Project" increases.

13.7.1 Impact on Actual Fraction of Man-Day on Project The dynamic behavior of the "Actual Fraction of a Man-Day on Project" for EXAMPLE is depicted in Figure 13.5. The two "spikes" in overwork occur as an *explicit* project milestone is approached. The first spike occurs towards the end of the development phase, and the second spike occurs towards the end of the only other explicit milestone in our model, the end of the system testing phase. This pattern was observed by Boehm and labelled the "Deadline Effect" phenomenon. Figure 13.6 shows his measured data on two projects with *three* major milestones: a plans and requirements review (PRR), a product design review (PDR), and an acceptance test [48]. It is clear that the Deadline Effect held strongly for both projects, generally producing a doubling of effort as each milestone approached.

With a simulation model such as ours, one need not guess at the cause of, say, a spike in a particular variable. Simulation experiments isolating and combining the effects of suspected factors can pinpoint the mechanism(s) responsible. In the remaining part of this section, we will trace the set of actions and reactions that lead to the behavior pattern of the "Actual Fraction of a Man-Day on Project" shown in Figure 13.5.

The "Perceived Shortage in Man-Days" is depicted in Figure 13.5. The shortage in man-days is perceived late in the development phase, around day 180. As project members perceive the shortage, they react by working harder, allocating more man-hours in an attempt to compensate for the perceived shortage and to bring the project back on schedule. Working harder translates in the model into the higher values of the "Actual Fraction of a Man-Day on Project," shown in Figure 13.5.

Even though the project members are working harder, the shortage in man-days keeps rising because as the development phase approaches its final stage, the degree of visibility increases rapidly, exposing even larger man-day shortages. By working harder, project members a only cutting into not eliminating the man-day shortage, whose real magnitude is becoming progressively apparent. To appreciate the significance of the work force's contributions, we also plotted curve (*), which depicts what the level of the "Perceived Shortage in Man-Days" would have been had the project members maintained their normal lower work rate.

13.7.2 Impact on Overwork Duration Threshold Project members are not willing to maintain an above-normal work rate indefinitely. Once people start working at a rate above their normal rate, their "Overwork Duration Threshold" decreases because people enjoy and need their slack time. As the "Overwork Duration Threshold" decreases, the maximum number of man-days of backlogged work that project members are willing to handle (in addition to their planned work) also decreases. If the "Maximum Shortage in Man-Days to be Handled" drops below the value of the "Perceived Shortage in Man-Days," only the maximum value would be handled through overwork, while arrangements with project management are made to adjust the project's man-days budget to handle what exceeds the "Maximum Shortage in Man-Days to be Handled."

In EXAMPLE this is exactly what happens. The persistence of the man-day shortage eventually overwhelms the work force's intensified efforts, and around day 300 (at the end of the development phase) arrangements are made to handle those remaining shortages through adjustments to both the project's man-days budget and its schedule.

The same sequence of events recurs towards the end of the system testing phase. As testing progresses, the system's error proneness becomes more visible, and the project members become increasingly more able to perceive how productive (in testing) the work force has actually been. As this happens, any shortages in man-days (for the testing

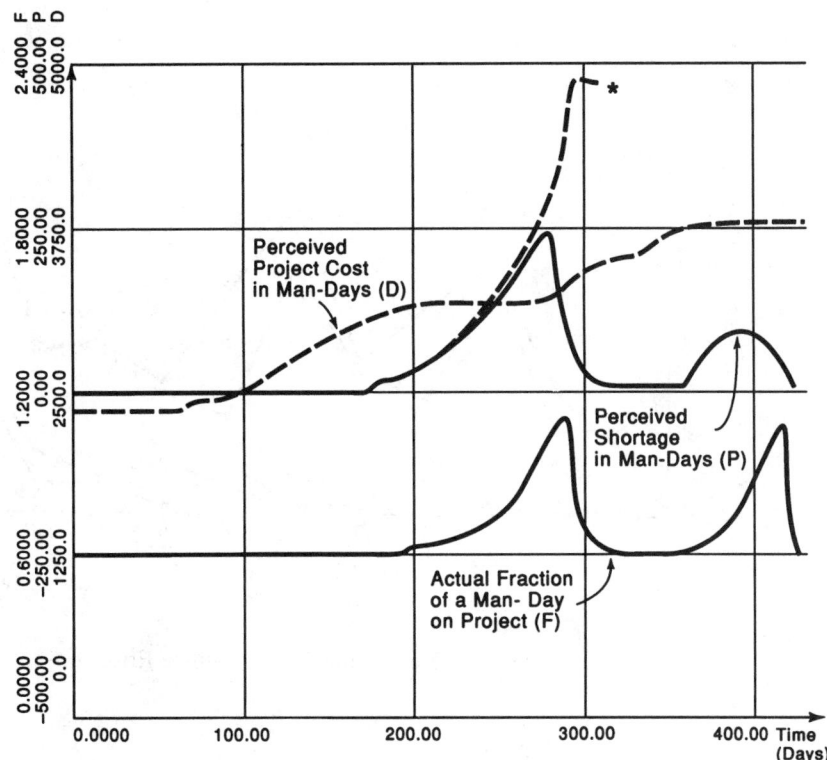

Figure 13.5   Work Intensity

phase) become more apparent. As Figure 13.5 indicates, such shortages are indeed perceived at an accelerating rate starting at day 370. Interestingly, no such shortages were experienced in the NASA project. This may seem counter-intuitive since in the NASA project only 15% of the project's man-days was allocated to the systems testing phase, where as in EXAMPLE 20% was allocated. The answer lies in NASA's exceptionally high expenditures on Quality Assurance, which, as a fraction of the development effort, is almost double that of EXAMPLE. As a result, in the NASA project a larger fraction of

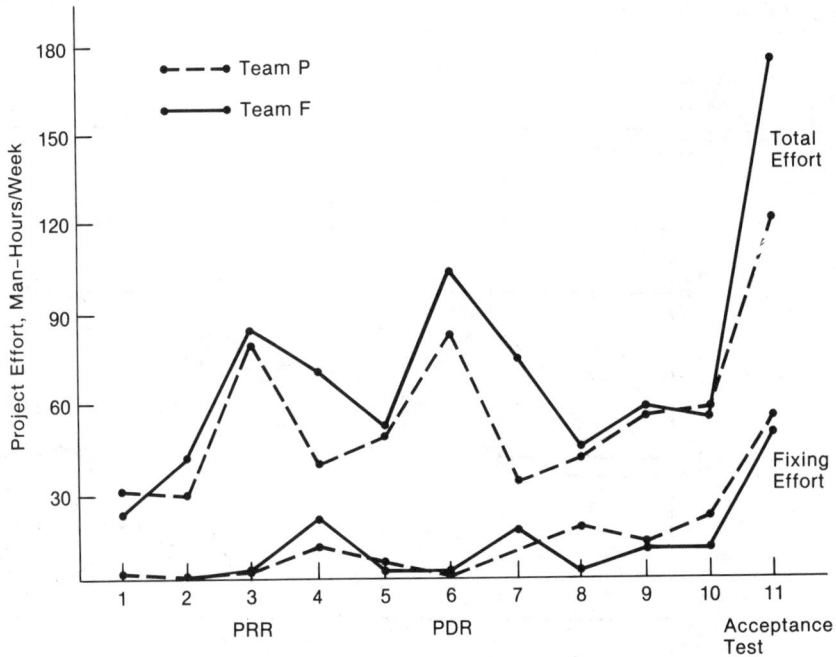

Figure 13.6 Examples of Deadline Effect

the errors is detected early in the development phase when errors are less costly to detect and correct. The workload of the system testing activity is dramatically reduced.

In Figure 13.5, as the man-day shortage is detected, the work force reacts by working harder, compressing slack time and increasing the "Actual Fraction of a Man-Day on Project." At this stage, however, the magnitude of the shortages is not as high as at the end of the development phase, when the man-day shortage has to be handled not only through a surge in productivity but also through additions to the project's man-days budget. Here, though, the shortage in man-days is sufficiently low and can be handled solely through a final surge in productivity.

13.8 Concluding Comments on the Model of the EXAMPLE Project

The objective of this chapter was to define the experimental setting within which to conduct our experimentation and analysis of the dynamics of software development. The EXAMPLE software project serves as the prototype. The model to simulate EXAMPLE was run, and the behavior of several project variables were presented, explained, and found to replicate those reported in the literature.

We are now ready to use the model as a laboratory tool to study the dynamic implications of an array of managerial actions, policies, and procedures in the areas of scheduling, controlling, quality assurance, and staffing.

14

ON THE ACCURACY OF
SOFTWARE ESTIMATION

14.1 Software Cost and Schedule Estimation

For many years, estimation of software project development time and cost had been an intuitive process based on experience and analogy [200]. More recently, several quantitative software estimation models have been developed. They range from highly theoretical ones, such as Putman's [212], to empirical ones, such as the Walston and Felix's [257], and Boehm's COCOMO [49]. An empirical model uses data from previous projects to evaluate a current project. A theoretical model uses formulae based on global assumptions, such as the rate at which people solve problems or the number of problems available for solutions at a given time.

Still, software cost schedule estimation continues to be a major problem for the management of software development. "Even today, almost no model can estimate the true cost of software with any degree of accuracy" [130]. Farquhar [95] articulates the significance of the issue as follows:

> Unable to estimate accurately, the manager can know with certainty neither what resources to commit to an effort nor, in retrospect, how well these resources were used. The lack of a firm foundation for these two judgments can reduce programming management to a random process in that positive control is next to impossible. This situation often results in the budget overruns and schedule slippages that are all too common today.

Several reasons for the difficulty have been suggested in the literature, including:

1. Software development is a process that is not yet fully understood by "estimators" [200].

2. The phases and functions that constitute the software development process are influenced by a large number of ill defined variables [85, 210].

3. Most of the activities within the process are still primarily human rather than mechanical, and therefore prone to all the subjective factors that affect human performance [200, 208, 210].

Identifying the causes of a difficulty or a problem is an important first step towards resolving it. The next step is to identify a strategy for handling it. For the software estimation problem, a strategy that has been frequently quoted in the literature was articulated by Pietrasanta more than two decades ago:

> The serious student of estimating must first be willing to probe deeply into the fascinating and complex system development process, to uncover the phases and functions of the process, to highlight the subtle interrelationships of the program system being developed and the project organization doing the developing. ... relationships is precisely what is required if estimates are ever to be improved. Only then can we do meaningful quantitative research and scientific analysis of resource requirements [207].

Having captured within our integrative system dynamics model "influence variables of software development and their causal relationships," we embark on a quantitative analysis of software cost and schedule estimation.

14.2 On the Accuracy of Software Estimation

In this chapter we will show, first, why a software estimation tool cannot be adequately judged based only on how accurately it matches *historical* project results and, second, why a more accurate estimate is not necessarily a "better" estimate.

Consider the following situation: A 64 KDSI software project that has initially been estimated using a method A to be 2,359 man-days ends up actually consuming at completion 3,795 man-days. The project's characteristics (e.g., its size and complexity) are then fed into a method B, which is being considered by management; its results are compared to the project's *actual* performance. Let us assume that method B produces a 5,900 man-day estimate. If we define "the percentage of relative error" in estimating man-days (MD) as

$$\% \ Error = 100 \times \frac{ABS\,[MD_{ACT} - MD_{EST}]}{MD_{ACT}} \tag{14.1}$$

then, for method A

$$\% \ Error_A = 100 \times \frac{ABS\,[3,795 - 2,359]}{3,795} = 38\%$$

and for method B

$$\% \ Error_B = 100 \times \frac{ABS\,[3,795 - 5,900]}{3,795} = 55\%$$

Can one conclude that method B would have provided a less accurate estimate of the project's man-days had it been used instead of method A?

The answer is NO. The reason we cannot make such a conclusion is that we cannot assume that had the project been initiated with B's 5,900 man-day estimate instead of A's 2,359, it *still* would have actually consumed exactly 3,795 man-days. In fact the project could result in consuming many more or fewer than 3,795 man-days. Before such a determination can be made, no valid assessment of the relative accuracy of the two methods can be made.

14.3 A Different Estimate Creates a Different Project

The critical point is that *a different estimate creates a different project*. This phenomenon is somewhat analogous to the "General Heisenberg" principle in experimentation: "When experimenting with a system about which we are trying to obtain knowledge, we create a new system" [150]. Koolhass gives a fine example: "A man inquires through the door of the bedroom where his friend is sick, 'How are you?' whereupon his friend replies 'Fine,' and the effort kills him."

By imposing different estimates on a software project we create different projects.

Research clearly indicates that the decisions that people make in projects and the actions they take are significantly influenced by the pressures and perceptions produced by the project's schedule [57, 109, 125, 224, 236]. Our model captures such schedule influences. The most significant influences are depicted in the causal loop diagram of Figure 14.1.

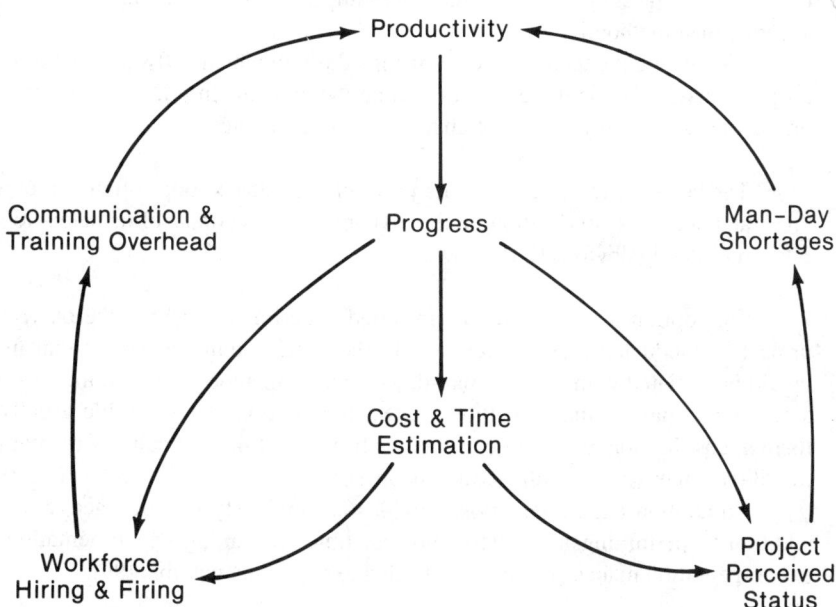

Figure 14.1 Causal model of key schedule influences

Schedules have a direct influence on the hiring and firing decisions throughout the life of a software project. As shown earlier, in TRW's COCOMO model the project's staff size is determined by dividing the man-days estimate (MD) by the development time estimate (TDEV). Thus, for example, a tight time schedule (i.e., a low TDEV value) means a larger work force. A higher work force level generally means more communication and training overhead, which in turn affect productivity negatively.

Scheduling can dramatically change the manpower loading throughout the life of a project. For example, the work force level shot upwards toward the end of the NASA project because of NASA's strict constraints on schedule. This situation did not occur in EXAMPLE.

Productivity is also influenced by man-day shortages. For example, if the project is perceived to be behind schedule, software developers tend to work harder, such as by allocating more man-hours to the project, in an attempt to compensate for the perceived shortage and to bring the project back on schedule. Man-day shortages are obviously more prone to occur when the project is initially underestimated. Conversely, if project management initially overestimates the project, man-day "excesses" could arise. When the project is perceived to be ahead of schedule, "Parkinson's Law indicates that people will use the extra time for ... personal activities, catching up on the mail, etc." [49]. This, of course, means that they become less productive.

14.4 Need for Simulation Experimentation

Having identified how software project estimation can influence project behavior, we can return to the question raised at the beginning of this chapter: Is method A truly more accurate than method B?

Identifying the feedback relationships through which software estimation influences project behavior is one thing and discerning the dynamic implications of such interactions on the total system is another. Richardson and Pugh note:

> The behavior of systems of interconnected feedback loops often confounds intuition and analysis, even though the dynamic implications of isolated loops may be reasonably obvious [221].

One option is to conduct a controlled experiment whereby the 64 KDSI software project is conducted twice under exactly the same conditions except that in one case it would be initiated with a 2,359 man-day estimate (method A) and in the second case with a 5,900 man-day estimate (method B). Such an option is not feasible usually because of its high cost in money and time as well as because of the difficulty of recreating the same initial resources (e.g., equally skilled people).

Simulation experimentation provides an obviously more attractive alternative. In addition to permitting less costly and less time consuming experimentation, simulation experimentation makes perfectly controlled experiments possible [99].

14.5 Case Study of Safety Factor Policy

Rather than conduct a limited experiment simply to investigate methods A and B, we conduct instead an experiment that answers a broader set of issues raised in the interviews at one organization.

In that organization project managers were rewarded on how closely their projects actually met their initially estimated man-days budget. The estimation procedure that they *informally* used was as follows:

1. Use basic COCOMO to estimate the number of man-days (MD):

$$MD = 2.4 \times 19 \times (KDSI)^{1.05} \ man-days \tag{14.2}$$

2. Multiply this estimate by a safety factor to account for undiscovered tasks. The safety factor ranged from 25% to 50%.

3. Use the new value of man-days (MD′) to calculate the development time (TDEV) using COCOMO:

$$TDEV = 47.5 \times (MD' / 19)^{0.38} \ days \tag{14.3}$$

It is important to note that the "Safety Factor Philosophy" is not unique to this one organization. For example, in a study of the software cost estimation process at the Electronic System Division of the Air Force Systems Command, Devenny found that most program managers budget additional funds for software as a "management reserve." He also found that these management reserves ranged from 5% to 50% of the estimated software cost with a mean of 18%. As with our organization, the policy was an informal one: "Frequently the reserve was created by the program office with funds not placed on any particular contract. Most of the respondents indicated that the reserve was not identified as such to prevent its loss during a budget cut" [85].

To test the efficacy of that informal policy we will run a number of simulations of EXAMPLE with different values for the safety factor. We will experiment with values ranging from 0% to 100%. For example, for a safety factor of 50% the project would be initialized with the following estimates:

1. First, calculate MD,
$$MD = 2.4 \times 19 \times 42.88^{1.05} = 2,359 \ man-days$$

2. Second, calculate MD′
$$MD' = MD \times (1 + Safety-Factor / 100)$$
$$= MD \times 1.5 = 3.538.5 \ man-days$$

3. Finally, calculate TDEV
$$TDEV = 47.5 \times (MD' / 19)^{0.38} = 346 \ days$$

The results of the experiment are exhibited in Figures 14.2 through 14.5.

14.5.1 Impact of Safety Factor on Relative Error In Figure 14.2 the percentage of the relative error in estimating man-days is plotted against different values of the safety factor. The "Safety Factor Policy" seems to be working. The larger the safety factor the smaller the estimation error. In particular in the 25-50% range, which was used in the organization, the estimation error drops from being approximately 40% in the base run to values in the upper twenties. In fact, Figure 14.2 suggests that by using a safety factor in the 25-50% range the project manager might not be going far enough since a 100% safety factor, for example, would drop the estimation error down to 12%.

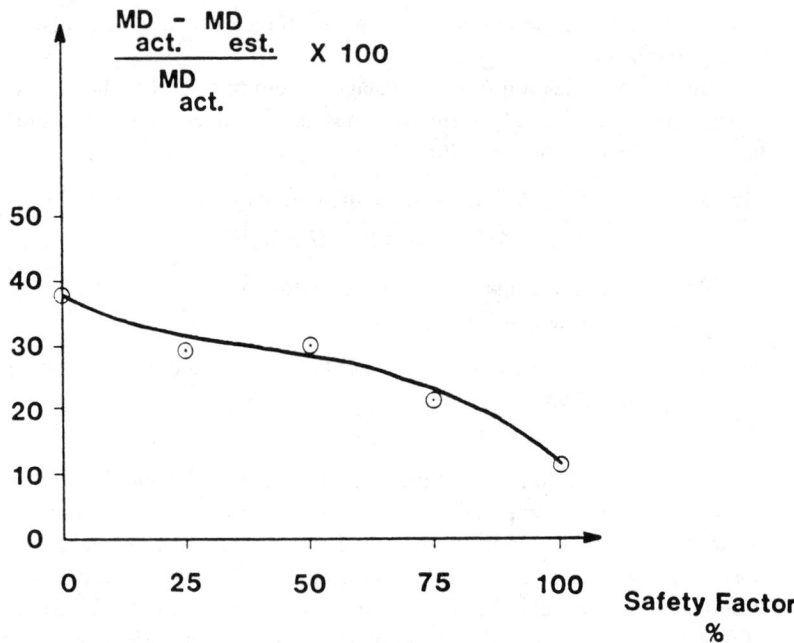

Figure 14.2   Relative error as function of safety factor %

14.5.2 Assumptions Implied in Safety Factor Policy   The rationale or justification for using a safety factor stated by the interviewees in that organization is based on the following assumptions:

1. Past experiences indicate a strong bias by software developers to underestimate the scope of a software project.

2. "[One] might think that a bias would be the easiest kind of estimating problem to rectify, since it involves an error that is always in the same direction. ... [But biases] are, almost by definition, invisible. The same psychological mechanism (e.g., optimism of software developers) that creates the bias works to conceal it" [81].

3. To rectify this bias on the part of software developers, project management must use a safety factor. When the project manager " ... adds a contingency factor (25%? 50%? 100%?) he is, in effect, saying that: much more is going to happen that I don't know about, so I'll estimate the rest as a percentage of that which I do know something about" [207].

    In other words, the safety factor is simply a mechanism to bring the initial man-days estimate closer to the project's *true* size in man-days as shown in Figure 14.3.

14.5.3 Actual Effect of Safety Factor Policy   The assumptions of Figure 14.3 cannot be contested solely on the basis of Figure 14.2, which provides only part of the story. A more complete picture is provided by Figure 14.4 which plots the actual man-days that

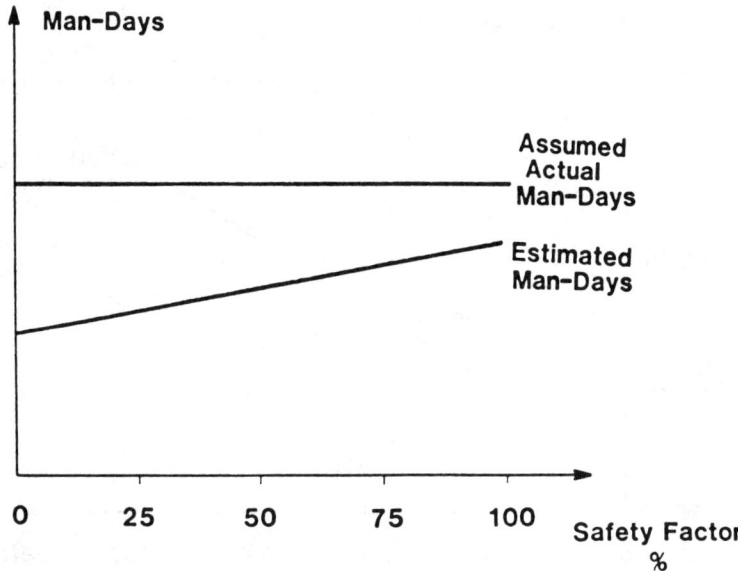

Figure 14.3   Assumed Effect of Safety Factor Policy

would be consumed by EXAMPLE, when different safety factors are applied to its initial estimate. The assumption of Figure 14.3 is obviously invalid. As higher safety factors are used, leading to more and more generous initial man-day allocations, the *actual* number of man-days consumed does not remain at some inherently-defined value. For example, in the base run, EXAMPLE would be initiated with a man-day estimate of 2,359 man-days and would end up consuming 3,795 man-days. A safety factor of 50% leads to a 3,538 man-day initial estimate, EXAMPLE ends up consuming not 3,795 man-days but 5,080 man-days. To reiterate a point made earlier: *A different estimate creates a different project.*

This happens, as explained earlier, because the project's initial estimates create pressures and perceptions that affect how people behave on the project. In particular, an overestimate of the project's man-days can lead to a larger buildup of the project's work force, leading to higher communication and training overheads, which in turn affect productivity negatively. In addition, overestimating a project often leads to an expansion of the project members' slack time activities, which leads to further reductions in productivity.

14.5.4 Impact of Safety Factor on Productivity   Figure 14.5 is a plot of "Gross Productivity" defined as the project size in DSI (i.e., 64,000 DSI) divided by the actual number of man-days expended, for the different safety factor situations. Gross productivity drops from a value of 16.8 DSI/Man-Day in the base run to as low as 12 when a 100% safety factor is used.

The drop in productivity is initially significant and then levels off for higher safety factors. The reason is that when the safety factor increases from 0% in the base run to a relatively small value (e.g., 25%), most of the man-day excesses that result are absorbed

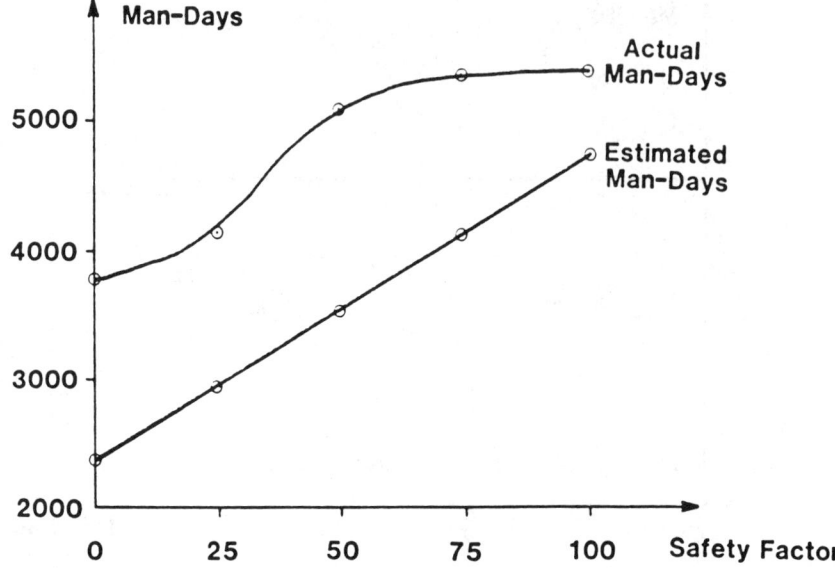

Figure 14.4 Actual Effect of Safety Factor Policy

by the employees as less overworking and more slack time. In EXAMPLE man-day backlogs occurred toward the end of both the development phase and the system testing phase and led to periods of overwork. When a small safety factor is used, however, such backlogs decrease, leading to shorter overwork durations. As the safety factor increases, man-day excesses rather than backlogs result. When excesses are small, they tend to be absorbed as expanded slack activities. However, there is a limit on how much "fat" employees are willing or allowed to absorb. Beyond those limits man-day excesses become translated into cuts in the project's work force, schedule, or both. Thus, as the safety factor increases, losses in productivity due to slack time activities decreases, leading to smaller drops in gross productivity.

14.6 Return to Issue of Software Estimation Accuracy

Our own project EXAMPLE used Method A and produced a 2,359 man-day estimate in the base run. Since EXAMPLE ended up actually consuming 3,795 man-days, the percentage of relative absolute error in estimating man-days is 38%. Would method B, which produces a 5,900 man-day estimate for EXAMPLE (i.e., an estimate that is 55% higher than EXAMPLE's actual man-day expenditures of 3,795), have provided a less accurate estimate?

Method B's estimate of 5,900 man-days is 150% higher than A's 2,359 estimate; method B is *equivalent* to a "Safety Factor Policy" in which the safety factor is 150%. To check the behavior of project EXAMPLE had it been estimated using Method B, we re-ran the model with an initialized value of the man-days estimate (MD) equal to 5,900. The results of the run, together with those of the base case, are shown in Table 14.1.

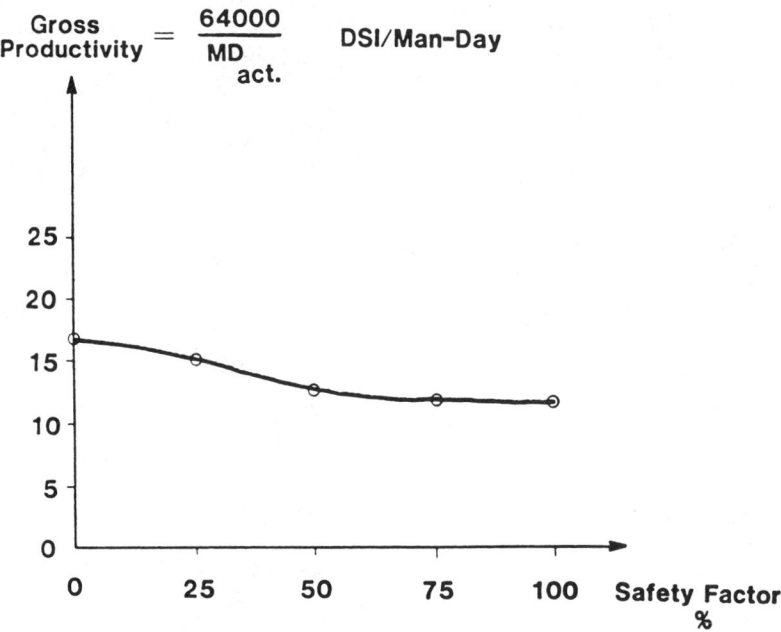

Figure 14.5   Gross productivity as a function of safety factor %

TABLE 14.1. COMPARISON OF SOFTWARE ESTIMATIONS

	Method B	Method A (Base Case)
MD_{EST}	5,900	2,359
MD_{ACT}	5,412	3,795
% Error	9 %	38 %

The results are quite interesting. Method B turns out to be a more accurate estimator. However, the improved accuracy is attained at a high cost. The project consumes 43% more man-days!

14.6.1 Implications and Insights For the organization we interviewed, the message is the same. The "Safety Factor Policy" does achieve its intended objective: more accurate estimates. However, the organization pays dearly for this. As Figure 14.4 indicates, a safety factor in the 25-50% range results in a 15-35% increase in the project's cost in man-days.

To conclude this chapter we restate the two basic insights we gained:

1. A different estimate creates a different project. The important implication is that a new software estimation model cannot be adequately judged solely on the basis of how accurately it can estimate historical projects. Because of the significant influence that a schedule has on the behavior of a software project, the only guaranteed test of an estimation method is to try it.

2. A more accurate estimate is not necessarily a better estimate. An estimation method should be judged not only on how accurate it is but also on how costly the projects it *"creates"* are.

15

PORTABILITY OF
ESTIMATION MODELS

15.1 Quantitative Software Estimation Models

Many different kinds of quantitative software estimation models have been developed. These models vary in what they provide (e.g., total cost and manning schedule) and what factors they use to calculate their estimates. The formulae and parameters they incorporate also vary. In almost all cases the model is based either directly or indirectly on historical data [236]. Sometimes the collected data are translated into tables or graphs indicating productivity (instructions per man-day, man-month, or man-year). Another approach is to formulate a parametric model, a mathematical function of several variables suggested by previous experimentation and engineering judgment. Statistical techniques are then applied to the data to reduce the number of variables and to compute the constants.

However, "even today, almost no model can estimate the true cost of software with any degree of accuracy" [184]. For example, the Basic COCOMO estimates come within a factor of 1.3 of the actual development figures for the projects in the COCOMO data base only 28% of the time and within a factor of 2 only 60% of the time [49]. The 1965 SDC model had a standard deviation larger than the mean estimate [196]. The analysis of the IBM-FSD model in [257] reported a standard deviation of a factor of 1.71 (mean of 274 instructions/man-month; range about the mean of 160-470 instructions/man-month).

15.2 Portability of Estimation Models

Of particular interest to us is the *portability* of the models — the ability to use them effectively in companies different from the one(s) in which they were developed. Portability has proven to be especially poor [43, 49, 144, 184].

Both the accuracy and the portability of software estimation models can be significantly improved by taking into consideration not only the technical aspects of the software development environment, as is the case with the current models, but also the managerial and organizational characteristics of the environment. We will identify

several managerial and organizational variables that most current models fail to
"acknowledge" but that significantly influence the cost of software development.

15.2.1 Weaknesses of Current Models To set the stage for our analysis we will first
report on an interesting experiment by Mohanty, which cleverly demonstrates the two
weaknesses in current models [184].

Mohanty's objective was to examine the extent to which the available quantitative
software estimation models produce the same cost estimate for a given project. The
following models were included in the exercise: (1) The Farr and Zagorski Model, (2)
The Kustanowitz Model, (3) The Wolverton Model, (4) The Walston-Felix Model, (5)
The Aerospace Model, (6) The Aaron Model, (7) The GRC Model, (8) The Naval Air
Development Center Model, (9) The Doty Model, (10) The SDC Model, (11) The
Schneider Model, and (12) The Price-S Model.

Mohanty's first identified the full set of factors that are incorporated in the 12
models. He was then able to define his hypothetical software project. Forty-nine factors
were identified. They involved system size, data base, system complexity, type of
program, documentation, environment (e.g., requirements definition, security, and
computer access), and "other," a category that includes such items as miles traveled,
reliability, and growth requirements. However, none of the cost models described uses all
the factors. Cost models developed before 1974, for example, emphasized productivity
without considering the quality of the finished product. Newer models consider quality
but do not include it explicitly.

Mohanty made his hypothetical software project 36,000 machine-language
executable instructions. The resulting 12 cost estimates for the project are exhibited in
Figure 15.1. (Note: the estimates cover only the design, coding, and testing phases, as
does our model.) As the figure indicates, the estimated cost varies from a low of
$362,500 (the Farr and Zagorski Model) to a high of $2,766,667 (the Kustanowitz Model)
for the *same* software project. In other words, the highest estimate is over 650% higher
than the lowest.

Since the size of the project and cost per instruction were the same for the different
models, the variations in cost are obviously caused by other factors. Two sources of
variation were suggested by Mohanty. The first related to the quality of the final product.
For example, when the costs of highly reliable software are collected into a cost data base,
a model that uses this data base will estimate the cost of a reliable product. On the other
hand, if the data base reflects software products with low reliability, any model based on it
would invariably estimate the cost of a less reliable product. Since the cost data bases
used in developing the cost models are different, embodying software with different
qualities, one source of variation in estimated cost is the quality of the final product.

The second source of variation suggested by Mohanty is environmental:

> Each model was developed for a cost data base collected in a given company
> environment. This data base thus embodies the specific nature of the organizational
> problems, work patterns, and management approaches and practices. Where this
> data base is regressed to derive coefficients for use in a given model, the model
> reflects that company's environment only [184].

His assertion is supported by others in the literature [35, 65, 203, 207, 244]. A few
researchers have even suggested some managerial/organizational factors that they feel

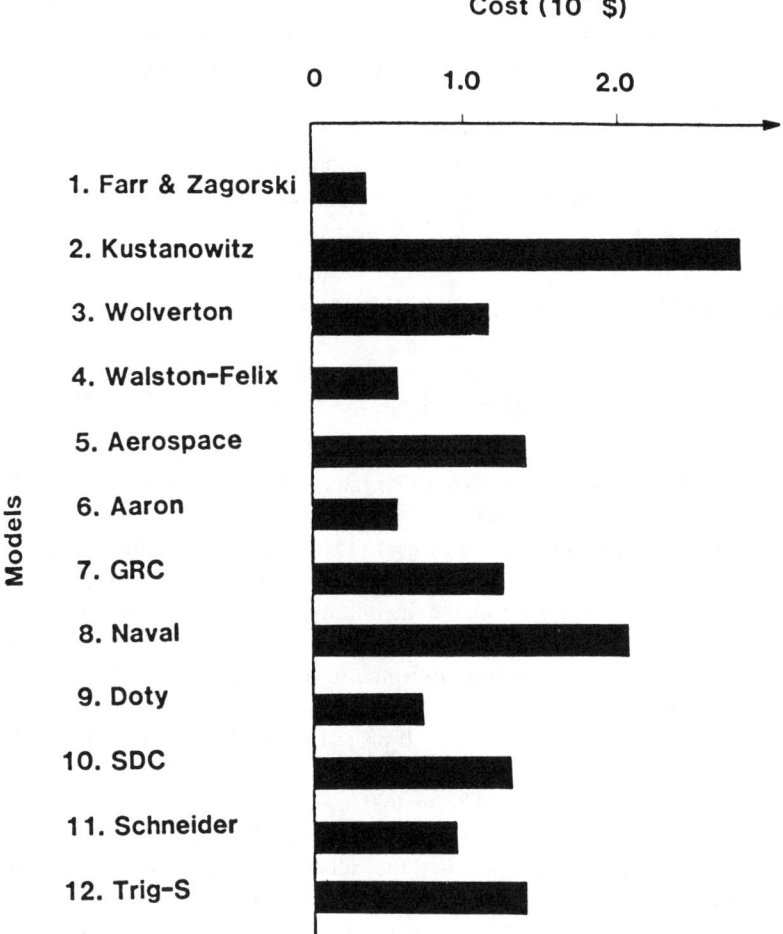

Figure 15.1   Cost estimates for same project

need to be accounted for in software cost estimation. For example, Tausworthe discusses the importance of accounting for manpower turnover while Clapp argues for the consideration of managerial policy on the acquisition of manpower and the distribution of effort among the software development activities. [65, 244]

15.2.2 Impact of Managerial Variables We will discuss the results of a simulation experiment conducted to quantify the impact of four managerial variables on the cost of software development. Two of the variables address manpower-acquisition and staffing policy issues while the other two concern issues of effort distribution among the software development activities. The four variables were selected based on two criteria proposed in Boehm and Wolverton: (1) objectivity and (2) prospectiveness. According to Boehm and Wolverton, software cost estimation models should include only objective variables to avoid allocating the software cost variance to poorly calibrated subjective factors such as complexity) [53]. The inclusion only of objective variables makes it harder to jiggle the model to obtain any result that one wants. Furthermore, a software cost estimation model should avoid the use of variables whose values cannot be determined until the project is complete.

We will examine the impact of each of the four variables individually. This will then be followed by an experiment to evaluate the impact of the four variables combined. The result is significant: based on just these four managerial variables, EXAMPLE's cost varies by a factor of two.

15.3 Staffing and Manpower-Acquisition Variables

Two model variables that address staffing and manpower-acquisition policy issues will be examined: (1) ''Average Daily Manpower per Staff'' and (2) the ''Willingness to Change Work Force.''

15.3.1 Project Staffing Policies
Our interviews at GM and Digital revealed a difference in the two organizations' software project staffing policies. At GM project members were assigned full-time to a single project (15)† whereas at Digital it was more common to assign software people to more than one project (usually two) (11), (16). The two policies have also been reported in the literature [148]. In the model, this staffing issue is represented by the variable ''Average Daily Manpower per Staff.'' For example, when project members are assigned full-time to the project, the value of the ''Average Daily Manpower per Staff'' is set at 1 because each project member contributes 1 man-day every working day to the project. If project members allocate on the average only 50% of their time to the project, as at the Digital groups studied, the value of the ''Average Daily Manpower per Staff'' would be set to 0.5.

To examine the impact of these two different staffing policies on project cost we ran project EXAMPLE twice; first the value of the ''Average Daily Manpower per Staff'' was set at 1 and then it was set at 0.5. The measure of project cost is simply the value of the total number of man-days expended to complete the project. The results are shown in Table 15.1.

TABLE 15.1

Average Daily Manpower per Staff	Man-Days
1.0	3,795
0.5	4,641

The policy of allocating project members half-time to the project results in a cost that is 22% higher. The reason is two-fold. First, there is a loss in productivity due to the increased communication overhead. This factor accounts for approximately 90% of the

---

† Reminder, a reference citation in the form (i) where ''i'' is a number between 1 and 27, refers to one of the 27 interviews of Table 4.1.

increase in the project's cost. As explained earlier,

$$Staffing\ Level\ (full-time\ employees) = \frac{MD}{TDEV} \qquad (15.1)$$

If the "Average Daily Manpower per Staff" is less than 1, adjustments would then be made to determine the actual number of employees needed. For example, if MD = 1000 man-days and TDEV = 200 days, the average staffing level is 5. If employees are assigned only half-time to the project, then the actual staffing level is 10 employees. With 10 people rather than 5 involved in developing the system the communication overhead increases, and the group's overall productivity decreases. More time is lost on human communication, for example, to resolve questions about design and testing [244]. Moreover, the amount of work itself usually increases in the form of more documentation, modules, and interfaces [69, 109].

The second reason for the increased cost is an increase in training overhead, which accounts for 10% of the increase. When new project members are recruited (from within the organization or from the outside), they pass through an orientation to learn the project's ground rules, the goals of the effort, the plan of the work, and all the details of the system. Newcomers are usually trained by the "old timers." "While (the old-timer) is helping the new employee learn the job, his own productivity on his other work is reduced" [62]. Training overhead is a function of the number of newcomers, *not* of the number simply of full-time newcomers. For example, in [118] when project members were assigned half-time on the project, team size doubled; as a result training overhead doubled. When the "Average Daily Manpower per Staff" is less than 1, more training overhead is incurred because a larger work force is required.

15.3.2 Manpower Acquisition Policies It is important to recall that the variable "Willingness to Change Work Force," the manpower-acquisition variable, is an expression of a *policy* for managing projects. Thus a range of functions are possible here, capturing different strategies for how to balance work force and schedule adjustments throughout the project to minimize overruns and costs. Our objective now is to examine the sensitivity of the project's cost to this variable. In particular, we will examine two different manpower acquisition policies.

Policy A can be defined as follows: At the initiation of the project, estimates are made for the project's total effort in man-days (MD) and its development time (TDEV). The project's desired staffing level is determined by dividing MD by TDEV. People are hired, complementing the core of project members on hand at the initiation of the project, until the desired staffing level is reached and then maintained. That is, new people are hired only to replace those who either quit or are transferred out.

Such a policy was reported by Devenny in his study of software cost estimation at the Electronic Systems Division of the Air Force Systems Command. He observed:

> The data indicate that none of the ten contractors ever significantly altered the size of the original software team. The contractor will normally keep the initially formed team working until the software is eventually completed. [85]

In EXAMPLE Policy A will be operationalized as follows: Estimates for the total effort in man-days, the development time, and the staffing level will be calculated exactly as in chapter 13. These values turn out, respectively, to be 2,359 man-days, 296 days, and

8 people. We will assume that at the project's initiation only half the desired number of people (i.e., 4) are on board. Four more people are then recruited. The desired level of eight people is maintained until the end of the project: new people would be hired only to replace those who either quit or are transferred out. The results of Policy A and the base run are shown in Table 15.2.

TABLE 15.2. POLICY A COMPARISON

Manpower Acquisition Policy	Man-Days	Duration
Base Case	3,795	430
A	3,559	488

Policy A leads to a 6% drop in cost compared with the base case. The drop, however, is achieved at the cost of a large schedule slip since EXAMPLE takes 13.5% more time to complete. Whether this tradeoff is made explicitly and willingly by the Electronic Systems Division contractors is not clear. However, by not adjusting the work force level to correct any initial errors in estimating the scope of the project, the policy leaves little room to accommodate any initial underestimate except as a software schedule slip. (Remember, EXAMPLE's size is initially underestimated by 33%.) In the base case, on the other hand, as the project's "Undiscovered Job Tasks" are discovered and project management comes to realize that the scope is larger than what has been expected, adjustments are made (see chapter 13) not only to the schedule but to the work force level as well.

The point here is that the different policies affect what the project's cost will end up being *and should therefore be explicitly considered when project cost estimates are made*.

Under Policy B, project management is willing to adjust the work force level for any initial underestimation throughout the life cycle (that is, further than in the base case).

In the *base case*, the "Willingness to Change Work Force" was the sum of the "Hiring Delay" and the "Average Assimilation Delay." In the early stages of the project when "Time Remaining" was generally much larger than the sum of the "Hiring Delay" and the "Average Assimilation Delay," management was willing to adjust the work force level to meet the completion date. As the number of days perceived remaining drops below $1.5 \times$ (Hiring Delay + Average Assimilation Delay), though, management starts demurring. For example, if the "Hiring Delay" is 40 working days and the "Average Assimilation Delay" is 80 days, then as "Time Remaining" drops below 180 days, management starts becoming reluctant to hire new people even though the time and effort perceived remaining imply that more people are needed. The reluctance stems from the realization that most of those remaining 180 days would be "wasted" in the hiring, orientation, and training. When the "Time Remaining" eventually drops below $0.3 \times$ (Hiring Delay + Average Assimilation Delay), no more additions are made to the project's work force; the hiring rate falls to zero. If the project is behind schedule, management has little choice but to push back the completion date.

While the above formulation expresses a representative policy for manpower acquisition, it is by no means the only policy. A range of policies is possible here, representing different strategies for adjusting work force and schedule throughout the project to minimize overruns costs.

Policy B is one such policy. It is adopted by at least one group in a Massachusetts-based software development/consulting company. Policy B is similar to Policy A; the only difference is that the "Willingness to Change Work Force" is equal to just the "Hiring Delay." Policy B is more aggressive in acquiring people. In the base case policy management starts becoming reluctant to increase the work force level when the perceived number of days remaining to complete the project drops below $1.5 \times$ (Hiring Delay + Average Assimilation Delay), i.e., below $1.5 \times (40 + 80) = 180$ days. Under policy B this happens much farther into the project's life cycle, i.e., when only $1.5 \times 40 = 60$ working days are perceived remaining. The aggressive policy is justified, we were told, by the firm's impressive growth rate, which is fueled by a sizable backlog of assignments. The WCWF1 table function for policy B is shown in Figure 15.2.

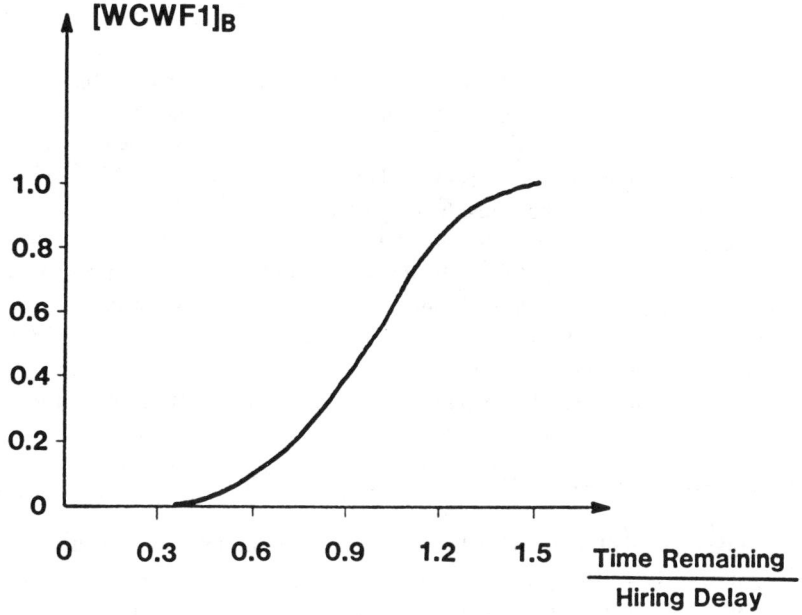

Figure 15.2 Function of WCWF1 used

The results of the base case and Policies A and B in EXAMPLE are shown in Table 15.3.

TABLE 15.3. COMPARISON OF POLICIES A AND B

Manpower Acquisition Policy	Man-Days	Duration
Base Case	3,795	430
A	3,559	488
B	4,321	373

Policy B's cost is 14% higher than the base case and 21% higher than Policy A's. But under policy B the project takes 13% less time than the base case and almost 25%

less time than Policy A. Both the increase in the cost and the decrease in the duration can be attributed to a higher work force level. But more people on the project means more work gets done. It also means that the project team's overall productivity is lower because of the increased communication and training overheads.

The objective of this exercise is *not* to decide which policy is better, but merely to establish that manpower acquisition policy does have an impact on what the project's costs will end up being *and should therefore be explicitly considered when project cost estimates are made.*

Establishing a particular factor for cost estimation is not enough. The factor must also be quantified before it can be used in a quantitative cost estimation model. According to Clapp:

> Variables used in cost estimation tend to be those which are easier to measure, quantify, and estimate, even if they are not the most significant. [65]

We feel that our "Willingness to Change Work Force" table function formulation provides a valid, easily calculable measure of manpower acquisition policy. We must note, however, that this measure is not original for us, for it has been previously used in other system dynamics models of R&D project management [223].

A final note: These results may seem to contradict Brooks' Law, which states that "Adding manpower to a late software project makes it later" [57]. The most aggressive of the three policies, Policy B, actually leads to the earliest completion date. Our model results indicate that "adding manpower to a late software project makes it more costly, but *not necessarily* later." An analysis of the implications of Brooks' Law under various situations is presented in chapter 19.

We turn next to the second category of variables: effort distribution.

15.4 Effort Distribution Variables

In planning a software project, management not only provides estimates for the project's total man-days effort but also plans the distribution of it among the project's phases [80, 123, 173]. Numerous authors have presented figures indicating life cycle resource distributions among phases. Sometimes the source of their information has been reported; in most instances it has gone unreported causing some difficulty with interpretation and application. In Table 3.5 a comparison of three authors' results done by McKeen indicates that substantial differences exist particularly in the coding and testing phases of development. Commenting on the situation McKeen wrote:

> A major conclusion is that we do not possess an adequate understanding of resource consumption behavior over the life cycle development phases. [172]

McKeen himself studied 32 software development projects. He found "no real support for 'typical' or 'dominant' development profiles at all" [172].

In this section our objective is to understand the impact of planned effort distribution among a project's phases on cost. Thibodeau and Dodson were the first to hypothesize the existence of such an impact:

Past attempts to establish mathematical expressions that can predict the life cycle cost components for software systems have achieved only qualified success. The mathematical models for these relationships included only variables that describe the software characteristics and related environmental factors. This paper presents the hypothesis that software cost estimating relationships must include the effects of resources consumed in one life cycle phase on other phases. Such a model is difficult to validate. This is mainly due to the need for greater quantities of data of greater precision than is usually available. [252]

In our view, the difficulty arises because of the phenomenon we discussed in detail in chapter 14: a different project estimate creates a different project. While all the arguments presented in chapter 14 were in terms of a project's *total* effort estimate, they apply equally to estimates at the phase level. We can therefore restate the above assertion as follows: *A different distribution of estimated effort among a project's phases creates a different project.* The impact of different effort distributions on the cost of a particular software project can be determined only by repeating the particular project under controlled conditions in which only the distribution of estimated effort among the project's phases is allowed to change.

In the remainder of this chapter we will use the model to conduct an experiment using EXAMPLE. The model has two effort distribution parameters. The first allocates the project's estimated man-days among the model's two explicit phases, development (which includes design and coding) and system testing. In the base case 80% of the effort is allocated to development and 20% to testing. The second effort distribution parameter is the "Planned Fraction of Manpower for QA," which is set at 15%. That is, 15% of the development effort is planned for QA activities during the design and coding stages. These values conform to the TRW software development environment. (See chapter 13).

15.4.1 Effort Distribution Alternative Policy The selection of another effort distribution profile to experiment with and compare to the base case distribution was in a sense both easy and difficult. It was easy because there was a large number of candidate profiles. There is a wide range of effort distribution profiles reported in the literature. However, the selection of one was difficult because of the many that are reported, none seemed to be "typical" or "dominant," as McKeen's study indicates [172]. We finally decided to make our selection based on the data collected in our interviews. We selected the case we felt provided the most interest. It involved one group at GM using the 40-20-40 effort distribution profile: 40% for preliminary and detailed design, 20% for coding, and 40% for testing. 40-20-40 is perhaps the most widely touted distribution of effort in software development projects [60, 135, 172, 200].

In terms of our model, this translates into a 60-40 distribution. That is, 60% of the total man-days are allocated to development and 40% to system testing. The GM group allocated to QA 20% of the development effort. This translates into a 0.20 value for "Planned Fraction of Manpower for QA" in the model.

15.4.2 Impact of Alternative Effort Distribution Policy The result of running EXAMPLE with this new effort distribution profile, Policy C, is shown in Table 15.4.

TABLE 15.4. POLICY C COMPARISON

Effort Distribution Policy	Man-Days
Base Case	3,795
C	4,443

A change in EXAMPLE's effort distribution from the base case to Policy C leads to a 17% increase in cost for four reasons. The first is the planned increase in the QA effort. Second, as a result, more errors are detected during development, leading to a larger rework effort expenditure. Third, the cost of development increases. The reason for this is, however, less obvious. Recall the sequence of steps followed in planning a project's various activities starting with the determination of total man-days. Based on this *total* value the project's schedule is calculated. Allocations to the development and testing activities are then made. Since this run's *total* man-day estimate is the same as that of the base case, the scheduled duration is also the same. However, since in the current case a lower fraction of the manpower is devoted to development work, a larger team is required to meet the schedule. A larger team means larger training and communication overheads and hence a larger development cost. The fourth reason is an increase in the testing effort. The testing effort increases over the base case situation even though it "should" be lower. It should be lower because more effort is devoted to QA, leading to the detection of a larger fraction of the errors. The testing effort increases in spite of a lower testing workload (because of the lower errors) because of a lower testing productivity. In the base case project members had to over-work during the testing phase because there were more errors and less time. In the current case, on the other hand, there is more time, and the work expands to fill it.

The implication is that for a 40% testing phase, a 20% allocation to QA is excessive. Or conversely, for a 20% allocation to QA, a 40% testing phase is excessive. It would be useful to determine the "optimal" combination. This will be investigated in chapter 18.

15.5 An Experiment Combining the Effect of all Four Variables

Our objective in this chapter was to demonstrate the significant impact of several managerial variables on the cost of software development. We examined four managerial variables. Two variables are related to the acquisition and staffing of the project's work force: the "Average Daily Manpower per Staff" and the "Willingness to Change Work Force." The other two variables concern the distribution of effort among the project's different activities; development, testing, and QA. The *individual* impact of the different variables on the project's cost was evaluated in *separate* experiments (except for the two effort distribution variables, which were tested together). The results indicate that individually the variables can make as much as a 20% difference in EXAMPLE's total cost in man-days.

15.5.1 The Experiment In this final experiment, we would like to evaluate the *combined* effect of the four managerial variables on cost. And so we re-run EXAMPLE with the following four adjustments:

1. Set the value of the "Average Daily Manpower per Staff" at 0.5. (The base case value is 1.)

2. The "Willingness to Change Work Force" is formulated in terms of the "Hiring Delay," yielding a more aggressive manpower acquisition policy. (In the base case it is formulated in terms of the (Hiring Delay + Average Assimilation Delay).)

3. Allocation of effort among the development and testing phases is set at 60% development and 40% testing. (In the base case it is 80-20.)

4. The "Planned Fraction of Manpower for QA" is set at 20%. (In the base case it is 15%.)

15.5.2 The Results   The result of running EXAMPLE with this different set of managerial policies is a total cost of 7,316 man-days, *almost double the base case cost of 3,795 man-days.*

The implication is clear: Because the above four managerial policies vary from one software development organization to another, the portability of software cost estimation models can be improved significantly if such variables are accounted for.

Heretofore, the impact of a company's managerial environment on software development has not been quantified. The insights gained by the experiments in this chapter can be useful in three ways. First, the effect of these four managerial variables can modify the cost of a software project by a factor of 2. Second, by quantifying the impact, it is harder for the software engineering community to ignore the issue. Finally, there are four aspects of a company's managerial environment that are significant determinants of software development cost. They deserve further investigation.

16

ANALOGY METHOD OF SOFTWARE ESTIMATION

16.1 Estimation by Analogy

In previous chapters our focus was on quantitative software estimation methods. In this chapter we turn our attention to "Estimation by Analogy," probably the most commonly used method to estimate software projects

> Estimation by analogy involves reasoning by analogy with one or more completed projects to relate their actual costs to an estimate of the cost of a similar new project [49].

> To apply this method at least one project with similar features must have been completed previously. The new project must be clearly specified at least at the functional level, permitting comparison of similar elements [43].

> Oliver wrote: "The most common technique on making operational estimates is the use of experience gained on one or more similar projects" [200]. This assertion is supported by at least one empirical study. In his Ph.D. dissertation Thayer surveyed 60 software development projects in the aerospace industry and found that the analogy method was used in 60% of the cases, making it by far the most common estimation method [246].

In the previous chapters we argued that software project estimation affects project behavior. A project's estimate creates pressures and perceptions that directly influence the decisions people make and the actions they take throughout the project's life cycle. For example, the causal loop diagram of Figure 16.1 depicts the influence of project estimation on hiring/firing decisions, perceived project status, and productivity. It implies that the use of analogy in estimation results in a feedback loop as depicted in Figure 16.2. The estimation by analogy method produces project estimates and schedules that affect the decisions and actions of the technical performers and their managers, which in turn affect work performance, which would then eventually influence future estimations.

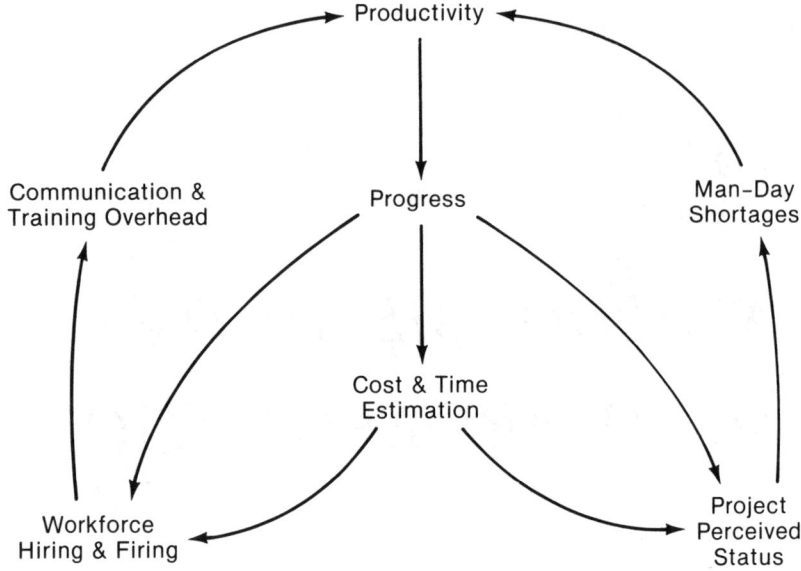

Figure 16.1   Influence of project estimation

Figure 16.2   Feedback loop resulting from estimation by analogy

16.2 Experiment to Evaluate Analogy Method

What does the existence of the estimation by analogy feedback loop mean? Is it good or bad? These are some of the questions we will attempt to answer in this chapter with several experiments.

The first involves a hypothetical situation in which a company undertakes a sequence of five *identical* software projects, all identical to EXAMPLE, our prototype project.

16.2.1 EXAMPLE1 EXAMPLE1 uses base case conditions. On EXAMPLE1, the company, lacking the benefit of previous experience, underestimates the size of the project by 33%: the company estimates the project's size to be only 48.22 KDSI, as in EXAMPLE's base case. The base case estimates for the project's man-days and duration were also the estimates used in EXAMPLE. That is, the project's man-days are estimated to be 2,359 and its development time to be 296 working days. As our base case analysis of chapter 13 indicates, after completing EXAMPLE1 we learn that it:

- Is really 64 KDSI.

- Consumes 3,795 man-days.

- Takes 430 days to complete.

16.2.2 EXAMPLE2 EXAMPLE2 is identical to EXAMPLE1 but it comes along later, and project management is in a better position to estimate its true size. We assume that EXAMPLE2's size is estimated perfectly to be 64 KDSI, to require 3,795 man-days, and to last 430 days. Based on these figures management estimates that a staff size of 3,795/430=9 (approx.) full-time people are required.

Conducting EXAMPLE2 under such circumstances produces the following results: actual man-days expended = 3,787 and actual duration = 454 days. While the project is almost perfectly on target in terms of the man-day expenditures, it *still* finishes late, approximately 6% beyond the estimated schedule.

This result is not only surprising but also disturbing. EXAMPLE2 overruns what amounts to a "perfect" schedule estimate.

16.2.3 EXAMPLE3, EXAMPLE4, EXAMPLE5 When we repeated the above sequence of actions and reactions three more times for EXAMPLE3, EXAMPLE4, and EXAMPLE5, the surprising behavior persisted: the schedule was overrun in each case. Management started each project with a slightly longer scheduled duration than the previous one. However, each still overran its schedule; management used an even longer schedule duration for the next project. The results for the five simulation runs are shown in Figure 16.3.

16.3 Analysis of Experiments

It is important to make one clarification. The objective of this experiment is *not* to investigate the behavior of a sequence of five *identical* software projects! Such a scenario is unrealistic. Choosing to conduct such an experiment *and being able to do so* is, however, one strength of simulation modeling. It allows us to conduct experimentation

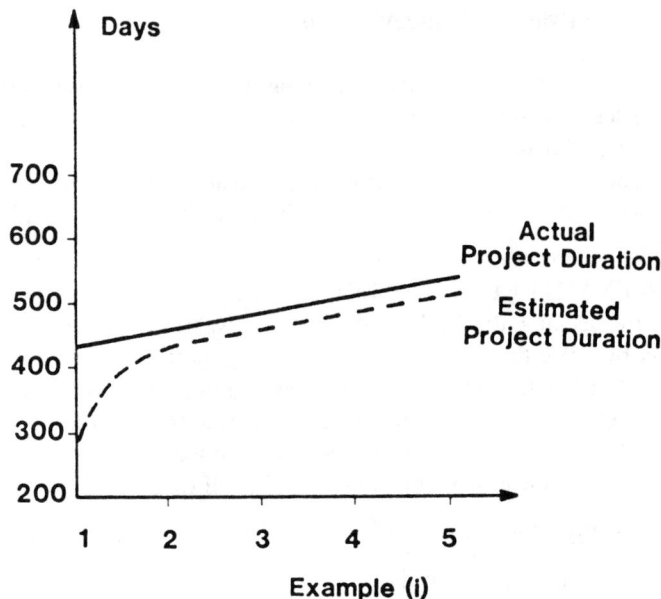

Figure 16.3 Simulation runs for EXAMPLE1 through EXAMPLE5

with absolute control over variables. Our objective is to study the effects of using estimation by analogy. Studying such relationships in a real setting where projects and managers vary can only *and unnecessarily* confuse the issues and complicate the analysis. For example, for EXAMPLE2 overruns, we can definitively rule out underscheduling as a cause and instead look for a better explanation. If, however, EXAMPLE2 had not been identical to EXAMPLE1, we would not have been able to make such an argument. Instead we would have had to investigate the differences in scope between the two projects.

We can now interpret the experiment's results. There are two. First, there appear to be inherent factors in the management of a software project that would cause it to overrun even with a "perfect" schedule estimate. The second more interesting result is that because of the inherent tendency to overshoot, the use of the analogy method in estimating injects a bias in scheduling, a bias that in the long-run generates longer than necessary schedules.

16.3.1 Schedule Overrun EXAMPLE2 overran a schedule that was perfectly adequate to complete EXAMPLE1, a project identical to it. Through further experimentation with the model it was possible to isolate the real cause of this persisting schedule-overrun problem: the interaction of two factors, the manpower-acquisition policy and the turnover of project personnel.

As explained in the preceding chapter, in the early stages of a project staffing is maintained at the level which is perceived to be necessary and sufficient to complete the project on schedule. As the project proceeds towards its final stages, management becomes increasingly reluctant to hire new people. Thus, if at that stage the project runs into schedule problems, management would react not by adding more people but rather by pushing the schedule completion date back.

A project runs into scheduling problems whenever the "Man-Days Perceived Still Needed" to complete the project exceeds the "Man-Days Remaining." In previous chapters we discussed how this can develop due to an increase in the former. For example, if the project's size was under-estimated, the value of the "Man-Days Perceived Still Needed" could rise as the undiscovered tasks are discovered. In EXAMPLE2, though, this will not occur. We assume that the experience gained on EXAMPLE1 will lead to a "perfect" estimate of EXAMPLE2's size. What can happen, however, is that the value of the "Man-Days Remaining" for EXAMPLE2 drops below the value of the "Man-Days Perceived Still Needed," and when this happens, EXAMPLE2 runs into scheduling problems. The value of the "Man-Days Remaining" is simply the product of the work force level (in full-time equivalent employees) and the time remaining in the schedule. Any drop in the work force level because of turnover will in turn decrease the value of the man-days remaining, creating a scheduling problem. When this happens towards the end of the project — when management is reluctant to add new people — the adjustment will be to push the completion date back, resulting in a schedule overrun.

16.3.2 Tendency to Overshoot Thus far we have addressed only the first result of our experiment, that a software project can still overrun a "perfect" schedule estimate. The second result of the experiment can be stated as follows: because of the inherent tendency to overshoot, the use of the analogy method in estimating injects a bias in an organization's scheduling, a bias that in the long term generates longer than necessary project schedules.

The phenomenon of projects consuming longer and longer schedules is one that has been frequently encountered in system dynamics studies of organizational behavior [241]. It has been termed "The Policy Resistance of Social Systems," "Shifting the Burden to the Intervenor," and "Addiction," among other things. A simple example of such a phenomenon is that of caffeine addiction: an addict has to consume a certain amount of caffeine per day to maintain a certain level of alertness. As time goes on, the burden of maintaining alertness shifts from the normal physiological body processes to the externally supplied caffeine dose. The result, of course, is that higher and higher doses are required to maintain the *same* level of alertness.

Richardson and Pugh provide an explanation for why social systems have this tendency to resist policies designed to improve behavior (e.g., why a software project tends to resist the policy of estimation by analogy, which is designed to solve the schedule overrun problem yet continues to overrun its schedule):

(The) compensating feedback is a property of real systems, as well as system dynamics models, and is the reason real systems tend to be resistant to policies designed to improve behavior ... .

(A) parameter change may weaken or strengthen a feedback loop, but the multi-loop nature of a system dynamics model naturally strengthens or weakens other loops to compensate. The result is often little or no overall change in model behavior [221].

In our experiments, this is exactly what happens. To see how, let us first recall the steps followed to estimate a project. First, the estimates of the project's man-days and its duration are made. These can be made using analogy or another estimation technique such as COCOMO. The project's average staffing level is calculated by dividing the man-days estimate by the estimate for the development time. For example, in EXAMPLE2 the estimates were MD = 3,795, TDEV = 430 and the average staffing level = 3,795/430 = 8.8 full-time employees. We also know that EXAMPLE2's *actual* man-days and duration end up being 3,787 and 454, respectively. EXAMPLE2's *actual* average staffing level is 3,787/454 = 8.3 full-time employees. When the analogy method is then used to estimate EXAMPLE3, EXAMPLE2's actual values are used, yielding: MD = 3,787, TDEV = 454, and an average staffing level of 8.3 full-time equivalent employees. Notice what is happening: EXAMPLE2's *actual* average staffing level ends up slightly less than what was *planned* for, i.e., 8.3 instead of 8.8. This is caused by the turnover problem. The actual (lower) value is the one passed over to the next project.

Extending the project's schedule from 430 to 454 days weakens the schedule pressure in the system, and the hiring loop simply compensates by causing the project to start with a smaller work force. Such compensating behavior is often invisible to the participants. It is unlikely that EXAMPLE3's project managers notice the compensating behavior because the 8.8 figure is only a planning (not an actual) figure for EXAMPLE2. Quite possibly, it would not be preserved in any project records. Even if it is, it is unlikely that EXAMPLE3's manager will use it; after all, by concentrating on EXAMPLE2's *actual* data, the manager would be behaving in what appears to be the rational way.

This managerial dilemma is not at all unique to the management of software projects. According to Forrester:

> ... social systems are inherently insensitive to most policy changes that people select in an effort to alter the behavior of the system. In fact, a social system tends to draw our attention to the very points at which an attempt to intervene will fail. Our experience, which has been developed from contact with simple systems, leads us to look close to the symptoms of trouble for a cause. When we look, we discover that the social system presents us with an apparent cause that is plausible according to what we have learned from simple systems. But this apparent cause is usually a coincident occurrence that, like the trouble symptom itself, is being produced by the feedback-loop dynamic of a larger system [100].

When a software development project overruns its schedule there is an apparent cause: the project was poorly estimated. After all, software estimation is not yet an exact science. Significantly, it is often impossible in a real life situation to demonstrate that underestimation was *not* in fact the cause. By using our simulation model, we can exclude changes in requirements from our analysis.

16.4 Summary

A number of conclusions can be drawn from our experiments:

- A software development project can still overrun what amounts to a ''perfect'' schedule estimate.

- Research on the causes of schedule overrun problems must be extended beyond merely software estimation accuracy. One such cause is the interaction of the manpower-acquisition policy and personnel turnover.

- Estimating by analogy injects a bias in an organization's scheduling process, a bias that generates in the long run longer than necessary project schedules.

17

THE 90% SYNDROME

17.1 Description of the 90% Syndrome

This chapter focuses on a control problem faced by many software project managers: the "90% syndrome" problem. Our aim is to provide some insights into its causes.

There is ample evidence in the literature to support the pervasiveness of the "90% syndrome" in the management of software development projects (see [28, 81, 85, 89, 242]). Baber provides the following description of the problem:

> ... estimates of the fraction of work completed (increase) as originally planned until a level of about 80-90% is reached. The programmer's individual estimates then increase only very slowly until the task is actually completed [28].

17.2 Model Reproduction of the 90 Syndrome

To examine the model's capacity to generate the "90% syndrome," we simulated EXAMPLE with three different initial conditions:

1. The base case where the size is initially underestimated by 33%:

$$SIZE = 42.88 \ (and \ not \ 64) \ KDSI$$
$$MD = 2,359 \ man-days$$
$$TDEV = 296 \ days$$

2. The case where its size is properly estimated but its man-days requirements are underestimated by 33%. Such a situation might arise because of an underestimate of the project's complexity or an overestimate of the team's productivity or both. As was mentioned before, COCOMO exists in a hierarchy of increasingly detailed forms. In its more detailed versions the estimate of a project's man-day requirements can be adjusted by multipliers to account for factors such as complexity, required reliability, and team capability. For example, for a project perceived to have a "very low" complexity rating, the man-days estimate would be 30% below the "nominal" case. Thus if a project is incorrectly perceived at its initiation as being "very low" in complexity when in fact it is not, an underestimate of its man-day requirements will result.

Thus, for this second case:

$$SIZE = 64\ KDSI$$

$$\begin{aligned}
MD &= 0.67 \times MD_{NOMINAL}\\
&= 0.67 \times [2.4 \times 19 \times 64^{1.05}]\\
&= 2{,}407\ man-days
\end{aligned}$$

$$\begin{aligned}
TDEV &= 47.5 \times (2{,}407\ /\ 19)^{0.38}\\
&= 299\ days
\end{aligned}$$

3. The case where neither size nor man-day requirements are underestimated:

$$SIZE = 64\ KDSI$$
$$MD = 2.4 \times 19 \times 64^{1.05} = 3{,}593\ man-days$$
$$TDEV = 47.5 \times (3{,}593\ /\ 19)^{0.38} = 348\ days$$

The results of the three simulation runs are shown in Figures 17.1 through 17.3.

17.2.1 Case 1: Size Underestimation As might be expected, the "90% syndrome" arises when a software project is initially underestimated. Progress generally lacks visibility in the earlier phases of development; it is measured by the rate of expenditure of resources rather than by of actual accomplishments, and status reporting ends up being nothing more than an echo of the project's plan. This creates the "illusion" that the project is on target. However, as the project approaches its final stages (when 80-90% of the resources are consumed), discrepancies between the percentage of tasks accomplished and the percentage of resources expended become increasingly apparent. At the same time, project members become increasingly able to perceive how productive the work force has actually been. Management and work force can better appreciate the amount of effort actually remaining. As appreciation develops, it in effect discounts the project's progress rate. Thus even as the project members proceed towards the final stages of the project, perhaps at a higher work rate, they discover that more and more work needs to be done and that their effective progress toward completion is reduced. The diminution of progress continues until the project is completed.

17.2.2 Case 2: Man-Day Underestimation We did not expect the significant difference in the acuteness of the problem between the two types of underestimates. The "90% syndrome" is much more acute when man-days requirements are underestimated than it is when size is. With a little reflection we can see why. When *man-days* requirements are underestimated the problem often remains undetected until the final stages when most of the budgeted man-days are consumed and the project members can perceive how productive the work force has actually been. On the other hand, when size is underestimated, the situation is less severe because the problem tends to be detected faster. In both the NASA case study and the EXAMPLE base case, for example, the "Undiscovered Job Tasks" do not remain undiscovered until the last stages of the project; instead they start to be discovered during the detailed design phase. When such tasks are discovered, adjustments to the project's man-days are often made. As a result, the project arrives at its final stages with its initial underestimate largely detected, which reduces the severity of the "90% syndrome."

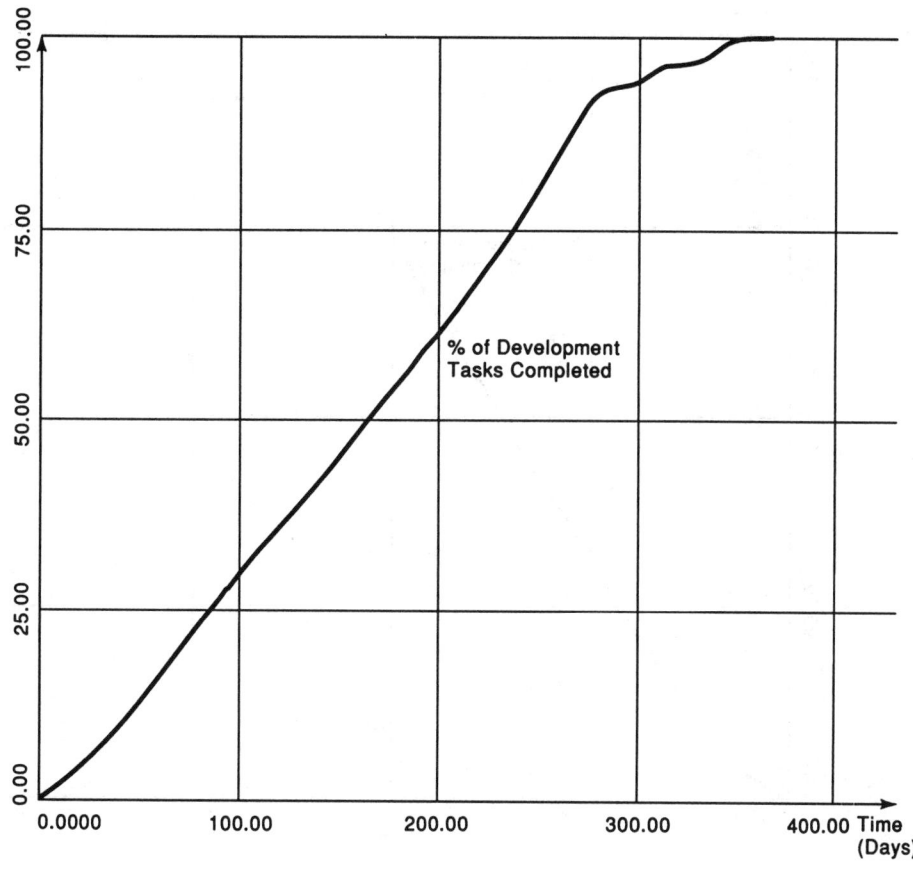

Figure 17.1 Case 1: Size underestimation

17.3 Implications of the 90 Syndrome

The "90% syndrome" arises because of the interaction of two factors: underestimation and imprecise measurement of progress. The reason progress tends to be imprecisely measured is that imprecise surrogates are used to measure it. "A surrogate is a substitute measure of some phenomenon that is used because it is not feasible to measure the phenomenon directly" [22]. For software, consumption of resources is the surrogate often used to measure progress. In this section we will discuss implications of the 90% syndrome and focus on the impact of better monitoring tools.

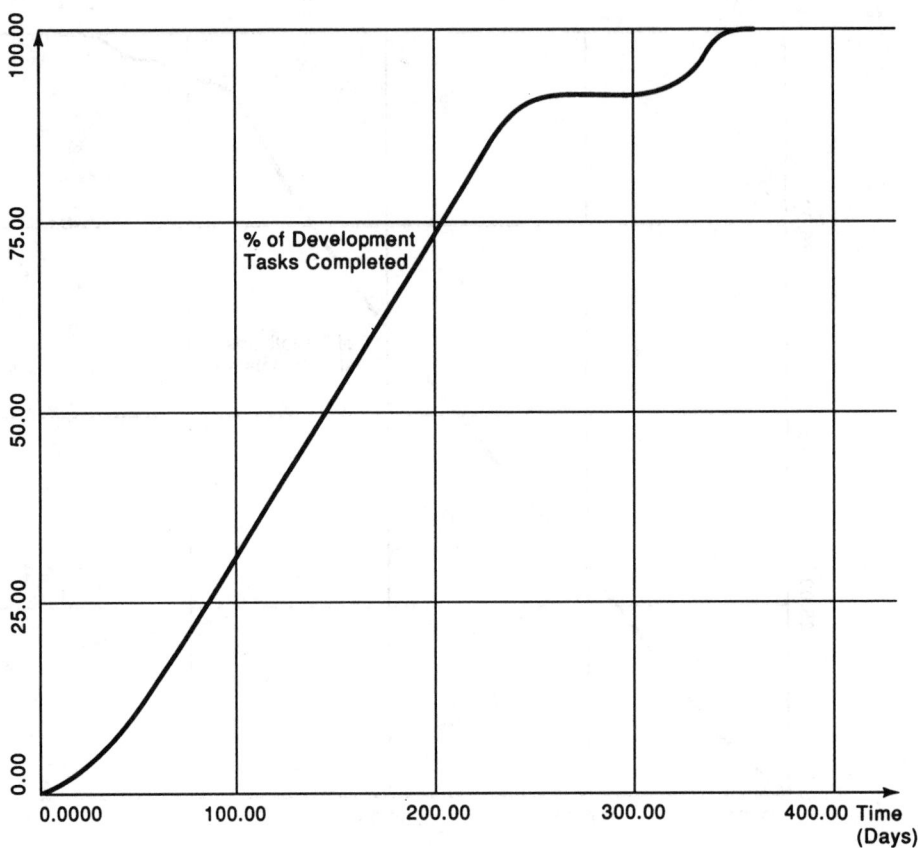

Figure 17.2 Case 2: Man-Days underestimation

17.3.1 Better Monitoring Tools Attempts have been made to develop more precise tools that would directly measure progress in a software project, e.g., automated monitoring systems such as SIMON [98].

17.3.2 Persistence of Problem However, primarily because such tools address only one aspect of the problem — the imprecise measurement of progress, not the underestimation aspect — their use could have unintended and dysfunctional consequences. Consider for example an effective measurement tool in a typical environment, where projects tend to be underestimated at their initiation. The better the measurement tool the earlier it will detect that progress is not keeping up with the underestimated schedule. When a

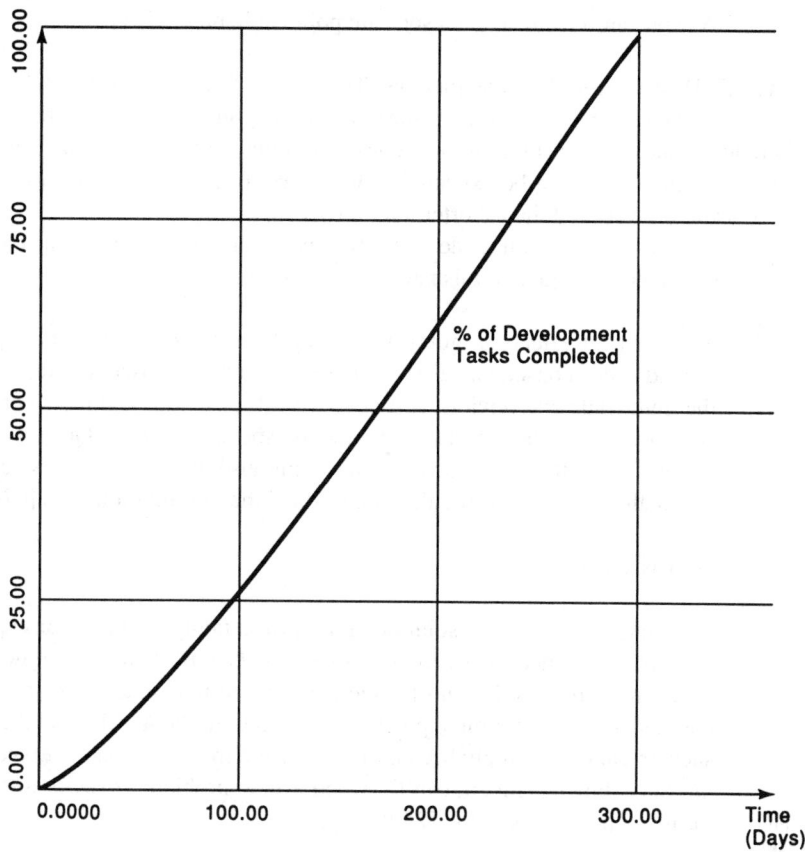

Figure 17.3   Case 3: No underestimation

discrepancy is detected early in the development cycle, management usually reacts by adding more people rather than by adjusting the schedule. This happens, according to DeMarco, for political reasons:

> Once an original estimate is made, it's all too tempting to pass up subsequent opportunities to estimate by simply sticking with your previous numbers. This often happens even when you know your old estimates are substantially off. There are a few different possible explanations for this effect: "It's too early to show slip. ... If I re-estimate now, I risk having to do it again later (and looking bad twice)."

As you can see, all such reasons are political in nature [81].

17.3.3 Dysfunctional Consequences The result of sticking with a schedule that is too tight is often an increase in the project's cost [49] due to a large work force level. This could produce a project that is erroneously compressed in duration and inflated in cost, an outcome that might not be expected or welcomed (e.g., in an organization where smaller costs are more critical than shorter durations).

The scenario of unintended and dysfunctional consequences caused by managerial intervention is not unique to this particular situation:

> The chain of effects in going from a problem to immediate consequences then to second-order-consequences (i.e., those that appear subsequent to, or as a result of, the immediate and obvious consequences of an action) and newly created problems is a pervasive characteristic of modern social systems. Quite literally, in such systems everything depends on everything else and often in ways so complex and round about that it is difficult to understand the interrelationships [67].

And as a result,

> ... apparently logical solutions may prove faulty as their consequences ramify. Furthermore, since the consequences of a decision often occur much later than the decision itself, it is difficult for the members to trace backward from the disruptive consequences to determine precisely what caused them. The members cannot make such an analysis, simply because there are too many competing explanations. Thus, the only thing members can do when a new problem arises is to engage in more localized problem-solving [259].

The reader might recall that the preceding argument was used in chapter 1 to support an *integrative* perspective to the study of software project management. Indeed, even though the issues we are raising here on the dysfunctional consequences of measurement tools are beyond the scope of this book, we feel that a general integrative approach provides the viable basis for addressing them.

18

THE ECONOMICS OF
QUALITY ASSURANCE

18.1 Quality Assurance Concern and Methodologies

Quality Assurance (QA) is a set of activities performed in the development of a software product to reduce doubts and risks about the performance of the product in the target environment [210]. The rationale for QA was summarized in chapter 8.

18.1.1 Quality Assurance Methodologies Software quality assurance is approached by two distinct and complementary methodologies. The first is to assure that the quality is initially built into the product. This methodology emphasizes that a coherent, complete, unambiguous, and nonconflicting set of requirements be designed early in the project. The second is to review and test the product as the product is designed and coded [84].

18.1.2 Methodologies for Review and Testing As indicated in section 2.4 (''Model Boundary''), our model's development phase includes both design and coding activities but *excludes* the development of the requirements. Thus, for our analysis, we will focus on the second QA methodology. We will start our investigation at the ''successful completion'' of a software requirements review and assume that there will be no subsequent changes or modifications in the system's requirements.

Several specific techniques are available for reviewing and testing the software product as it is designed and coded: structured walk-throughs and technical reviews [105], inspections [94], code reading (a process where code logic and code format are scrutinized by a programmer other than the original designer) [260] and integration testing [78, 141]. Not included in this activity is module or unit testing, which is commonly considered to be part of the coding process [172].

18.2 Economics of Quality Assurance

In this chapter we focus on economics rather than on technical aspects of QA. We investigate the tradeoff between the benefits and costs of QA in terms of the total project cost.

QA tools and techniques add cost to the development of software. For example, man-hours are expended in developing test cases, running test cases, and conducting structured walk-throughs. The added cost is

> ... a source of concern to everyone associated with the program, particularly the program manager and the customer. ...
> A (more) pressing concern to the software quality manager is how cost efficient are the QA operations during the development cycle. The QA organization, just as all elements of the development process, will and should be subject to detailed and continuing scrutiny regarding the cost of doing business [146].

This "pressing concern" has not, however, been addressed in the literature: there are no published studies investigating "how cost efficient are the QA operations during the development cycle." Three possible reasons for this deficiency are: (1) It is a managerial issue. Like many other aspects of software production, managerial considerations tend to attract less research attention. "Perhaps this is so because computer scientists believe that management per se is not their business" [70]. (2) The emphasis has been on "selling" QA to managers; hence the emphasis on stressing the benefits (e.g., see [93, 72]). (3) The high cost of controlled experimentation in software engineering has made it difficult to perform such research [117, 191].

The question is not whether QA is justified but *how much* of it is justified. To find an answer we simulate EXAMPLE under different levels of manpower commitments to QA and observe the benefits and costs in each case.

18.2.1 Cost Savings of QA The primary goal of QA is "that errors be detected and corrected as early as possible and only a minimal amount of problems be allowed to slip from one phase of the development to the next" [256]. Several studies have established the significant savings gained by the early detection and correction of errors. McClure reports that Shooman determined that detecting and correcting a design error during the design phase required one-tenth the effort that would have been needed to detect and correct it during the system testing phase because of the additional inventory of specifications, code, user and maintenance manuals, and so on that would also have required correction [166].

An important relationship is therefore the one between the QA effort expended and the percentage of errors detected during development. The relationship produced in our experiment is exhibited in Figure 18.1.

18.2.2 Diminishing Returns of QA A significant feature of the relationship shown in Figure 18.1 is the diminishing returns as QA expenditures exceed 20-30% of development effort. Shooman observed that "in any sizable program, it is impossible to remove all errors (during development). ... some errors manifest themselves, and can be exhibited only after system integration" [236]. A compilation of *single* point studies reported by Boehm [49] and shown in Figure 18.2 illustrates the relationship between QA effort and unit-level error-removal.

18.2.3 Tradeoff Between QA Savings and Costs Figure 18.1 suggests that the savings in the cost of rework and testing from the application of QA flattens out as QA expenditures exceed 20-30% of development effort. (See Figure 18.3.) On the other hand, increasing QA as a percentage of the development effort results in an *exponential* increase

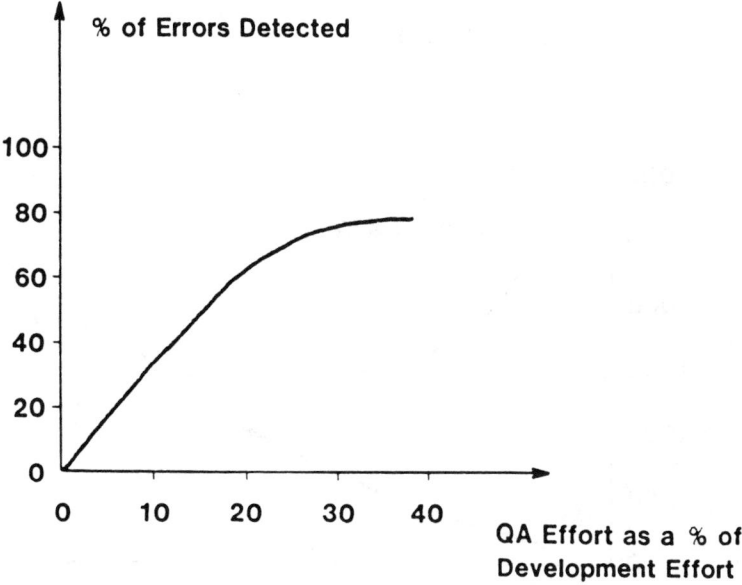

Figure 18.1   Errors detected by various levels of QA effort

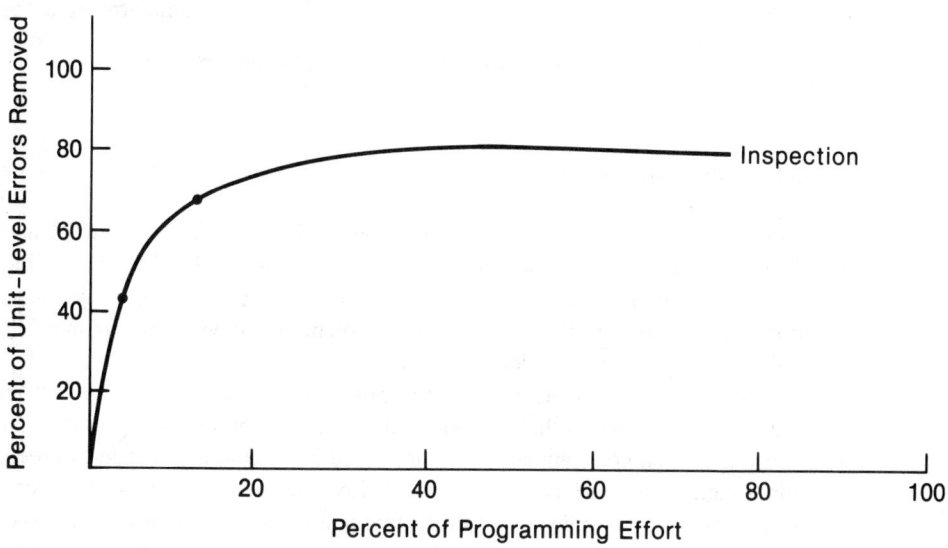

Figure 18.2   Boehm's summary of QA studies

in QA's absolute cost in man-days. As a larger fraction of the development effort is allocated to QA, the development effort itself increases because as more man-days are allocated to QA (without corresponding reductions in Rework + Testing man-days), the project's size in man-days goes up. This leads to the acquisition of a larger work force. A larger work force means a less productive work force, as we have already seen.

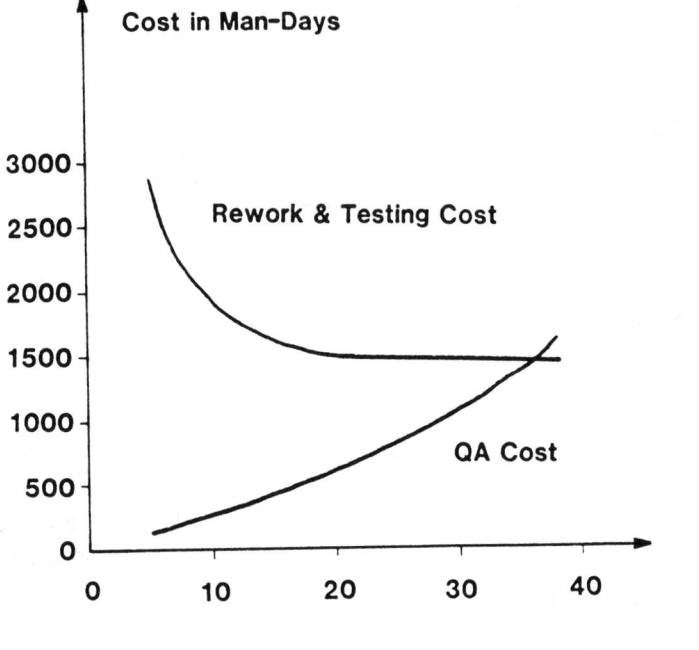

Figure 18.3 QA effort impact on costs

18.3 Optimal Quality Assurance Effort

In Figure 18.3, as the QA costs rise, the benefits (i.e., reduction in rework and testing cost) decline. What is the "optimal" QA effort expenditure? For EXAMPLE the answer is shown in Figure 18.4, which plots EXAMPLE's *total* cost (in man-days) against QA effort defined in terms of percentage of development man-days: the "optimal" QA effort expenditure is 16% of the development man-days.

Two important conclusions can be drawn from Figure 18.4. The first and more generalizable conclusion is that QA policy does have a significant impact on total project cost. EXAMPLE's cost ranges from a low of 3,770 man-days to values around 5,000 man-days, i.e., values that are 33% higher. At low values of QA expenditures the increase in cost results from the large cost of the testing phase. At high values of QA expenditures excessive QA expenditures are themselves the culprit. The second result is the optimal QA expenditure level of 16%. What is significant about the result is not its value, since this cannot be generalized beyond EXAMPLE, but rather the process of deriving it, namely, our integrative system dynamics approach. Beyond controlled experimentation (which is too costly and time consuming to be feasible) our model, as far as we know, provides the first capability to analyze quantitatively the costs and benefits of QA for software production. The model is generalizable because one can customize models for different software development projects.

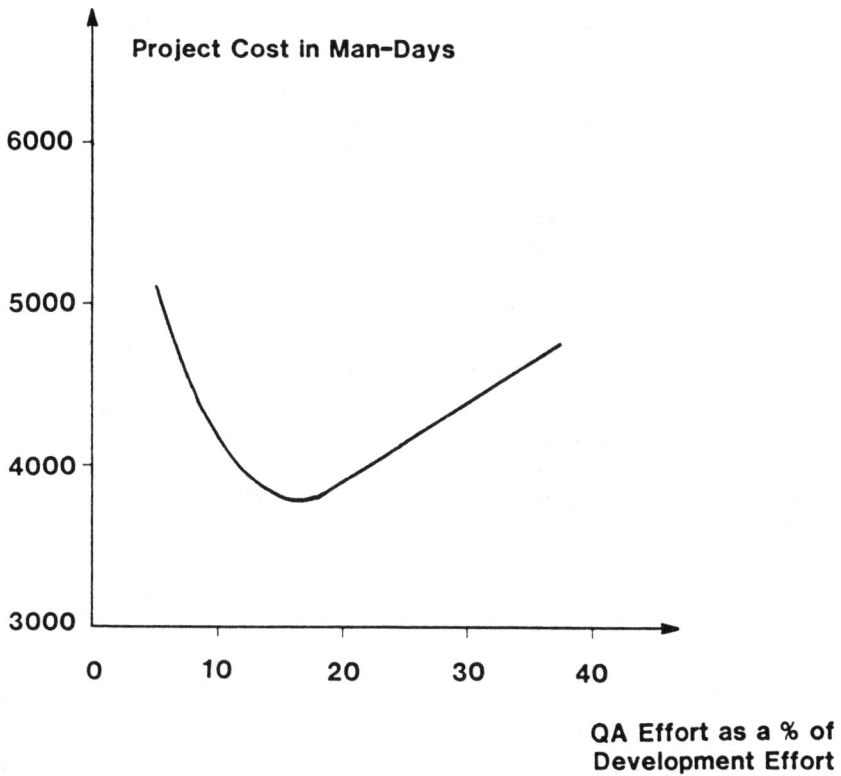

Figure 18.4   Optimal QA effort for project EXAMPLE

18.4 Generality of Optimality

Why is the optimal value of 16% derived above not generalizable? To answer the question we will test two project variables that can change from project to project and from organization to organization. Such an investigation will have two useful outcomes: First, we will derive results of the form "An increase in factor X warrants a greater QA expenditure" which will be generalizable beyond EXAMPLE. Such results could, for example, be useful "rules-of-thumb" for organizations. Second, using the "rules-of-thumb," we can adapt and adjust our own results, increasing their generalizability.

18.4.1 Experiment #1: Distribution of Effort Between Development and Testing In planning a software project management not only estimates the project's total effort in man-days but also allocates that effort among the project's phases [123]. Substantial differences in opinion exist on how the distribution is or should be made [173]. In EXAMPLE's base case we assumed a distribution of 80% for development (design and coding) and 20% for testing, values chosen to conform to the TRW software development environment.

We will now examine the effect on QA of the 40-20-40 effort distribution: 40% for preliminary and detailed design, 20% for coding, and 40% for testing. This particular distribution reflects perhaps the most widely touted rule-of-thumb on distribution of effort among the phases of software development projects [60, 135, 172, 200]. In our model, 40-2-40 translates into a 60-40 distribution. That is, 60% of the total man-days are allocated to design and coding, and 40% to testing.

Notice that we are trying to compute how much effort to allocate to QA by examing effort in the testing phase. It *appears* as though we have confused the independent and dependent variables. After all, QA is used not only in the development phase but also to minimize the cost of the testing phase. Our experiment's seemingly lopsided set-up, however, is really a reflection of what the state-of-the-art is in software project management. Both in the literature (e.g., [49]) and in the organizations we interviewed (e.g., based on discussions (3), (10), (11), (12), and (15)) the sequence of steps for allocating man-day expenditures is as follows: First the total project's effort is estimated. Then the effort is distributed among the life-cycle phases (e.g., using the 40-20-40 rule). *And then* effort is allocated to QA as a percentage of the development effort. For example, in Boehm's *Software Engineering Economics* he uses a case study titled "The Hunt National Bank EFT System" to outline how COCOMO would be used to estimate and allocate a project's man-day expenditures. The following sequence of steps is followed:

1. COCOMO's effort and schedule equations are used to estimate the project's man-days and development time.

2. Next, according to a distribution plan such as 40-20-40, man-days are allocated to development and testing.

3. *Finally*, effort is allocated to QA according to guidelines expressing QA as a percentage of development man-days [49].

This approach to planning is a reflection of how young software engineering is. First no explicit development life cycle existed. Emphasis was almost totally on the programming phase of a project. Next we realized the value of breaking the development process into distinct life cycle phases and emphasizing its earlier requirements and design phases. Only recently have we also come to realize the importance of emphasizing quality *during* the development of a software project. However, what the above planning sequence suggests is that the field has *not* yet grown to full maturity.

Running EXAMPLE where 40% of the man-days are allocated to testing unlike the base case's 20%, produced the result shown in Figure 18.5 (for experiment #1). The optimal QA expenditure level drops to 11% of development effort.

The fundamental reason is that effort expenditures are a function not only of the actual workload but also of *planned* expenditures. This phenomenon was explained in detail in chapter 15. Allocating more to testing expands the testing effort even though the workload itself might not. In other words, since the testing effort will expand as a result of management's increased allocation to testing, it makes sense to reap the greatest return from the increased investment in testing. That return would of course be achieved by decreasing the investment in QA. Note that the 11% allocation to QA is still within the range of QA expenditures reported both in the literature and in the organizations we studied (See chapter 6.)

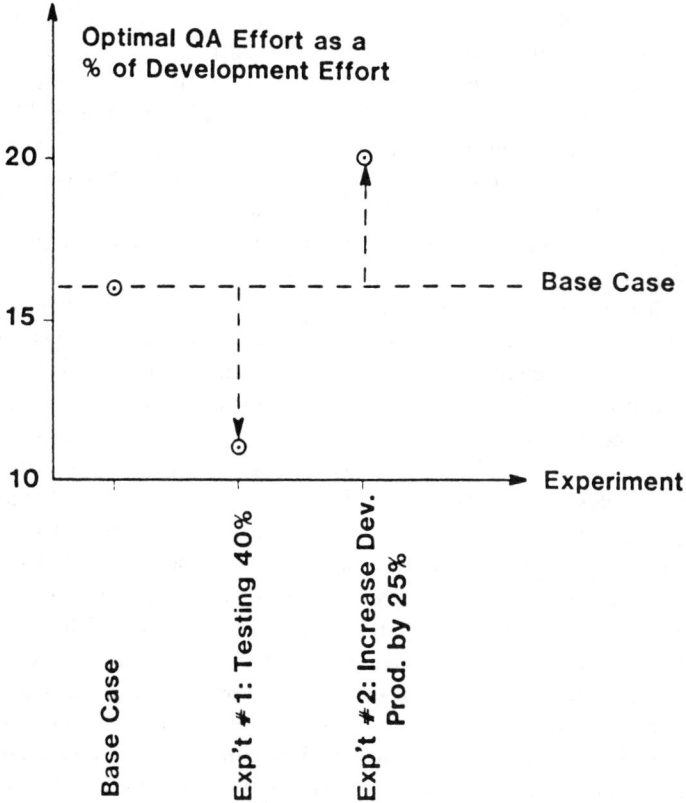

Figure 18.5   Optimal QA effort under various conditions

18.4.2 Experiment #2: Software Development Productivity We made a clear distinction between two sets of factors that can affect how productive people will be on a software project. The first set included factors that affect productivity dynamically throughout the development of a single project: for example, work force experience, learning, motivation, and communication. The second set included environmental factors that tend to remain invariant during the life of a single project: for example, availability of software tools, computer-hardware characteristics, programming language, and product complexity. Because the second set does not play a dynamic role during the life of a single project, we were able to represent it by a single parameter, the project's "Nominal Potential Productivity." Here we investigate the effect on the optimal QA expenditure due to changes in potential productivity caused by changes in the software development environment.

In chapter 13 we set EXAMPLE's "Nominal Potential Productivity" at 60 DSI/man-day — actually it was set to 1 Task/man-day, where a task was defined to be 60 DSI — to conform to the TRW software development environment. In experiment #2 we examine the effect of increasing the value of "Nominal Potential Productivity" by 25% to 75 DSI/man-day. Notice that such an increase affects only the productivity of software *development*. Such an increase has no direct effect on the productivity of processing errors (i.e., detecting them and correcting them). Of course, one could argue that there can be some correlation between the two productivities because higher quality people would be more productive in producing code and in detecting and correcting errors. We therefore might need to make corresponding adjustments to the error processing productivities in the model. While perfectly feasible, such adjustments would defeat the purpose of the experiment, which we can now elaborate more precisely: We would like to examine the effects of increasing the differential between *development* productivity and *error-processing* productivity in an organization.

The results of the experiment, shown in Figure 18.5, indicate that an increase in *development* productivity warrants an increase in QA expenditures *relative* to development expenditures. Higher development productivities mean that each man-day expended on the development of software yields more software. As a result more QA effort is required to handle the increased output. The increased output will not by itself trigger adjustments in the QA expended. *The required increases in QA must therefore be explicitly planned for.* The reason for this has to do with the "Parkinsonian" execution of QA. As discussed in chapter 8 both our own findings and findings reported in the literature suggest that the QA rate is often independent of the QA effort allocated. What usually happens is that the QA effort is planned and allocated according to a fixed schedule of periodic group functions [183]. For example, a 2-hour walk-through for the 5 members of a team is scheduled for every Friday. During each QA review, all tasks developed since the previous review are supposed to be processed. What we found and explained in chapter 8 was an almost perfect realization of Parkinson's Law: no matter of how many tasks need to be processed within a QA review, each QA almost always processes all tasks. No backlogs develop in the QA pipeline. Even when QA is relaxed or suspended because of schedule pressure, no backlogs develop: when walk-throughs are suspended for a while on a project, the *requirement* for a walk-through is also suspended, *not* postponed [125].

18.4.3 The Search for Optimal QA Effort   There are two conclusions from the experiments described in this chapter. The first is that QA policy has a significant impact on total project cost. The second is that although the optimal QA percentage is dependent on the environment (e.g., varying from 11% to 20% in the experiments of Figure 18.5), it is possible to represent the characteristics of the environment in our model to ascertain the appropriate QA allocation for a specific project.

19

MODEL ENHANCEMENT AND BROOKS' LAW

19.1 Model Enhancements

Our model has increased our understanding of and enabled us to make predictions about the management of software development and established the viability of the system dynamics methodology as an effective research vehicle.

> From the system dynamics perspective, a model is developed to address a specific set of questions. One models problems, not systems. We emphasize the point because the purpose of a model helps guide its formulation. The problem to be addressed, the audience for the results of the study, the policies one wishes to experiment with, the implementation desired, all influence the content of the model [221].

Most of the research suggested in chapter 20 involves significant enhancements to our model. For the enthusiastic reader, we recommend an approach in which less ambitious, more limited enhancements are tackled before the more complex ones. Our objective in this chapter is to illustrate this process by examining a limited model enhancement by investigating Brooks' Law.

19.2 Brooks' Law

Brooks' Law was first publicized in Dr. Fred Brooks' 1975 book, *The Mythical Man-Month: Essays on Software Engineering*. The book embodies many insights into the management of large software projects gained through Brooks' experience in managing the development of IBM's OS/360. As explained by Brooks [57]:

> After leaving IBM in 1965 to come to Chapel Hill as originally agreed when I took over OS/360, I began to analyze the OS/360 experience to see what management and technical lessons were to be learned. ...

My own conclusions are embodied in the essays that follow, which are intended for professional programmers, professional managers, and especially professional managers of programmers.

Brooks' Law is stated as follows: "Adding manpower to a late software project makes it later" [57].

The lack of interchangeability between men and months was recognized by Brooks as being caused by training and intercommunication overheads:

Each worker must be trained in the technology, the goals of the effort, the overall strategy, and the plan of work. This training cannot be partitioned, so this part of the added effort varies linearly with the number of workers.

Intercommunication is worse. If each part of the task must be separately coordinated with each other, the effort increases as $n(n-1)/2$. Three workers require three times as much pairwise intercommunication as two; four require six times as much as two. ...

Since software construction is inherently a systems effort ... an exercise in complex interrelationships ... communication effort is great ... Adding more men then lengthens, not shortens, the schedule [57].

Brooks' Law has been widely endorsed in the literature (see [49, 135, 201, 210, 242]). It has often been used indiscriminately for large and small projects, for systems programming projects and applications software systems even though Brooks explicitly applied his Law to "Jumbo" systems programming projects. For example, Pressman [210] extends Brooks' Law to 6-10 man-year projects while Jensen and Tonies [135] and Synnott and Gruber [242] extended it to applications software systems.

Interestingly, the widespread endorsement of Brooks' Law has taken place even though it has not been formally verified. In this chapter we will investigate whether Brooks' Law applies to medium-sized applications projects developed in a familiar, in-house development environment, that is, to our prototype project EXAMPLE.

19.3 Model Enhancements to Highlight Brooks´ Law

Many studies have demonstrated the negative impacts of communication and training overheads on software development productivity. (See chapter 5.) What is the net impact on productivity of adding manpower to a late project? How does that affect the dynamics of hiring and training and ultimately the actual completion time?

To answer the questions we need to enhance the formulation of manpower assimilation in the model. The current formulation is shown in Figure 19.1, which is a simplification of Figure 5.10. Newly hired workforce is represented as the level variable "WFNEW."

The potential productivity of WFNEW was set at one-half that of the Experienced Workforce (WFEXP). Assigning all newly hired employees to a *single* level with the same average productivity value is obviously a simplification, but it served our original purposes.

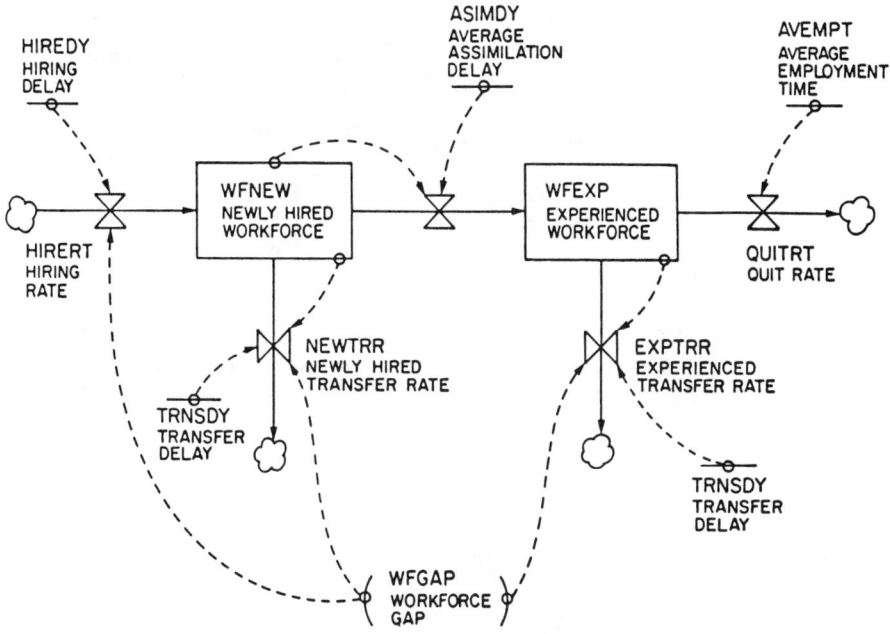

Figure 19.1 Original model of manpower assimilation (hiring and training)

In reality, while the *average* productivity of new hirees may be half that of experienced team members, their productivity is low at hiring and increases with training. The initial low productivity of new hirees is important to represent in a study of Brooks' Law, since *immediately* after new people are added, the *net* impact on productivity might be *negative*. In a production environment where the progress of product development is perfectly visible, information flow is instantaneous, management's reactions are immediate, and management's policy is to add more people when the project falls behind schedule, such a negative impact could lead to a vicious cycle: net negative productivity creates delays, which cause additional hiring, which leads to more severe losses in productivity, further delays, more hiring, and on and on. What effects will an immediate but not persistent net negative impact on productivity have on a more realistic project environment where visibility is not perfect, delays occur, and management's policy is not *always* to hire more people when the project falls behind schedule? Before answering the question we need to discuss the necessary model reformulations.

19.3.1 Multiple Levels of Manpower Assimilation Our more detailed structure for the newly hired workforce is shown in Figure 19.2. Instead of one level "WFNEW," we now have 3 levels: "WFNEW1," "WFNEW2," and "WFNEW3." Separating the newly hired workforce into these three levels allows us to capture the productivity differential that exists between the time of hiring and the end of training. We assume that productivity increases throughout training, with the values shown in Table 19.1.

TABLE 19.1. Increases in productivity due to training

Workforce	Nominal Potential Productivity (Tasks/Man-Day)
WFNEW1	0.1
WFNEW2	0.5
WFNEW3	0.9
WFEXP	1.0

Thus, the *average* nominal potential productivity for newly hired workforce is still 0.5 Task/Man-Day (i.e., half that of the experienced workforce), the value used in our current model.

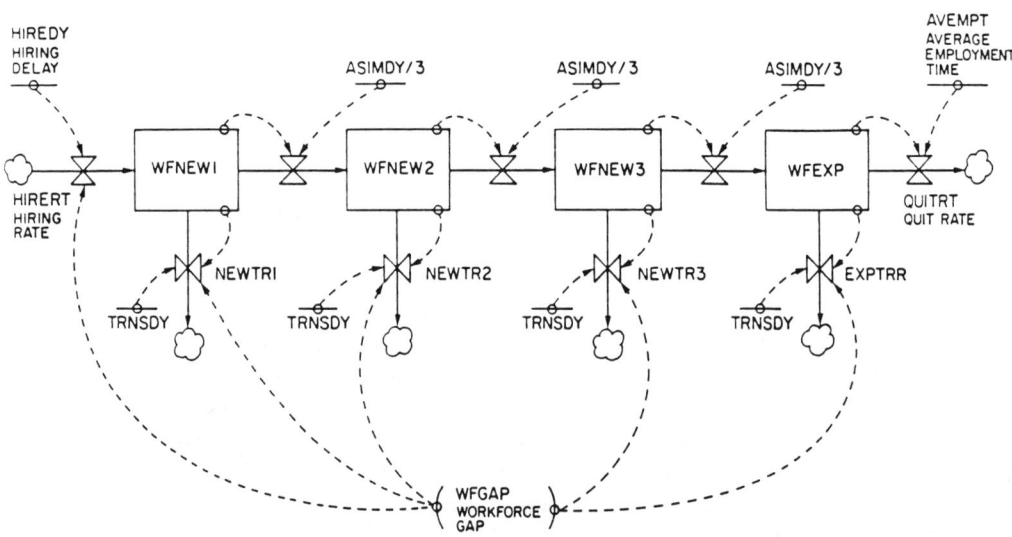

Figure 19.2 Enhanced model of manpower assimilation (hiring and training)

19.3.2 Reformulation of Average Nominal Potential Productivity Four different Nominal Potential Productivities instead of two in the original model means that we have to adjust the formulation of the Average Nominal Potential Productivity (ANPPRD) variable. The current formulation is:

$$ANPPRD = \frac{WFEXP \times NPWPEX}{TOTWF} + \frac{WFNEW \times NPWPNE}{TOTWF} \qquad (19.1)$$

where,

$WFEXP$ $= Experienced\ Workforce$

$WFNEW$ $= Newly\ Hired\ Workforce$

$TOTWF$ $= Total\ Workforce$

$NPWPEX = Nominal\ Potential\ Productivity\ of\ Experienced\ Employes$
$= 1\ Task/Man\text{-}Day$

$NPWPNE = Nominal\ Potential\ Producitivty\ of\ New\ Emplyess$
$= 0.5\ Task/Man\text{-}Day$

The new formulation is:

$$ANPPRD = \frac{WFEXP \times NPWPEX}{TOTWF} + \frac{WFNEW1 \times NPWPN1}{TOTWF} +$$

$$\frac{WFNEW2 \times NPWPN2}{TOTWF} + \frac{WFNEW3 \times NPWPN3}{TOTWF} \qquad (19.2)$$

where,

$NPWPN1 = Nominal\ Potential\ Productivity\ of\ WFNEW1$
$= 0.1\ Tasks/Man\text{-}Day$

$NPWPN2 = Nominal\ Potential\ Productivity\ of\ WFNEW2$
$= 0.5\ Tasks/Man\text{-}Day$

$NPWPN3 = Nominal\ Potential\ Productivity\ of\ WFNEW3$
$= 0.9\ Tasks/Man\text{-}Day$

19.3.3 Reformulation of Nominal Testing Manpower Needed per Error   Another productivity-related reformation needs to be made. In the current model, the effort needed to detect and correct errors in the testing phase is formulated as the product of the ''Error Density'' and the ''Nominal Testing Manpower Needed per Error.'' The value of the latter was set at 0.15 Man-days/Error.

The formulation for the ''Nominal Testing Manpower Needed per Error'' (i.e., TMPNPE = 0.15) does not *seem* to account for the experience mix of the workforce. That is, TMPNPE equals 0.15 Man-days/Error whether the project's workforce is all experienced, all inexperienced, or somewhere between. This is so not because we had assumed that TMPNPE is not affected by the experience mix of the workforce, but because we assumed that as the project approaches the testing phase management becomes unwilling to hire new employees and as a result, during testing the workforce consists of mostly experienced personnel. The simplified TMPNPE formulation is equivalent to:

$$TMPNPW = \frac{0.15}{AMPPRD}$$

where

$$ANPPRD = Average\ Nominal\ Potential\ Productivity$$
$$= 1\ Task/Man\text{-}Day$$

(where we assume that at the testing phase all staff are experienced).

To investigate Brooks' Law, we need to allow for the hiring of new staff even toward the final stages of the project. In such a case, the above assumption does not hold. We therefore change the formulation of TMPNPE from:

$$TMPNPE = 0.15\ Man\text{-}Day/Error$$

to:

$$TMPNPE = \frac{0.15}{ANPPRD}\ Man\text{-}Day/Error.$$

If management refrains from adding new staff in the testing phase,

$$TMPNPE = \frac{0.15}{1} = 0.15\ Man\text{-}Day/Error$$

as we had originally formulated.

But if management hires new staff in the testing phase, then ANPPRD will be less than 1 Task/Man-Day. The result will be a ''Nominal Testing Manpower Needed per Error'' greater than 0.15 Man-Day/Error: a loss in testing productivity due to the lower average experience of the workforce.

19.3.4 Adjustments to Assimilation Delay and Staff Transfers There are two ''house-keeping'' changes in Figure 19.2. The first concerns the ''Average Assimilation Delay.'' Each of the three new average assimilation delays in Figure 19.2 is set at ASIMDY/3. ASIMDY is the ''Average Assimilation Delay'' in the original model. The average assimilation period for the newly hired staff in the new formulation is still equal to 80 days, the value of ASIMDY in the original formulation.

The second change concerns the transferring of staff out of the project. Project personnel are transferred out of the project whenever the ''Workforce Level Sought'' is less than the current ''Total Workforce Level.'' In the original formulation, we assumed that new recruits still in training will be the first transferred out. Additional transfers would come from the ''Experienced Workforce'' pool. This basic policy assumption will be maintained in our new formulation. The only modeling change is to accommodate three newly-hired workforce levels by a four-step transfer-out policy instead of the original two-step one. In our new formulation, the *newest* of the ''new recruits,'' the WFNEW1, will be the first to leave, followed by WFNEW2, followed by WFNEW3. If still more transfers are needed, they would be made from the ''Experienced Workforce'' pool.

19.4 Model Experimentation

19.4.1 Establishment of Baseline Model Behavior First we need to establish our baseline or starting point for EXAMPLE, given the enhancements to the model's structure. This is shown in Figure 19.3. A comparison of the simulation results of Figure 19.3 with the equivalent base-case behavior of Figure 13.1 (our original model) indicates

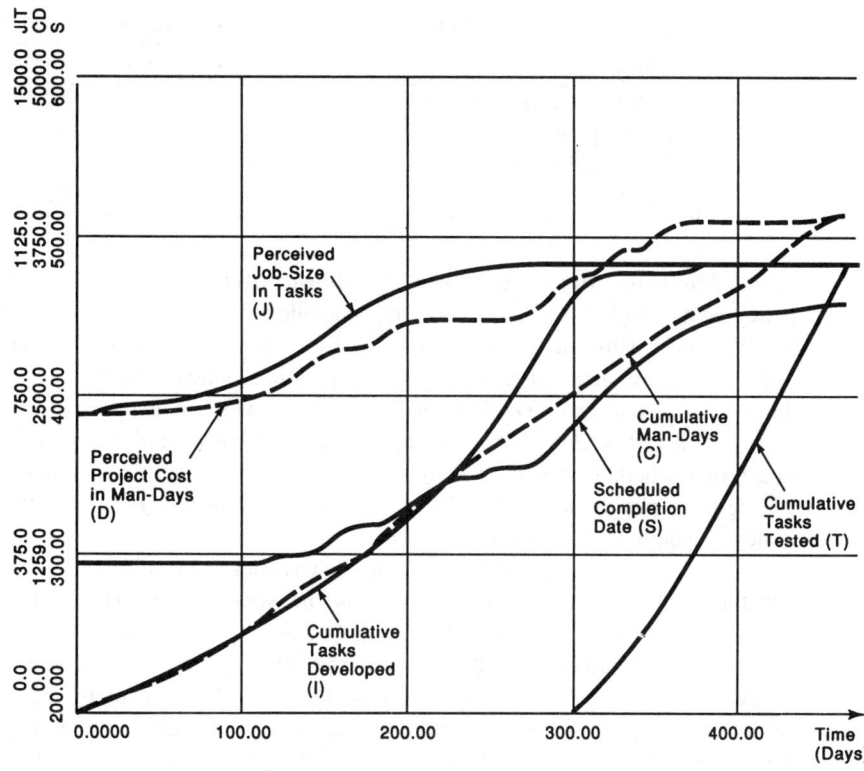

Figure 19.3   Baseline model behavior

a minimal impact. In fact, the project variables are almost identical. A comparison of some of the key project variables is shown in Table 19.2.

As we saw, EXAMPLE's size is initially underestimated. As a result the project experiences scheduling problems and overshoots its original schedule. (See chapter 13.) When the project's scheduling problems surface, management reacts first by adjusting the project's work force level and adding more people. However, as the project proceeds and scheduling problems persist, management becomes increasingly reluctant because of work force stability considerations to add more people and reacts by adjusting the project's schedule.

TABLE 19.2. Baseline results from original and enhanced model

Variable	Original Model	Enhanced Model
Completion Time in Days	430	461
Development Man-days	2681	2667
Testing Man-days	1114	1286
Total Man-days	3795	3953

19.4.2 Modeling More Aggressive Manpower Acquisition Policies Management's policy on how to balance work force and schedule adjustments is represented in the model by "Willingness to Change Work Force." By adjusting this variable we can examine the impact of more aggressive manpower acquisition policies on the project's cost and duration. We can examine whether Policy A, in which management continues adding more people to EXAMPLE even as the project proceeds toward the end of testing, results in a larger schedule overshoot than does Policy B, in which management refrains from adding more people near the end of the development phase. Brooks' Law suggests that Policy A would produce a longer project duration.

In the base case (and based on discussions with (23), (24), and (25)), the "Willingness to Change Work Force" is the sum of the "Hiring Delay" and the "Assimilation Delay." In the early stages of the project, when "Time Remaining" is generally much larger than the sum of the "Hiring Delay" and the "Assimilation Delay," management is willing to adjust the work force level to meet the project's scheduled completion date. As the number of days perceived remaining drops below $1.5 \times$ (Hiring Delay + Assimilation Delay), though, mangement starts becoming increasingly reluctant to increase the work force level.

The values of the "Hiring Delay" and the "Assimilation Delay" are 40 and 80 working days respectively in the base case. Thus, as "Time Remaining" drops below 180 days, management in the base case starts becoming reluctant to hire new people. When the "Time Remaining" drops below $0.3 \times$ (Hiring Delay + Assimilation Delay), or 48 working days, no more additions are made to the project's work force.

We can model more aggressive manpower acquisition policies by decreasing the value of "Willingness to Change Work Force." For example, if we set the parameter at 30 working days, management's willingness to add to the work force continues until much later into the project; management starts becoming reluctant to increase the work force level when the perceived number of days remaining to complete the project drops below 45 days and stops manpower additions completely at 9 working days before the perceived completion date.

19.4.3 Results of More Aggressive Manpower Acquisition Policies The results of adjusting the value of the time parameter are depicted in Figure 19.4.

The results do not totally support Brooks' Law. Adding more people to a late project always causes it to become more costly but does not *always* cause it to be completed later. The increase in the cost of the project is caused by the increased training and communication overheads, which in effect decrease the productivity of the average team member and thus increase the project's man-day requirements.

For the project's schedule to suffer, the drop in productivity must be large enough to render an additional person's *net cumulative* contribution to the project to be in effect

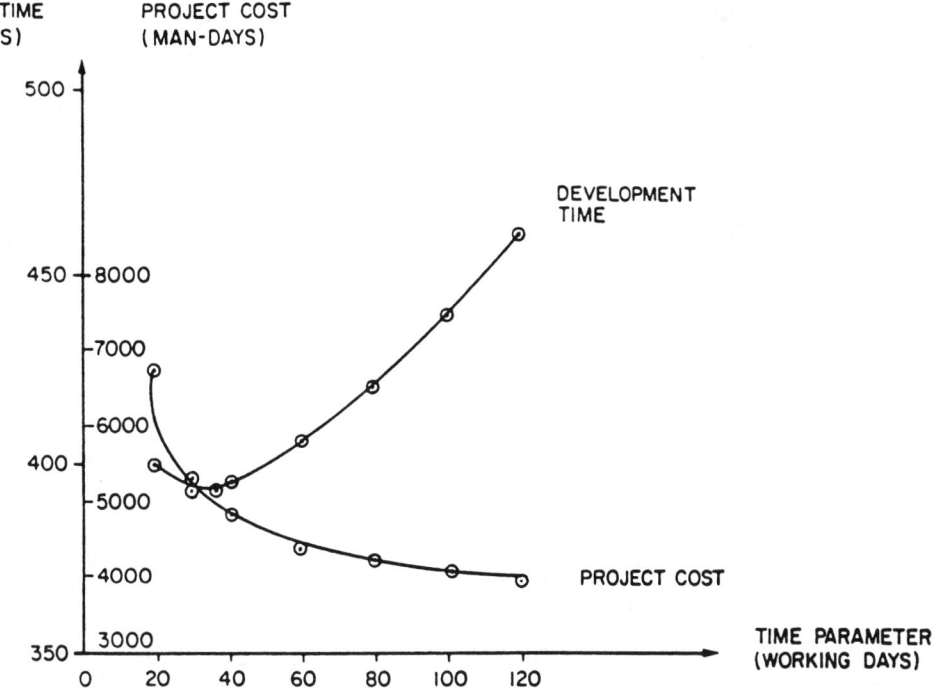

Figure 19.4 Impact of "Willingness to Change Work Force" on development time and project cost

negative: *net* because an additional person's contribution must be balanced against the lost opportunities of diverting experienced man-days from project work to training, and *cumulative* because a new hiree's immediate net contribution might be negative, and significantly so. As training takes place and his or her productivity increases, the net contribution becomes less and less negative, and eventually, given enough training, becomes positive. One needs to assess the cumulative effect of the new person's contribution from the time of hiring until project completion (or until the person leaves the project). Only when the cumulative impact is a negative one will the addition of the new staff number translate into a later project completion time.

The results of Figure 19.4 indicate that adding manpower to a late software project does not always cause a negative net cumulative contribution; it does not always make the project later. The results indicate that Brooks' Law holds only when the "Time Parameter" (TMPR) is fewer than 30 working days for EXAMPLE.

A smaller "Time Parameter" means that management's willingness to add more people to the project is maintained until later in the project's life cycle. When the Time Parameter is set at 30 working days, management is willing to add more people until it perceives that the time remaining to complete the project is fewer than $0.3 \times 30 = 9$ working days, that is, until the final stages of testing. It is with such extremely aggressive manpower acquisition policies that Brooks' Law holds in our EXAMPLE environment, the medium sized application project developed in a familiar in-house environment.

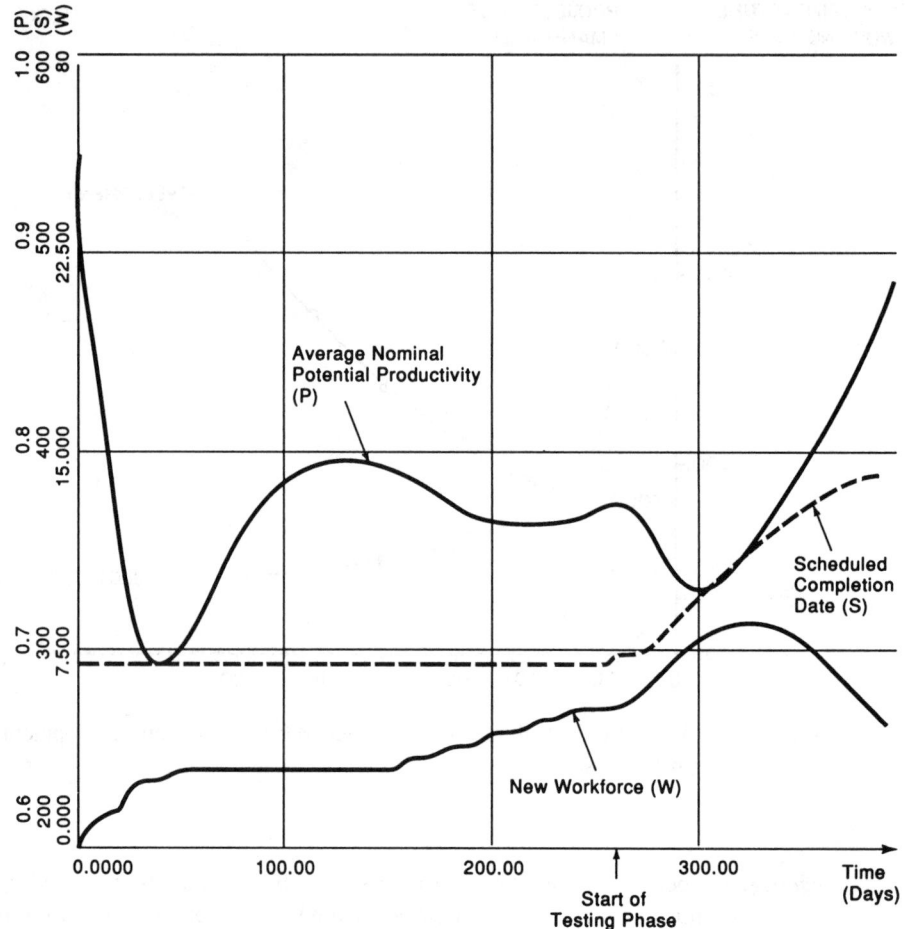

Figure 19.5 Aggressive manpower acquisition policy (TMPR = 30)

19.4.4 Impact of Aggressive Manpower Acquisition Policies on Productivity Figures
19.5 and 19.6 plot the workforce levels and Average Nominal Potential Productivity for
model runs with "Time Parameter" values of 30 and 20 working days, respectively.
These are "Time Parameter" values for which Brooks' Law applies. The results shed
some light on why the extremely aggressive manpower acquisition policy induced
through a "Time Parameter" value of 20 delays the completion date of the project as
opposed to the *relatively* less aggressive manpower acquisition policy of a "Time
Parameter" value of 30. In both cases the significant rise in the number of new hirees in
the testing phase causes an immediate and significant dip in the value of the Average
Nominal Potential Productivity. However, in Figure 19.6, more new personnel continues
to be hired until later in the life cycle — the result of a lower "Time Parameter" value.

     Why a larger number is hired is less obvious. By the time the testing phase is
reached in EXAMPLE, management has realized that the project is behind schedule.
Available options are to hire more people, extend the schedule, or do a combination of
both. Under more aggressive manpower acquisition policies (i.e., smaller "Time

Parameter'' values), management is less reluctant to add manpower to minimize schedule disruptions. In Figure 19.6 management "sticks" with the project's *original* "Scheduled Completion Date" slightly longer than in Figure 19.5. Choosing to work under a tighter schedule leaves no alternative but to increase the workforce. A larger workforce, however, means more training and communication overheads, which lead to lower productivity, which in turn creates the need for even larger workforce levels.

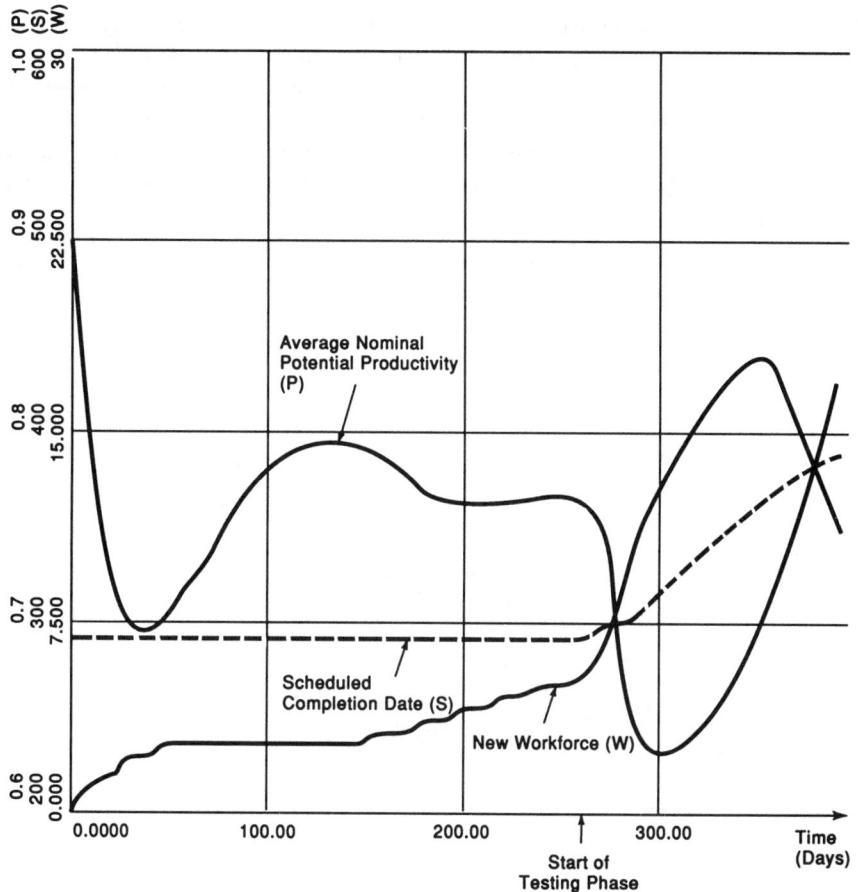

Figure 19.6 Very aggressive manpower acquisition policy (TMPR = 20)

The fact that more new people are hired later in the life cycle explains why the dip in the "Average Nominal Potential Productivity" in Figure 19.6 is both more severe and more lagging. The dip in productivity is severe and delayed enough to prevent the new hirees from reaching a high level of productivity, and from converting a negative net cumulative project contribution to a positive one within the remaining time. Thus their contribution remains a net negative.

19.5 Summary

Our objective in this chapter was to provide the reader with a feel for why and how to enhance the model's formulation when investigating new issues of software project management that lie beyond the purpose and scope of the original model.

Our experimental results provide insight into Brooks' Law. Adding more people to a late project always causes it to become more costly, but it does not *always* cause it to be completed later. The increase in the cost of the project is caused by the increased training and communication overheads, which in effect decrease the average productivity of the workforce and increase the project's man-day requirements. For the project's schedule to suffer, the drop in productivity must be severe and delayed enough to render an additional person's net cumulative contribution to the project to be a negative contribution. This happens only under extremely aggressive manpower acquisition policies, where management's willingness to add new staff members persists until the final stages of the testing phase.

20

CONCLUSIONS AND
FUTURE DIRECTIONS

20.1 Summary of Results

The objective of this book is to enhance our understanding of and gain insight into the general process by which software development is managed. We developed an integrative system dynamics model of software development project management, conducted a case study to test the model, and used the model to study and predict the dynamic implications of an array of managerial policies and procedures.

20.1.1 The Model The model integrates our knowledge of the micro components of software development project management (e.g., programming, productivity, planning, and controlling) into an integrated, continuous view of the software development process.

Before we can say that we have a *complete* understanding of any such activity, "... it is necessary to show that our knowledge of the individual components can be put together in a total system, i.e., an organization can be synthesized, which allows for the interactions of all the relevant variables and all the structural components" [68].

An integrated approach helps us achieve an overall understanding. It is also useful in two more "tactical" ways: problem diagnoses and solution evaluation. In Brooks' words: "... no one thing seems to cause the difficulty (in software projects) ... but the accumulation of simultaneous and interacting factors... " [57]. An integrated approach is useful because it both "prompts" and "facilitates" the search for the multiple and potentially diffused set of factors interacting to cause software development problems. For example, the schedule overshoot problem can arise not only because of schedule underestimation, but also because of management's hiring/firing policies.

Managerial intervention often leads to second- and third-order consequences. Our analysis of the "Safety Factor Policy" in scheduling software projects showed that while such a policy succeeds in producing more accurate project estimates, it tends to "create" more costly projects.

The model identifies feedback mechanisms and uses them to structure and clarify relationships in software project management. While the significance and applicability of the feedback systems concept to the study of managerial systems has been substantiated in many studies outside software engineering, it remains largely foreign to the software engineering project management community. We hope our work begins to remedy this deficit.

The mathematical formulation of a system dynamics model requires that the structural relationships between variables be explicitly and precisely defined. As such, the model lays the foundation for a theory of software project management. As suggested by Dubin:

> A theory is the attempt of a man to model some aspects of the empirical world. ... A theory tries to make sense out of the observable world by ordering the relationships among 'things' that constitute the theorist's focus of attention in the work 'out there' The process of putting things or units together in lawful relation to each other establishes the fundamental building blocks out of which a theory is constructed [90].

The high degree of explication required in the model helped us ferret out "knowledge gaps" in the literature. A set of 27 interviews with software development managers in 5 organizations helped us fill the gaps. The model therefore incorporates new findings about the management of software project management (e.g., on manpower acquisition policies under different scheduling considerations).

20.1.2 Case Study After the model was developed, we conducted a case study in a sixth organization, namely, the Systems Development Section of NASA's Goddard Space Flight Center. The objective of the case-study was to examine the model's ability to reproduce the dynamic behavior of a completed software project.

The DE-A project was selected for the case study by NASA. This project was selected to satisfy three criteria: (1) medium in size; (2) recent; and (3) typical: one that would be considered as having been developed in a familiar in-house software development environment.

To simulate the DE-A project, the model was first parameterized. The process involved setting 14 model parameters (e.g., "Hiring Delay" and "Turnover Rate") that represent the particular DE-A project environment. The parameter values were obtained from interviews at NASA and project documentation. The 14 model parameters do *not* involve any changes in the formulation of the model's policy structures. They merely define the DE-A environment within which the policies are exercised. This is significant, since the dynamic behavior is largely a result of the interaction of the model's unchanged policy structures.

The model was highly accurate in reproducing the actual development history of the DE-A software project. Specifically, it reproduced the dynamic behavior of the project's completion-date estimates, man-day estimates, cost in man-days, and work force loading.

20.1.3 Experimentation If "understanding" is the intellectual outcome of a theoretical model, then "prediction" is its practical outcome [90]. The model was used as an experimentation vehicle to study an array of managerial policies and procedures. Three areas were studied:

1. *Software cost and schedule estimation.* Three experiments were conducted. In the first, we examined the impact that schedules have on project performance. We

showed that "a different schedule creates a different project." An important implication is that a software estimation model cannot be judged solely based on how accurately it estimates historical projects. Furthermore, it is important to consider not only how accurate an estimation method is but also how costly the projects it "creates" are.

The second experiment concerned the portability of quantitative software estimation tools. Evidence in the literature indicates that currently available quantitative software estimation tools are not particularly portable from the company in which they were developed to another (e.g., see [43, 49]). Almost all the current models fail to account explicitly for the managerial characteristics of the software producing organization, which tend to vary significantly from one organization to another [184]. A major stumbling block has heretofore been the inability to quantify the impact of managerial-type factors on the cost of software development. Our experiment takes a first step towards rectifying the situation. We identified four aspects of a company's managerial environment (manpower acquisition, manpower allocation, effort distribution, and QA allocation) that significantly affect the cost of software development. We quantified their impact on cost. Because the four areas are variables that the project manager can objectively evaluate at the beginning of a software project, it should be feasible to incorporate them in future cost estimation models. This, we feel, will improve both the accuracy as well as the portability of such models.

The third experiment concerned the analogy method of software estimation. The experiment generated two interesting insights: first, that there are inherent factors in the management of a software project (resulting from the interaction of manpower acquisition policies and personnel turnover) that cause it to over-run even what would amount to be a "perfect" schedule estimate; second, that because of the inherent tendency to overshoot, the use of the analogy method injects a bias in the scheduling process, a bias that generates longer than necessary project schedules.

2. *The economics of quality assurance (QA).* Two sets of experiments were conducted on QA. The objective of the first was to investigate not whether but *how much* QA is justified. To do this we first examined the relationship between QA expended and the percentage of errors detected during development. A significant feature of this relationship is the "diminishing returns" of QA as QA expenditures extend beyond 20-30% of development effort. We then derived the "optimal" QA expenditure level, the level that minimizes total project cost. The "optimal" QA effort expenditure level for our prototype project was 16% of the development man-days. The significance of this result is not its value, since this cannot be generalized beyond the specific project used in our experiment, but rather the process of deriving it. Beyond controlled experimentation, which is too costly and time consuming to be practically feasible, our model, as far as we know, provides the first capability to analyze the costs/benefits of QA policy for software production quantitatively. This capability is generalizable in the sense that one can customize models for different software development environments to determine the optimal environment-specific conditions.

The results of the first set of QA experiments have also clearly demonstrated that QA policy does have a significant impact on total project cost. QA expenditures significantly lower *or* significantly higher than the "optimal" can cause a significant increase in the project's total cost. Low QA expenditures increase the cost of testing. High QA expenditures themselves consume high percentages of the project's cost.

The objective of the second set of QA experiments was to examine the sensitivity of the results to two project variables: the distribution of effort between the development and testing phases, and software development productivity. The findings constitute "rules-of-thumb" that organizations can use to adapt published results or results from other organizations to their own environment.

3. *Staffing.* We tested the applicability of Brooks' Law to the domain of "medium-sized applications projects developed in a familiar, in-house development environment."

Since its "enactment," Brooks' Law has been widely cited in the literature (e.g., see [49, 135, 201, 210, 242]). Furthermore, it has often been endorsed indiscriminately not only for large, but also for small projects, not only for systems programming projects, but also for applications software systems. Brooks explicitly specified the domain of applicability of his Law to "Jumbo" systems programming projects.

Our experimental results do *not* support Brooks' Law for the type of project studied in our research. Adding more people to a late project causes it to become more costly but not to be completed later unless hiring continues to the end of the project's testing phase.

Brooks' Law does not universally apply to all software development environments. It does not seem to apply to the medium sized application project developed in a familiar, in-house development environment. It is therefore not necessarily an invalidation of *Brooks'* "Brooks' Law," but rather a disqualification of the notion (implied not by Brooks but by the writings of others in the literature) that "Brooks' Law" is a universal law of software development.

20.2 Suggestions for Future Directions

According to Nobel Prize Winner Alfred Kastler "All knowledge is provisional --- never final." We believe that our work has pointed up several areas requiring more intensive research.

20.2.1 Model Enhancement Further research needs to be performed on our existing model. We propose the following set of extensions:

1. *Requirements definition/analysis phase.* It is important to incorporate the requirements definition/analysis phase into the model's life cycle since "the technology of defining the requirements for a software system is an area in most urgent need for improvement and itself constitutes a major portion of the so-called 'software-bottleneck' " [30]. Many in the field have hypothesized about the disruptive effects of changes in system requirements on software production and on the direct link between such disruptions and cost and schedule slippages [49]. Our modeling approach provides a powerful vehicle to test such hypotheses quantitatively.

2. *Multiple projects.* The current model does not accommodate multiple projects — two software projects developed in parallel. In such an environment competition for company resources becomes a significant dimension, affecting resource allocation policies such as manpower resource.

3. *Large-scale project environments.* It would be particularly interesting to extend our model to other environments such as large DOD software projects — projects that are more than 1 million lines of code in size. Such an extension requires several enhancements to the model. The development phase would be separated into ''finer'' phases (e.g., preliminary design, detailed design, and coding), with a set of formal milestones separating the phases (e.g., preliminary design review and critical design review). Interesting questions to investigate here are the cost/benefits of such milestones (e.g., administrative overhead versus visibility benefits), how and when serially planned phases overlap under schedule pressures, and how such *unplanned* overlapping affects the project. A second enhancement would be to restructure QA, which in such projects tends to be conducted by an independent organization. A third enhancement would be to incorporate the deep vertical structures that characterize the management of ''jumbo'' projects, to represent the paths of communication within the organization and the various levels of information filtering and processing and of decision-making.

4. *Quality.* Another interesting extension is the quality of the produced software product. First, the measure(s) of software quality (e.g., usability and maintainability) has to be determined; the work done in the software metrics field may be useful here [206]. Second, several model enhancements would be required. For example, software errors could be separated into different types according to seriousness. A more challenging enhancement would be to capture the effects of motivational factors on quality. Experiments have shown that explicit project goals (e.g., ''produce code as fast as you can'' versus ''produce maintainable code'') significantly affect productivity, error rates, and so on [263]. Motivation is particularly interesting because different software development objectives conflict with each other in practice. For example, concentrating purely on minimizing the software development budget and schedule is likely to have negative effects on software quality, and vice versa [49].

20.2.2 New Modeling Applications Rather than continuing to focus on software development *projects* per se, the modeling approach described here can be extended to investigate a broader set of issues pertaining to the software development *organization*. Rather than trace the life cycle(s) of one or more software projects, one may focus instead on the operations of a software development department as software products are developed, placed into operation, and maintained. A number of research questions are ripe for investigation:

1. The efficacy of different organizational structures (e.g., project, functional, and matrix) in different software development environments.

2. Personnel turnover, its costs (e.g., recruiting and training overheads), its benefits (e.g., access to new ideas and methodologies), and its causes (e.g., schedule pressures and maintenance load).

3. The impact of management approaches such as Management By Objectives (MBO) in both the short-term and the long-term (a system dynamics study in the *R & D* area showed that the short-run effect of MBO on increasing motivation and productivity may be reversed in the long-run if social interaction and communication are allowed to erode).

4. The organizational/environmental determinants of productivity (e.g., standards, software tools, use of librarians, and documentation requirements). One needs to investigate both short-term as well as long-term applications. For example, the software industry develops its own production tools; an investment in developing powerful software development tools (e.g., compilers and automated testing tools), might hamper productivity in the short-run, but often leads to better software, which usually leads to even more powerful tools.

20.3 Finale

It has been said that "a journey of a thousand miles starts with a single step." It has been our intention to provide some of these key steps that will ultimately lead to the long-sought destination of effective software project management.

BIBLIOGRAPHY

1. Abdel-Hamid, T. K. and Abdel-Hamid, N. T., "Improving Software Development Productivity: A Challenge and an Opportunity for Developing Nations." *The First International Information Conference in Egypt*, (December 1982).

2. Abdel-Hamid, T. K., "The Economics of Software Quality Assurance: A Simulation-Based Study." *MIS Quarterly*, (September 1988).

3. Abdel-Hamid, T. K., "Understanding the '90% Syndrome' in Software Project Management: A Simulation-Based Case Study." *Journal of Systems & Software*, (September 1988).

4. Abdel-Hamid, T. K., "An Integrative System Dynamics Perspective of Software Project Management: Examples of Project Estimation and Scheduling Experiments." *The 1989 Society for Computer Simulation Western Multiconference*, (January 4-6, 1989).

5. Abdel-Hamid, T. K., "The Dynamics of Software Project Staffing: A System Dynamics Based Simulation Approach." *IEEE Transactions on Software Engineering*, (February 1989).

6. Abdel-Hamid, T. K., "A Study of Staff Turnover, Aquisition, and Assimilation and their Impact on Software Development Cost and Schedule." *Journal of Management Information Systems*, (September 1989).

7. Abdel-Hamid, T. K., "On the Utility of Historical Project Statistics for Cost & Schedule Estimation." *Journal of Systems & Software*, 1990

8. Abdel-Hamid, T. K. and Madnick, S. E., "The System Dynamics Approach to Designing Software Project Planning and Control Systems: A Research Proposal." Technical Report, MIT, Sloan School of Management, (January 1982).

9. Abdel-Hamid, T. K. and Madnick, S. E., "A Model of Software Project Management Dynamics." *The 6th International Computer Software and Applications Conference (COMPSAC)*, (November 1982).

10. Abdel-Hamid, T. K. and Madnick, S. E., "An Integrative Approach to Modeling the Software Management Process: A Basis for Identifying Problems and Evaluating Tools and Techniques." *IEEE Computer Society Workshop on Software Engineering Technology Transfer*, (April 1983).

11. Abdel-Hamid, T. K. and Madnick, S. E., "The Dynamics of Software Project Scheduling: A System Dynamics Perspective." *Communications of the ACM*, (May 1983), 340-346.

12. Abdel-Hamid, T. K. and Madnick, S. E., "Impact of Schedule Estimation on Software Project Behavior." *IEEE Software*, (May 1986).

13. Abdel-Hamid, T. K. and Madnick, S. E., "On the Portability of Quantitative Software Estimation Models." *Information & Management*, Vol. 13, No. 1, (August 1987), 1-10.

14. Abdel-Hamid, T. K. and Madnick, S. E., "The Economics of Software Quality Assurance: A Systems Dynamics Based Simulation Approach." *The Annals of the Society of Logistics Engineers*, Vol. 1, No. 2, (October 1987), 8-32.

15. Abdel-Hamid, T. K. and Madnick, S. E., "Software Productivity: Potential, Actual, and Perceived." *System Dynamics Review*, (Summer 1989).

16. Abdel-Hamid, T. K. and Madnick, S. E., "Lessons Learned from Modeling the Dynamics of Software Project Management." *Communications of the ACM*, (December 1989).

17. Abdel-Hamid, T. K. and Madnick, S. E., "The Elusive Silver Lining: How we Fail to Learn from Failure in Software Development." *The Sloan Management Review*, 1990.

18. Adrion, W. R. et al., "Validation, Verification, and Testing of Computer Software." *ACM Computer Surveys*, Vol. 14, No. 2, (June 1982), 159-192.

19. Alberts, D. S., "The Economics of Software Quality Assurance." *National Computer Conference*, 1976.

20. Albrecht, A. J., "Measuring Application Development Productivity." *Proceedings of the Joint SHARE/GUIDE/IBM Application Development Symposium*, (October 1979).

21. Anthony, R. N., *Planning and Control Systems: A Framework for Analysis*. Cambridge, MA: Harvard University Press, 1979.

22. Anthony, R. N. and Dearden, J., *Management Control Systems*. Chicago, IL: Richard D. Irwin, Inc., 1980.

23. Aron, J. D., "Estimating Reasons for Large Programming Systems." *Software Engineering: Concepts and Techniques*. Edited by J. M. Buxton, P. Naur and B. Randell. Litton Educational Publishing, Inc., 1976.

24. Arseven, S. M., "A System to Monitor and Control the Development and Documentation of a Computer programming Project." Unpublished Ph.D. dissertation, Texas A&M University, 1975.

25. Artzer, S. P. and Neidrauer, R. A., "Software Engineering Basics: A Primer for the Project Manager." Unpublished thesis, Naval Postgraduate School, Monterey, CA, 1982.

26. Ashenurst, R. L., ed., "Curriculum Recommendations for Gradute Professional Programs in Information Systems." *Communications of the ACM*, Vol. 15, No. 15, (May 1972), 363-398.

27. Ashton, R. H., "Deviation-Amplifying Feedback and Unintended Consequences of Management Accounting Systems." *Accounting, Organization and Society*, Vol. 1, No. 4, (1976).

28. Baber, R. L., *Software Reflected*. New York, NY: North Holland Publishing Company, 1982.

29. Baker, C. and Silverberg, D., *Defense News*. Vol. 4, No. 51, (December 18, 1989).

30. Bacon, G. , "Software." *Science*, Vol. 215, (February 1982), 775-779.

31. Bailey, J. W. and Basili, V. R., "A Meta-Model for Software Development Resource Expenditures." *Proceedings, 5th International Conference on Software Engineering*, IEEE/ACM/NBS, (March 1981), 107-116.

32. Baker, F. T., "Chief Programmer Team Management of Production Programming." *IBM Systems Journal*, Vol. 11, No. 1, 1972.

33. Barbacci, M. R., Habermann, A. N. and Shaw, M., "The Software Engineering Institute: Bridging Practice and Potential." *IEEE Software*, (November 1985), 4-21.

34. Bartol, K. M., "Professionalism as a Predictor of Organizational Commitment, Role, Stress, and Turnover: A Multidimensional Approach." *Academy of Mgmt Journal*, Vol. 22, No. 4, (December 1979), 815-821.

35. Bartol, K. M. and Martin, D. C., "Managing Information Systems Personnel: A Review of the Literature and Managerial Implications." *MIS Quarterly*, (December 1982), 49-70.

36. Basili, V. R., "Improving Methodology and Productivity Through Practical Measurement." A Lecture at the Wang Institute of Graduate Studies, Lowell, MA, (November 1982).

37. Basili, V. R. and Weiss, D. M., "Evaluation of a Software Requirements Document by Means of Change Data." *Proceedings of the 5th International Conference on Software Engineering*, IEEE, (March 1981).

38. Basili, V. R. and Weiss, D. M., *Evaluating Software Development by Analysis of Changes: The Data From the Software Engineering Laboratory*. Computer Science Technical Report Series, TR-1236. College Park, MD, University of Maryland, (December 1982).

39. Basili, V. R. and Zelkowitz, M. V., "Measuring Software Development Characteristics in the Local Environment." *Computer & Structures*, Vol 10,(1979), 39-43.

40. Bauer, F. L., "A Trend for the Next 10 Years of Software Engineering." *Software Engineering*. Edited by H. Freeman and P. M. Lewis II. New York, NY: Academic Press, Inc., 1980.

41. Beck, L. L. and Perkins, T. E., "A Survey of Software Engineering Practice: Tools, Methods, and Results." *IEEE Transactions on Software Engineering*, Vol. SE-9, No. 5, (September 1983).

42. Belford, P. C., et al., "An Evaluation of the Effectiveness of Software Engineering Techniques." *IEEE COMPCON*, (Fall 1977).

43. Benbasat, I. and Vessey, I., "Programmer and Analyst Time/Cost Estimation." *MIS Quarterly*, Vol. 4, No. 2, (June 1980), 31-43.

44. Boebert, W. E., "Software Quality Through Software Management." *Software Quality Management*. Edited by J. D. Cooper and M. J. Fisher. New York, NY: Petrocelli Books, Inc., 1979.

45. Boehm, B. W., "Software and its Impact: A Quantitative Assessment." *Datamation*, (May 1973), 48-59.

46. Boehm, B. W., "Software Engineering." *IEEE Transactions on Computers*, (December 1976).

47. Boehm, B. W., "Software Engineering." *Software Engineering*. Edited by H. Freeman and P. M. Lewis II. New York, NY: Academic Press, Inc., 1980.

48. Boehm, B. W., "An Experiment in Small-Scale Application Software Engineering." *IEEE Transactions on Software Engineering*, Vol. SE-7, No. 5 (September 1981), 482-493.

49. Boehm, B. W., *Software Engineering Economics*. Englewood Cliffs, NJ: Prentice-Hall, Inc., 1981.

50. Boehm, B. W., "Improving Software Productivity." *Computer*, (September 1987), 43-50.

51. Boehm, B. W. and Papaccio, P. N., "Understanding and Controlling Software Costs." *IEEE Transactions on Software Engineering*, Vol. 14, No. 10, (October 1988), 1462-1477.

52. Boehm, B. W. and Ross, R., "Theory-W Software Project Management: Principles and Examples." *IEEE Transactions on Software Engineering*, Vol. 15, No. 7, (July 1989).

53. Boehm, B. W. and Wolverton, R. W., "Software Cost Modeling: Some Lessons Learned." *Journal of Systems and Software*, Vol. 1, No. 3, 1980.

54. Boehm, B. W., et al., "Some Experience with Automated Aids to the Design of Large-Scale Reliable Software." *Proceedings of the International Conference on Reliable Software*, (April 1975).

55. Bott, H. S., "The Personnel Crunch." *Perspectives on Information Management*. Edited by J. B. Rochester. New York, NY: John Wiley & Sons, Inc., 1982.

56. Brandon, D. H., "The Economics of Computer Programming." *On The Management Of Computer Programming*. Edited by G. Weinwurm. Princeton, NJ: Auerbach Publishing, Inc., 1970.

57. Brooks, F. P. Jr. *The Mythical Man-Month*. Reading, MA: Addison-Wesley Publishing Co., 1978.

58. Brooks, F. P. Jr., "No Silver Bullet: Essence and Accidents of Software Engineering." *Computer*, (April 1987), 10-19.

59. Brooks, F. P. Jr., *Report of the Defense Science Board Task Force on Military Software*. Department of Defense, Office of the Under Secretary of Defense for Acquisition, (September, 1987).

60. Bruce, P. and Pederson, S. M., *The Software Development Project: Planning and Management*. New York, NY: John Wiley & Sons, Inc., 1982.

61. Burchett, R., "Avoiding Disaster in Project Control." *Data Processing Digest*, Vol. 28, No. 6, (June 1982), 1-3.

62. Canning, R. G., "Progress in Project Management." *EDP Analyzer*, (December 1977), 1-11.

63. Carroll, P. B., "Creating New Software Was Agonizing Task for Mitch Kapor Firm." *The Wall Street Journal*, Vol. CCXV, No. 93, (May 11, 1990), A1, A7.

64. Chrysler, E., "The Impact of Program and Programmer Characteristics on Program Size." *National Computer Conference*, (1978), 581-587.

65. Clapp, J. A., "A Review of Software Cost Estimation Methods." *MITRE Technical Report*, (June 1976), 1-55.

66. Cleland, D. I. and King, W. R., *Management: A Systems Approach*. New York, NY: McGraw-Hill Book, Inc., 1972.

67. Cleland, D. I. and King, W. R., *Systems Analysis and Project Management*. New York, NY: McGraw-Hill, 1975.

68. Cohen, K. J. and Cyert, R. M., "Simulation of Organizational Behavior." *Handbook of Organizations*. Edited by J. G. March. Chicago, IL: Rand McNally & Co., 1965.

69. Conway, M. E., "How Do Committees Invent?" *Datamation*, (April 1968), 28-31.

70. Cooper, J. D., "Software Engineering: R & D Trends and Defense Needs." *Research Directions in Software Technology*. Edited by P. Wegner. Cambridge, MA: The M.I.T. Press, 1979.

71. Cooper, J. D., "Corporate Level Software Management." *IEEE Transactions on Software Engineering*, Vol. SE-4, No. 4, (July 1978).

72. Cooper, J. D. and Fisher, M. J., eds., *Software Quality Management*. New York, NY: Petrocelli Books, Inc., 1979.

73. Cooper, K. G., "Naval Ship Production: Acclaim Settled and a Framework Built." *Interfaces*, Vol 10, No. 6, (December 1980).

74. Corbato, F. J. and Clingen, C. T., "A Managerial View of the Multics System Development." *Research Directions in Software Technology*. Edited by P. Wegner. Cambridge, MA: The M.I.T. Press, 1979.

75. Cougar, J. D. and Zawacki, R. A., *Motivating and Managing Computer Personnel*. New York, NY: John Wiley & Sons, Inc., 1980.

76. Crowley J. D., "The Application Development Process: What's Wrong With it?" *JDC Associates.* Walnut Creek, CA, 1979.

77. Curtis, B., Krasner, H., and Iscoe, N., "A Field Study of the Software Design Process for Large Systems." *Communications of the ACM*, Vol. 31, No. 11, (November 1988), 1268-1287.

78. Daly, E. B., "Management of Software Development." *IEEE Transactions on Software Engineering*, (May 1977).

79. Daly, E. B., "Organizational Philosophies Used in Software Development." *The Economics of Information Processing.* Edited by R. Goldberg and H. Lorin. New York, NY: John Wiley & Sons, Inc., 1982.

80. Davis, G. B., *Management Information System: Conceptual Foundations, Structure and Development.* New York, NY: McGraw-Hill, Inc., 1974.

81. DeMarco, T., *Controlling Software Projects.* New York, NY: Yourdon Press, Inc., 1982.

82. DeMarco, T. and Lister, T., *Peopleware: Productive Projects and Teams.* New York, NY: Dorset House Publishing Company, 1987.

83. DeRose, B. C. and Nyman, T. H., "The Software Life Cycle." *Research Directions in Software Technology.*, Edited by P. Wegner. Cambridge, MA: The M.I.T. Press, 1979.

84. Deutsch, M. S., "Verification and Validation." *Software Engineering.* Edited by R. W. Jensen and C. C. Tonies. Englewood Cliffs, NJ: Prentice-Hall, Inc., 1979.

85. Devenny, T. J., "An Exploration Study of Software Cost Estimating at the Electronic Systems Division." NTIS, U.S. Dept. of Commerce, (July 1976).

86. Distaso, J. R., "Software Management - A Survey of the Practice in 1980." *Proceedings of the IEEE*, Vol. 68, No. 9, (September 1980), 1103-1119.

87. DOD., *Strategy for a DOD Software Initiative.* Dept. of Defense, 1982.

88. Donelson, W. S., "Project Planning and Control." *Datamation*, (June 1976).

89. Driscoll, A. J., "Software Visibility and the Program Manager." *Defense Systems Management Review*, Vol. I, No. 2, 1977, 12-27.

90. Dubin, R., *The Organization, Management and Tactics of Social Research.* Edited by R. O'Toole. Cambridge, MA: Schenkman Publishing Co., Inc., 1971.

91. Edelman, R. M., "Engineering Manpower Resource Management in a Multi-Project Environment." Unpublished S.M. Thesis, M.I.T., Sloan School of Management, Cambridge, MA, 1975.

92. Endres, A. B., "An Analysis of Errors and their Causes in System Programs." *IEEE Transactions on Software Engineering.* (June 1975), 140-149.

93. Ergott, H. L. Jr., "Introduction: Software Quality Management as a Discipline." *Software Quality Management.* Edited by J. D. Cooper and M. J. Fisher. New York, NY: Petrocelli Books, Inc., 1979.

94. Fagan, M. E., "Design and Code Inspections to Reduce Errors in Program Development." *IBM Systems Journal*, Vol. 15, No. 3, 1976.

95. Farquhar, J. A., *A Preliminary Inquiry into the Software Estimation Process.* Technical Report, AD F12 052, Defense Documentation Center, Alexandria, VA, (August 1970).

96. Finkelstein, A., " 'Not Waving But Drowning': Representation Schemes for Modelling Software Development." *11th International Conference on Software Engineering*, Pittsburgh, PA, (May 15-18, 1989), 402-403.

97. Fitz-enz, J., "Who is the DP Professional?" *Datamation*, (September 1978), 125-128.

98. Fleischer, R. J. and Spitler, R. W., "Simon: A Project Management System for Software Development." *Computer Software Engineering*, (April 1976).

99. Forrester, J. W., *Industrial Dynamics.* Cambridge, MA: The M.I.T. Press, 1961.

100. Forrester, J. W., "Counter Intuitive Behavior of Social System." *Technology Review*, Vol 74, No. 3, (January 1971).

101. Forrester, J. W., *System Dynamics - Future Opportunities.* D-3108-1, (July 1979).

102. Fox, J., ed., *Computer Software Engineering.* New York, NY: Polytechnic Press of the Polytechnic Institute of New York, 1976.

103. Frank, W. L., *Critical Issues in Software: A Guide to Software Economics, Strategy, and Profitability.* New York, NY: John Wiley & Sons, Inc., 1983.

104. Freedland, M., "What You Should Know About Programmers." *Datamation*, (March 15, 1987), 131-134.

105. Freedman, D. P. and Weinberg, G. M., *Handbook of Walkthroughs, Inspections, and Technical Reviews.* Boston, MA: Little, Brown and Co., Inc., 1982.

106. Fries, M. J., *Software Error Data Acquisition.* Boeing Aerospace Co., Seattle, WA, AD/A-039 9 16, (April 1977).

107. Gaffeny, J. E., "Maximize Design Effort and Minimize Program Control Complexity To Maximize Software Development Productivity." *IEEE COMPSAC*, (October 1980).

108. Gaffeny, J. E., "A Macro-Analysis Methodology for Assessment of Software Development Costs." *The Economics of Information Processing. Vol. 2: Operations, Programming, and Software Models.* Edited by R. Goldberg and H. Lorin. New York, NY: John Wiley & Sons, Inc., 1982.

109. Gagliardi, U., Classnotes, Harvard University, Cambridge, MA, 1981.

110. Gansler, J. S., "Keynote: Software Management." *The Symposium on Computer Software Engineering.* Polytechnic Institute of New York, (April 1976).

111. Gehring, P. F. Jr., "A Quantitative Analysis of Estimating Accuracy in Software Development." Unpublished Ph.D. dissertation, Texas A&M University, 1976.

112. Gehring, P. F. Jr. and Pooch, V. W., "Software Development Management." *Data Management*, (February 1977), 14-38.

113. General Research Corp., "Cost Reporting Elements and Activity Cost Tradeoffs for Defense System Software." Santa Clara, CA, (May 1977).

114. Gilb, T., *Software Metrics*. Winthrop, Cambridge, MA, 1977.

115. Gilb, T., *Principles of Software Engineering Management*. Reading, MA: Addison-Wesley Publishing Company, 1988.

116. Glass, R. L., *Software Reliability Guidebook*. Englewood Cliffs, NJ: Prentice-Hall, 1979.

117. Glass, R. L., *Modern Programming Practices: A Report From Industry*. Englewood Cliffs, NJ: Prentice-Hall, 1982.

118. Gordon, R. L. and Lamb, J. C., "A Close Look at Brooks' Law." *Datamation*, (June 1977), 81-86.

119. Grady, R. B. and Caswell, D. L., *Software Metrics: Establishing a Company-wide Program*. Englewood Cliffs, New Jersey: Prentice-Hall, Inc., 1987.

120. Graham, A. K., "Parameter Estimation in System Dynamics Modeling." *Elements of the Systems Dynamics Methods*. Edited by J. Randers. Cambridge, MA: The M.I.T. Press, 1980.

121. Green, L. H., "Organizing for Project Management." *Systems Development Management*. Edited by J. Hannan. Princeton, NJ: Auerbach Publishers, Inc., 1982.

122. Green, P. E. and Tull, D. S., *Research for Marketing Decisions*. Englewood Cliffs, NJ: Prentice-Hall, Inc., 1978.

123. Gunther, R. C., *Management Methodology for Software Product Engineering*. New York, NY: John Wiley & Sons, Inc., 1978.

124. Hales, K. A., "Software Management Lessons Learned - The Hard Way." *The 6th International Computer Software and Applications Conference (COMPSAC)*, (November 1982).

125. Hart, J. J., "The Effectiveness of Design and Code Walkthrough." *The 6th International Computer Software and Applications Conference (COMPSAC)*, (November 1982).

126. Hartwick, R. D., "Software Testing." *Advances in Computer Programming Management*. Edited by T. A. Rullo. Philadelphia, PA: Heyden & Sons, Inc., 1980.

127. Hausen, H. L. and Mullerburg, M., "Software Engineering Environment: State of the Art, Problems and Perspectives." *The 6th International Computer Software and Applications Conference (COMPSAC)*, (November 1982).

128. Herndon, M. A. and Lane, J. A., "Analysis of Software Errors for Cost Factors." American Institute of Aeronautics and Astronautics, Inc., 1977.

129. Hormer, J. B., "A Dynamic Model for Analyzing the Emergence of New Medical Technologies." Unpublished Ph.D. dissertation, M.I.T., Cambridge, MA, 1983.

130. Humphrey, W. S., *Managing the Software Process*. Reading, MA: Addison-Wesley Publishing Company, 1989.

131. Ibrahim, R. L., "Software Development Information System." *Journal of Systems Management*, (December 1978), 34-39.

132. Ingham, A. G., "The Ringelmann Effect: Studies of Group Size and Group Performance." *Journal of Experimental Social Psychology*. Vol. 10, (1974), 371-384.

133. Ingrassia, F. S., "The Unit Development Folder (UDF): An Effective Management Tool for Software Development." TRW Technical Report. TRW-SS-76-11, Redondo Beach, CA: TRW, 1979. (also in D.J. Reifer, editor, *Tutorial: Software Management*, IEEE Computer Society, 1989, 249-262).

134. Isaac, S. and Michael, W., *Handbook in Research and Evaluation*. San Diego, CA: Edits Publishers, 1971.

135. Jensen, R. W. and Tonies, C. C., *Software Engineering*. Englewood Cliffs, NJ: Prentice-Hall, 1979.

136. Jones, M. M. and McLean, E. R., "Management Problems in Large Scale Software Development Projects." *Industrial Management Review*, (Spring 1970), 1-15.

137. Jones, T. C., "Program Quality and Programmer Productivity." *IBM*, TR 02.764, 28, (January 1977).

138. Jones, T. C., "Measuring Programming Quality and Productivity." *IBM Systems Journal*, Vol. 17, No. 1, 1978, 39-63.

139. Jones, T. C., "A Survey of Programming Design and Specification Techniques." *Proceedings of the IEEE Specifications of Reliable Software Conference*, (March 1979).

140. Jones, T. C., "Defect Removal: A Look at the State of the Art." *ITT CommNet*, Vol. 1, No. 3, (December 1981).

141. Jones, T. C., "The Limits of Programming Productivity." *Proceedings of the 14th Annual Conference of the Society for Information Management*, Chicago, IL, (September 1982).

142. Keider, S. P., "Why Projects Fail." *Datamation*, (December 1974).

143. Kelly, T. J., "The Dynamics of R & D Project Management." Unpublished M.S. Thesis, M.I.T., Sloan School of Management, Cambridge, MA, 1970.

144. Kemerer, C. F., "An Empirical Validation of Software Cost Estimation Models." *Communications of the ACM*, Vol. 30, No. 5, (May 1987), 416-429.

145. Kirby, E. J., "The Systems Development Manager." *Systems Development Management.* Edited by J. Hannan. Princeton, NJ: Auerbach Publishers, Inc., 1982.

146. Knight, B. M., "Organizational Planning for Software Quality." *Software Quality Management.* Edited by J. D. Cooper and M. J. Fisher. New York, NY: Petrocelli Books, Inc., 1979.

147. Knuth, D. E., "The Errors of TEX*. "*Software-Practice and Experience*, Vol. 19, No. 7, (July 1989), 607-685.

148. Knutson, J., "Developing the Project Plan." *Advances in Computer Programming Management.* Philadelphia, PA: Heyden & Sons, Inc., 1980.

149. Kolence, K., "Software Engineering Management and Methodology." *Software Engineering: Report on a Conference Sponsored by the NATO Science Committee.* Edited by P. Naur and B. Randell. Vol. 13, (October 1968).

150. Koolhass, Z., *Organization Dissonance and Change.* New York, NY: John Wiley & Sons, Inc., 1982.

151. Kootz, H. and O'Donnel, C., *Principles of Management: An Analysis of Management Functions.* 5th ed. New York, NY: McGraw-Hill Books Co., 1972.

152. Kotter, J. P., *Organizational Dynamics: Diagnosis and Intervision.* Reading, MA: Addison-Wesley Publishing Co., Inc., 1978.

153. Kustanowitz, A. L., "System Life Cycle Estimation (Slice:) A New Approach to Estimating Resources for Application Program Development." *COMPSAC*, 1977.

154. Larkin, J. E., "The Psychology of DP Professional: A Career Planning Tool." *ComputerWorld*, (CW-0221), 1982.

155. Laudon, K. C. and Laudon, J. P., *Management Information Systems: A Contemporary Perspective.* New York, NY: Macmillan, 1988.

156. Lawler, E. E. and Rhode, J. G., *Information and Control in Organizations.* Pacific Palisades, CA: Goodyear Publishing Co., Inc., 1976.

157. Leavitt, H. J., *Managerial Psychologly.* 4th ed. Chicago, IL: The University of Chicago Press, 1978.

158. Lehman, J. H., "How Software Projects Are Really Managed." *Datamation*, (January 1979), 119-129.

159. Lehman, M. M., *Laws and Conservation in Large Program Evaluation.* Second Software Life Cycle Management Workshop. Atlanta, GA, (August 1978), 21-22.

160. Lientz, B. P. and Swanson, E. B., "Problems in Application Software Maintenance." *Comm of ACM*, Vol. 24, No. 11, (November 1981), 763-769.

161. Liu, L. and Horowitz, E., "A Formal Model for Software Project Management." *IEEE Transactions on Software Engineering*, Vol. 15, No. 10, (October 1989), 1280-1293.

162. Londeix, B., *Cost Estimation for Software Development*. Reading, MA: Addison-Wesley Publishing Company, 1987.

163. Maciariello, J. A., *Program - Management Control Systems*. New York, NY: John Wiley & Sons, Inc., 1978.

164. Mantei, M., "The Effort of Programming Team Structures on Programming Tasks." *Communications of the ACM*, Vol 24, No. 3, (March 1981), 106-113.

165. Martin, J., *Application Development Without Programmers*. Englewood Cliffs, NJ: Prentice-Hall, Inc., 1982.

166. McClure, C. L. , *Managing Software Development and Maintenance*. New York, NY: Van Nostrand Reinhold Company, 1981.

167. McFarlan, F. W., "Effective EDP Project Management." *Managing the Data Resource Function*. Edited by R. L. Nolan. St. Paul, MN: West Publishing Co., 1974.

168. McGarry, F. E., Personal Communications, 1983.

169. McGowan, C. L., "Management Planning for Large Software Projects." *IEEE*, 1978.

170. McGowan, C. L. and McHenry, R. C., "Software Management." *Research Directions in Software Technology*. Cambridge, MA: The M.I.T. Press, 1979.

171. McKeen, J. D., *The Nature of Inter-Activity Relationships Within the Systems Development Cycle*. Queen's University, Kingston, Ontario, Canada, (September 1981).

172. McKeen, J. D., "An Empirical Investigation of the Process and Product of Application System Development." Unpublished Ph.D. dissertation, University of Minnesota, 1981.

173. McKeen, J. D., "Successful Development Strategies for Business Application Systems." *MIS Quarterly*, Vol. 7, No. 3, (September 1983).

174. McLaughlin, R. A., "That Old Bugaboo, Turnover." *Datamation*, (October 1979), 97-101.

175. Mercer, B. D., "Weapon System Software Acquisition and Support: A Theory of System Structure and Behavior." Unpublished M.S. Thesis, Air Force Institute of Technology, 1982.

176. Merwin, R. E., "Software Management: We Must Find a Way." *IEEE*, 1978.

177. Metzger, P. W., *Managing a Programming Project*. 2nd ed. Englewood Cliffs, NJ: Prentice-Hall, Inc., 1981.

178. Miller, J. G., "Toward a General Theory for the Behavior Sciences." *The American Psychologist*, Vol. 10, (September 1955), 513-539.

179. Mills, H., "Top Down Programming in Large Systems." *Debugging Techniques in Large Systems*. Edited by R. Rustin. Englewood Cliffs, NJ: Prentice-Hall, 1971.

180. Mills, H. D., "Software Development." *IEEE Transactions on Software Engineering*, Vol. SE-2, No. 4, (December 1976).

181. Mills, H. D. *Software Productivity*. Canada: Little, Brown & Co., 1983.

182. Mills, H. D., "Software Engineering: Retrospect and Prospect." *The Twelfth Annual International Computer Software & Applications Conference (COMPSAC)*, (October 5-7, 1988), 89-96.

183. Mitchell, J. R., "Observations on the Use of Seven Structured Programming Techniques." *IEEE*, 1980.

184. Mohanty, S. N., "Software Cost Estimation: Present and Future." *Software - Practice and Experience*, Vol. 11, (1981), 103-121.

185. Moore, J. H., "A Framework for MIS Software Development Projects." *MIS Quarterly*, Vol. 3, No. 1, (March 1979), 29-38.

186. Morecroft, J. D. W., "A Critical Review of Diagramming Tools for Conceptualizing Feedback System Models." *The IEEE Conference on Cybernetics and Society*, 1980.

187. Morecroft, J. D. W. and Abdel-Hamid, T. K., "A Generic System Dynamics Model of Software Project Management." *The International System Dynamics Conference*, (July 1983).

188. Myers, G., *Estimating the Costs of a Programming System Development Project*. Systems Development Div., Poughkeepsie Lab., IBM. (May 1972).

189. Myers, G. J., *Software Reliability: Principles and Practices*. New York, NY: John Wiley & Sons, Inc., 1976.

190. Myers, G. J., "A Controlled Experiment in Program Testing and Code Walkthrough/Inspections." *Communications of the ACM*, Vol. 21, No. 9, (September 1978), 760-768.

191. Myers, W., "The Need for Software Engineering." *Computer*, (February 1978).

192. NASA, "Recommended Approach to Software Development." 1983.

193. NASA, "Software Development History for Dynamics Explorer (DE) Attitude Ground Support System (AGSS)." 1983.

194. NASA, "DE-A Resource Summary." 1983.

195. Nay, J. N., "Choice and Allocation in Multiple Markets: A Research and Development Systems Analysis." Unpublished M.S. Thesis, M.I.T., Dept. of Electric Engineering, Cambridge, MA, 1965.

196. Nelson, E. A., *Management Handbook for the Estimation of Computer Programmer Costs.* Ad-A648 750, Systems Development Corp., (October 1966).

197. Nelson, E. C., "Software Reliability, Verification and Validation." *Proceedings of the TRW Symposium on Reliable, Cost-Effective, Secure Software*, Redondo Beach, CA: TRW, Inc., 1974.

198. Norden, P. V., "Useful Tools for Project Management." *Operation Research in Research and Development.* Edited by B. V. Dean. New York, NY: John Wiley & Sons, Inc., 1963.

199. Okada, M., "Software Development Effort Estimation Study - A Model from CAD/CAM System Development Experiences." *The IEEE Computer's 6th International Computer Software & Applications Conference*, Chicago, IL, (November 1982).

200. Oliver,, "Estimating the Cost of Software." *Computer Programming Management.* Edited by J. Hannan. Princeton, NJ: Auerbach Publishers, Inc., 1982.

201. Paretta, R. L. and Clark, S. A., "Management of Software Development." *Journal of Systems Management*, (April 1976).

202. Parikh, G. and Zvegintzev, N., "The World of Software Maintenance." *IEEE Tutorial on Software Maintenance*, IEEE, 1983.

203. Park, R. E., "An Open Letter to Cost Model Evaluators." *Journal of Parametrics*, Vol. 9, No. 3, (October 1989), 6-10.

204. Parnas, D. L., "Information Distribution. Aspects of Design Methodology." *IFIP Congress Computer Software*, 1971, 26-30.

205. Perlis, A. J., "Software Engineering Education." *Software Engineering Techniques: Report on a Conference Sponsored by the Nate Science Committee.* Edited by J. N. Baxton and B. Randell. (October 1969).

206. Perlis, A. J., et al., *Software Metrics.* Cambridge, MA: The M.I.T. Press, 1981.

207. Pietrasanta, A. M., "Managing the Economics of Computer Programming." *Proceedings ACM National Conference*, 1968.

208. Pooch, U. W. and Gehring, P. F. Jr., "Toward a Management Philosophy for Software Development." *Advances in Computer Programming Management*, Vol. 1. Edited by T. A. Rullo, Philadelphia, PA: Heyden & Sons, Inc., 1980.

209. Powers, R. F. and Dickson, G. W., "MIS Project Management: Myths, Opinions, and Reality." *California Management Review*, Vol. XV, No. 3, (Spring 1973), 147-156.

210. Pressman, R. S., *Software Engineering: A Practitioner's Approach.* New York, NY: McGraw-Hill, Inc., 1982.

211. Pugh, A. L. III., *Dynamo Users' Manual.* 5th ed. Cambridge, MA: The M.I.T. Press, 1976.

212. Putnam, L., "A General Empirical Solution to the Macro Software Sizing and Estimating Problem." *IEEE Transactions on Software Engineering*, July 1978, 345-361.

213. Putnam, L. H. and Fitzsimmons, A., "Estimating Software Costs, Part I." *Datamation*, (September 1979).

214. Putnam, L. H., "The Real Metrics of Software Development." *EASCON 80*, 1980, 310.

215. Radice, A., "Productivity Measures in Software." *The Economics of Information Processing Vol. 2: Operations, Programming and Software Models*. Edited by R. Goldberg and H. Lorin. New York, NY: John Wiley & Sons, Inc., 1982.

216. Reed, E. A., "Time Sheet Accounting." *Journal of Systems Management*, (January 1979), 32-35.

217. Reifer, D. J., "The Nature of Software Management: A Primer." *Tutorial: Software Management*. Edited by D. J. Reifer. IEEE Computer Society, 1979.

218. Reihl, J. W., "An Examination of Management Practices in the Development of Business Information Systems." Unpublished Ph.D. dissertation, George Washington University, 1977.

219. Reynolds,, "What's Wrong With Computer Programming Management?" *On the Management of Computer Programming*. Edited by G. F. Weinwurm. Princeton, NJ: Auerbach Publishing, Inc., 1970.

220. Richardson, G. P., "Sources of Rising Product Development Times." Technical Report D-3321-1, SD Group, Cambridge, MA, M.I.T., 1982.

221. Richardson, G. P. and Pugh, G. L. III., *Introduction to Systems Dynamics Modeling and DYNAMO*. Cambridge, MA: The M.I.T. Press, 1981.

222. Richmond, D., "No Nonsense Recruitment." *Perspectives on Information Management: A Critical Selection of ComputerWorld Feature Articles*. Edited by J. B. Rochester. New York, NY: John Wiley & Sons, Inc., 1982.

223. Roberts, E. B., "The Dynamics of Research and Development." Published Ph.D. dissertation, M.I.T., Cambridge, MA, 1964.

224. Roberts, E. B., "A Simple Model of R & D Project Dynamics." *Managerial Applications of System Dynamics*. Edited by E. B. Roberts. Cambridge, MA: The M.I.T. Press, 1981.

225. Roberts, E. B., "System Dynamics — An Introduction." In *Managerial Applications of System Dynamics*, edited by E. B. Roberts. Cambridge, MA: The MIT Press, 1981.

226. Sampson, W. F., et al., "Organizational Strategies for Producing Better Software." *First International Computer Software and Applications Conference (COMPSAC)*, (November 1977), pp. 233-239.

227. Schein, E. H., *Organizational Psychology*. 3rd ed. Englewood Cliffs, NJ: Prentice-Hall, Inc., 1980.

228. Schlender, B. R., "How to Break the Software Logjam." *Fortune*, (September 25, 1989), 100-112.

229. Schultz, R. L. and Sullivan, E. M., "Developments in Simulation in Social and Administrative Science," in Guetzkow, H. S. et al. *Simulation in Social and Administrative Science: Overviews and Case-Examples*. Englewood Cliffs, NJ: Prentice-Hall, Inc., 1972.

230. Scott, R. F. and Simmons, D. B., "Programmer Productivity and the Delphi Technique." *Datamation*, (May 1974), 71-73.

231. Scott, R. F. and Simmons. D. B., "Predicting Programming Group Productivity - A Communications Model." *IEEE Transactions on Software Engineering*, Vol. SE-1, No. 4, (December 1975).

232. Selltiz, C., et al., *Research Methods in Social Relations*. 3rd ed. New York, NY: Holt, Rinehart & Winston, 1976.

233. Semprevivo, P. C., *Teams - In Information Systems Development*. New York, NY: Yourdon, Inc., 1980.

234. Shell, R. L., "Work Measurement for Computer Programming Operations." *Industrial Engineering*, (October 1972), 32-36.

235. Shneiderman, B., *Software Psychology - Human Factors in Computer and Information Systems*. Cambridge, MA: Winthrop Publishers, Inc., 1980.

236. Shooman, M. L., *Software Engineering - Design Reliability and Management*. New York, NY: McGraw-Hill, Inc., 1983.

237. Shooman, M. L. and Natarajan, S., "Effect of Manpower Development and Bug Generation on Software Error Models." Rome Air Development Center RADC-TR-76-400, (January 1977).

238. Snyder, T. R., "Rate Charting." *Datamation*, (November 1976), 44-47.

239. Stalnaker, A. W. and Mayer, D. B., "Selection and Evaluation of Computer Personnel." *Proceedings of 23rd ACM National Conference*, Brandon/Systems Press, Inc., 1968, 657-670.

240. Steiner, I. D., "Models for Inferring Relationships Between Group Size and Potential Group Productivity," *Behavioral Science*, 1966, pp. 273-283.

241. Sterman, J., Class Notes, M.I.T., Cambridge, MA, 1981.

242. Synnott, W. R. and Gruber, W. H., *Information Resource Management*. New York, NY: John Wiley & Sons, Inc., 1981.

243. Tanniru, M. R., et al., "Causes of Turnover Among DP Professionals." *Proceedings of the 8th Annual Computer Personnel Research Conference*, Miami, FL, (June 1981).

244. Tausworthe, R. C., *Standardized Development of Computer Science*. Englewood Cliffs, NJ: Prentice-Hall, Inc., 1977.

245. Tausworthe, R. C., "The Work Breakdown Structure in Software Project Management." *Journal of Systems and Software*, 1980, 181-186.

246. Thayer, R. H., "Modeling a Software Engineering Project Management System." Unpublished Ph.D. dissertation, University of California, Santa Barbara, CA, 1979.

247. Thayer, T. A., et al., *Software Reliability: A Study of Large Project Reality*. New York, NY: North Holland, 1978.

248. Thayer, R. H., et al., "The Challenge of Software Engineering Project Management." *Computer*, (August 1980).

249. Thayer, R. H., et al., "Major Issues in Software Engineering Project Management." *IEEE Transactions on Software Engineering*, Vol. SE-7, No. 4, (July, 1981).

250. Thayer, R. H., et al., "Validating Solutions to Major Problems in Software Engineering Project Management." *Computer*, (August 1982).

251. Thayer, R. H. and Lehman, J. H., *Software Engineering Project Management: A Survey Concerning U.S. Aerospace Industry Management of Software Development Projects*. Sacramento Air Logistics Center, McClellan Air Force Base, CA, (November 1977).

252. Thibodeau, R. and Dodson, E. N., "Life Cycle Phase Interrelationships." *Journal of Systems and Software*, Vol. 1, 1980, 203-211.

253. Thomsett, R., *People Project Management*. New York, NY: Yourdon Press, Inc., 1980.

254. Toellner, J., "Project Estimating." *Journal of Systems Management*, (May 1977), 6-9.

255. Tsichritzis, D., "Project Management." *Software Engineering*. Edited by F. L. Bauer. Berlin: Springer-Verlag, 1977.

256. Tsui, F. and Priven, L., "Implementation of Quality Control in Software development." *National Computer Conference*, 1976.

257. Walston, C. E. and Felix, C. P., "Method of Programming Measurement and Estimation." *IBM Systems Journal*, Vol. 16, No. 1, 1977.

258. Wegner, P., ed., *Research Directions in Software Technology*. Cambridge, MA: The M.I.T. Press, 1980.

259. Weick, K. E., *The Social Psychology of Organization*. 2nd ed. Reading, M:A Addison-Wesley Publishing Co., Inc., 1979.

260. Weinberg, G. M., *The Psychology of Computer Programming*. New York, NY: Litton Educational Publishing, Inc., 1971.

261. Weinberg, G. M., "Overstructured Management of Software Engineering." *Proceedings of the 6th International Conference on Software Engineering*, Tokyo, September 1982.

262. Weinberg, G. M., *Understanding the Professional Programmer*. Boston, MA: Little, Brown & Co., Inc., 1982.

263. Weinberg, G. M. and Schulman, E. L., "Goals and Performance in Computer Programming." *Human Factors*, Vol. 16, No. 1, 1974, 70-77.

264. Weinwurm, G. F., ed., *On the Management of Computer Programming*. Princeton, NJ: Auerbach Publishing, Inc., 1970.

265. Weiss, D. M., "Evaluating Software Development by Error Analysis." *Journal of Systems and Software*, Vol. 1, 1979, 57-70.

266. Weiss, H. M., "Project Control." *Journal of Systems Management*, (May 1973), 14-17.

267. Wender, P. H., "Vicious and Virtuous Circles: The Role of Deviation Amplifying Feedback in the Origin and Perception of Behavior." *Psychiatry*, Vol. 31., 1968.

268. Willoughby, T. C., "Computing Personnel Turnover: A Review of the Literature." *Computing Personnel*, Vol. 7, No. 1-2, (Autumn 1977), 11-13.

269. Winrow, B., *Acquiring Entry-level Programming Management*. Edited by J. Hannan. Princeton, NJ: Auerbach Publishers, Inc., 1982.

270. Wolverton, R. W., "The Cost of Developing Large-Scale Software." *IEEE Transactions on Computers*, (June, 1974).

271. Youker, R., "Organizational Alternatives for Project Management," *Management Review*, Vol. 16, No. 11, 46-53 (1977).

272. Yourdon, E., *Managing the System Life Cycle. A Software Development Methodology Overview*. New York, NY: Yourdon, Inc., 1982.

273. Zelkowitz, M. V., "Perspectives on Software Engineering." *Computing Surveys*, Vol. 10, No. 2, (June 1978).

274. Zelkowitz, M. V., et al., *Principles of Software Engineering and Design*. Englewood Cliffs, NJ: Prentice-Hall, Inc., 1979.

275. Zmud, R. W., "Management of Large Software Development Efforts." *MIS Quarterly*, Vol. 4, No. 2, (June 1980), 45-56.

276. Zolnowski, J. C. and Ting, P. D., "An Insider's Survey of Software Development." *Proceedings of the 6th International Conference on Software Engineering*, Tokyo, (September 1982).

APPENDIX: DYNAMO MODEL

```
* BASE.5 / BASE MODEL: VERSION 5
NOTE
NOTE **************
NOTE HUMAN RESOURCE MANAGEMENT SUBSYSTEM
NOTE **************
NOTE
L       WFNEW.K=WFNEW.J+DT*(HIRERT.JK-ASIMRT.JK-NEWTRR.J)
NOTE NEW WORKFORCE (PEOPLE)
N       WFNEW=0
R       HIRERT.KL=MAX(0,WFGAP.K/HIREDY)
NOTE HIRING RATE (PEOPLE/DAY)
C       HIREDY=40
NOTE HIRING DELAY (DAYS)
A       WFGAP.K=WFS.K-TOTWF.K
NOTE WORKFORCE GAP (PEOPLE)
A       NEWTRR.K=MIN(TRNFRT.K,WFNEW.K/DT)
NOTE NEW EMPLOYEES TRANSFER RATE OUT (PEOPLE/DAY)
A       TRNFRT.K=MAX(0,-WFGAP.K/TRNSDY)
NOTE TRANSFER RATE OF PEOPLE OUT OF PROJECT (PEOPLE/DAY)
C       TRNSDY=10
NOTE TIME DELAY TO TRANSFER PEOPLE OUT (DAYS)
R       ASIMRT.KL=WFNEW.K/ASIMDY
NOTE ASSIMILATION RATE OF NEW EMPLOYEES (PEOPLE/DAY)
C       ASIMDY=80
NOTE AVERAGE ASSIMILATION DELAY (DAYS)
A       DMPTRN.K=WFNEW.K*TRPNHR
NOTE DAILY MANPOWER FOR TRAINING (MAN-DAYS/DAY)
C       TRPNHR=0.2
NOTE NUMBER OF TRAINERS PER NEW EMPLOYEE (DIMENSIONLESS)
L       CMTRMD.K=CMTRMD.J+DT*DMPTRN.J
NOTE CUMULATIVE TRAINING MAN-DAYS
N       CMTRMD=0
L       WFEXP.K=WFEXP.J+DT*(ASIMRT.JK-EXPTRR.J-QUITRT.JK)
NOTE EXPERIENCED WORKFORCE (PEOPLE)
N       WFEXP=WFSTRT
NOTE INITIAL VALUE OF EXPERIENCED WORKFORCE LEVEL
A       EXPTRR.K=MIN(WFEXP.K/DT,TRNFRT.K-NEWTRR.K)
NOTE EXPERIENCED EMPLOYEES TRANSFER RATE (PEOPLE/DAY)
R       QUITRT.KL=WFEXP.K/AVEMPT
NOTE EXPERIENCED EMPLOYEES QUIT RATE (PEOPLE/DAY)
C       AVEMPT=673
NOTE AVERAGE EMPLOYMENT TIME (DAYS)
A       FTEXWF.K=WFEXP.K*ADMPPS
NOTE FULL-TIME-EQUIVALENT EXPERIENCED WF (MEN)
A       CELNWH.K=FTEXWF.K*MNHPXS
NOTE CEILING ON NEW HIREES (MEN)
C       MNHPXS=3
NOTE MOST NEW HIREES PER EXPERIENCED STAFF (MEN/MEN)
A       CELTWF.K=CELNWH.K+WFEXP.K
NOTE CEILING ON TOTAL WORKFORCE (PEOPLE)
A       WFS.K=MIN(CELTWF.K,WFNEED.K)
NOTE WF SOUGHT (PEOPLE)
A       TOTWF.K=WFNEW.K+WFEXP.K
```

NOTE TOTAL WF LEVEL (PEOPLE)

A   FTEQWF.K=TOTWF.K*ADMPPS

NOTE FULL TIME EQUIVALENT WF (EQUIVALENT PEOPLE)

A   FRWFEX.K=WFEXP.K/TOTWF.K

NOTE FRACTION OF WF THAT IS EXPERIENCED (DIMENSIONLESS)

NOTE

NOTE **************

NOTE SOFTWARE PRODUCTION SUSBSYSTEM

NOTE **************

NOTE

NOTE (A) MANPOWER ALLOCATION SECTOR

NOTE

A   TOTDMP.K=TOTWF.K*ADMPPS

NOTE TOTAL DAILY MANPOWER (MAN-DAYS/DAY)

C   ADMPPS=1

NOTE AVERAGE DAILY MANPOWER PER STAFF (DAY/DAY)

L   CUMMD.K=CUMMD.J+DT*TOTDMP.J

NOTE CUMULATIVE MAN-DAYS EXPENDED (MAN-DAYS)

N   CUMMD=.0001

A   DMPATR.K=TOTDMP.K-DMPTRN.K

NOTE DAILY MANPOWER AVAILABLE AFTER TRAINING (MAN-DAYS/DAY)

A   AFMPQA.K=PFMPQA.K*(1+ADJQA.K)

NOTE ACTUAL FRACTION

N   AFMPQA=PFMPQA

C   QO=0

NOTE QUALITY OBJECTIVE ... NORMAL QO = 0

A   PFMPQA.K=TABHL(TPFMQA,PJBAWK.K,0,1,.1)*(1+QO/100)

NOTE PLANNED FRACTION OF MANPOWER FOR QA (DIMENSIONLESS)

T   TPFMQA=.15/.15/.15/.15/.15/.15/.15/.15/.15/.15/0

A   ADJQA.K=TABHL(TADJQA,SCHPR.K,0,.5,.1)

NOTE % ADJUSTMENT IN PFMPQA (%)

T   TADJQA=0/-.025/-.15/-.35/-.475/-.5

A   DMPQA.K=MIN((AFMPQA.K*TOTDMP.K),.9*DMPATR.K)

NOTE DAILY MANPOWER ALLOCATED FOR QA (MAN-DAYS/DAY)

L   CMQAMD.K=CMQAMD.J+DT*DMPQA.J

NOTE CUMULATIVE QA MAN-DAYS (MAN-DAYS)

N   CMQAMD=0

A   DMPSWP.K=DMPATR.K-DMPQA.K

NOTE DAILY MANPOWER FOR SOFTWARE PRODUCTION (MAN-DAYS/DAY)

A   DESECR.K=DTCERR.K/DESRWD

NOTE DESIRED ERROR CORRECTION RATE (ERRORS/DAY)

N   DESECR=0

C   DESRWD=15

NOTE DESIRED REWORK DELAY (DAYS)

A   DMPRW.K=MIN((DESECR.K*PRWMPE.K),DMPSWP.K)

NOTE DAILY MANPOWER ALLOCATED FOR REWORK (MAN-DAYS/DAY)

N   DMPRW=0

L   PRWMPE.K=PRWMPE.J+(DT/TARMPE)(RWMPPE.J-PRWMPE.J)

NOTE PERCEIVED REWORK MANPOWER NEEDED PER ERROR (MAN-DAYS/ERROR)

N   PRWMPE=.5

C   TARMPE=10

NOTE TIME TO ADJUST PRWMPE (DAYS)

L   CMRWMD.K=CMRWMD.J+DT*DMPRW.J

NOTE CUMULATIVE REWORK MAN-DAYS (MAN-DAYS)

N   CMRWMD=0

A   DMPDVT.K=DMPSWP.K-DMPRW.K

NOTE DAILY MANPOWER FOR DEVELOPMENT/TESTING (MAN-DAYS/DAYS)

L   CMDVMD.K=CMDVMD.J+DT*DMPDVT.J*(1-FREFTS.K)
NOTE CUMULATIVE DEVELOPMENT MAN-DAYS (MAN-DAYS)
N   CMDVMD=0
NOTE
NOTE (B) SOFTWARE DEVELOPMENT SECTOR
NOTE
R   SDVRT.KL=MIN((DMPSDV.K*SDVPRD.K),TSKPRM.K/DT)
NOTE SOFTWARE DEVELOPMENT RATE (TASKS/DAY)
N   SDVRT=0
A   DMPSDV.K=DMPDVT.K*(1-FREFTS.K)
NOTE DAILY MANPOWER FOR SOFTWARE DEVELOPMENT (MAN-DAYS/DAY)
A   FREFTS.K=TABHL(TFEFTS,TSKPRM.K/PJBSZ.K,0,.2,.04)
NOTE FRACTION OF EFFORT FOR SYSTEM TESTING (DIMENSIONLESS)
T   TFEFTS=1/.5/.28/.15/.05/0
A   SDVPRD.K=POTPRD.K*MPDMCL.K
NOTE SOFTWARE DEVELOPMENT PRODUCTIVITY (TASKS/MAN-DAY)
A   POTPRD.K=ANPPRD.K*MPPTPD.K
NOTE POTENTIAL PRODUCTIVITY (TASKS/MAN-DAY)
A   ANPPRD.K=FRWFEX.K*NPWPEX+(1-FRWFEX.K)*NPWPNE
NOTE AVERAGE NOMINAL POTENTIAL PRODUCTIVITY (TASKS/MAN-DAY)
C   NPWPEX=1
NOTE NOMINAL POTENTIAL PRODUCTIVITY OF EXP EMPLOYEE (TSK/M-D)
C   NPWPNE=0.5
NOTE NOMINAL POTENTIAL PROD OF NEW EMPL. (TSK/M-D)
A   MPPTPD.K=TABHL(TMPTPD,PJBAWK.K,0,1,.1)
NOTE MULTIPLIER TO POTENTIAL PRODUCTIVITY DUE TO LEARNING (DIMENSIONLESS)
T   TMPTPD=1/1.0125/1.0325/1.055/1.09/1.15/1.2/1.22/1.245/1.25/1.25
A   MPDMCL.K=AFMDPJ.K*(1-COMMOH.K)
NOTE MULTIPLIER TO PRODUCTIVITY DUE TO MOTIVATION & COMM LOSSES (DIMENSIONLESS)
A   COMMOH.K=TABHL(TCOMOH,TOTWF.K,0,30,5)
NOTE COMMUNICATION OVERHEAD (DIMENSIONLESS)
T   TCOMOH=0/.015/.06/.135/.24/.375/.54
C   NFMDPJ=.6
NOTE NOMINAL FRACTION OF A MAN-DAY ON PROJECT (DIMENSIONLESS)
L   AFMDPJ.K=AFMDPJ.J+DT*WRADJR.JK
NOTE ACTUAL FRACTION OF A MAN-DAY ON PROJECT (DIMENSIONLESS)
N   AFMDPJ=NFMDPJ
R   WRADJR.KL=(WKRTS.K-AFMDPJ.K)/WKRADY.K
NOTE WORK RATE ADJUSTMENT RATE (1/DAY)
A   WKRADY.K=NWRADY.K*EWKRTS.K
NOTE WORK RATE ADJUSTMENT DELAY (DAYS)
A   NWRADY.K=TABHL(TNWRAD,TIMERM.K,0,30,5)
NOTE NORMAL WORK RATE ADJUSTMENT DELAY (DAYS)
T   TNWRAD=2/3.5/5/6.5/8/9.5/10
A   EWKRTS.K=CLIP(1,.75,WKRTS.K,AFMDPJ.K)
NOTE EFFECT OF WORK RATE SOUGHT (DIMENSIONLESS)
A   WKRTS.K=(1+PBWKRS.K)*NFMDPJ
NOTE WORK RATE SOUGHT (DIMENSIONLESS)
N   MAXMHR=1
NOTE MAXIMUM BOOST IN MAN-HOURS (DIMENSIONLESS)
A   PBWKRS.K=CLIP((MDHDL.K/(FTEQWF.K*(OVWDTH.K+.0001))),
X   (MDHDL.K/(TMDPSN.K-MDHDL.K+.0001)),PMDSHR.K,0)
NOTE % BOOST IN WORK RATE SOUGHT (%)
A   MDHDL.K=CLIP(MIN(MAXSHR.K,PMDSHR.K),-EXSABS.K,PMDSHR.K,0)*CTRLSW
NOTE MAN-DAYS THAT WILL BE HANDLED OR ABSORBED (MAN-DAYS)
C   CTRLSW=1
NOTE CONTROL SWITCH ... ALLOWS US TO TEST POLICY OF NO OVERWORK (0 OR 1)

A   EXSABS.K=MAX(0,(
X   TABHL(TEXABS,TMDPSN.K/MDRM.K,0,1,.1)*MDRM.K-TMDPSN.K))
NOTE MAN-DAY EXCESSES THAT WILL BE ABSOBED (MAN-DAYS)
T   TEXABS=0/.2/.4/.55/.7/.8/.9/.95/1/1/1
A   MAXSHR.K=(OVWDTH.K*FTEQWF.K*MAXMHR)*WTOVWK.K
NOTE MAXIMUM SHORTAGE IN MAN-DAYS THAT CAN BE HANDLED (MAN-DAYS)
A   WTOVWK.K=CLIP(1,0,TIME.K,BRKDTM.K+RLXTMC.K)
NOTE WILLINGNESS TO OVERWORK (0 OR 1)
L   BRKDTM.K=MAX(BRKDTM.J,SWITCH((TIME.J+DT),0,OVWDTH.K))
NOTE TIME OF LAST EXHAUSTION BREAKDOWN
N   BRKDTM=-1
L·   RLXTMC.K=RLXTMC.J*SWITCH(0,1,OVWDTH.K)+DT*
X   CLIP(1,-RLXTMC.J/DT,EXHLEV.K/MXEXHT,.1)
NOTE VARIABLE THAT CONTROLS TIME TO DE-EXHAUST
N   RLXTMC=0
A   OVWDTH.K=NOVWDT.K*MODTEX.K
NOTE OVERWORK DURATION THRESHOLD (DAYS)
A   NOVWDT.K=TABHL(TNOWDT,TIMERM.K,0,50,10)
NOTE NOMINAL OVERWORK DURATION THRESHOLD (DAYS)
T   TNOWDT=0/10/20/30/40/50
A   MODTEX.K=TABHL(TMODEX,EXHLEV.K/MXEXHT,0,1,.1)
NOTE EFFECT OF EXHAUSTION ON OVERWORK DURATION THRESHOLD (DIMENSIONLESS)
T   TMODEX=1/.9/.8/.7/.6/.5/.4/.3/.2/.1/0
L   EXHLEV.K=EXHLEV.J+DT*(RIEXHL.JK-RDEXHL.JK)
NOTE EXHAUSTION LEVEL (EXHAUST UNITS)
N   EXHLEV=0
R   RIEXHL.KL=TABHL(TRIXHL,(1-AFMDPJ.K)/(1-NFMDPJ),
X   -0.5,1,.1)
NOTE RATE OF INCREASE IN EXHAUSTION LEVEL (EXHAUST UNITS/DAY)
T   TRIXHL=2.5/2.2/1.9/1.6/1.3/1.15/.9/.8/.7/.6/.5/.4/.3/.2/0/0
R   RDEXHL.KL=CLIP(EXHLEV.K/EXHDDY,0,0,RIEXHL.JK)
NOTE RATE OF DEPLETION IN EXHAUSTION LEVEL (EXHAUST UNITS/DAY)
C   EXHDDY=20
NOTE EXHAUSTION DEPLETION DELAY TIME (DAYS)
C   MXEXHT=50
NOTE MAXIMUM TOLERABLE EXHAUSTION (EXHAUST UNITS)
NOTE
NOTE (C) QUALITY ASSURANCE AND REWORK SECTOR
NOTE
R   QART.KL=DELAY3(SDVRT.JK,AQADLY)
NOTE FOR QA RATE (TASKS/DAY)
L   TSKWK.K=TSKWK.J+DT*(SDVRT.JK-QART.JK)
NOTE TASKS WORKED (TASKS)
N   TSKWK=0
C   AQADLY=10
NOTE AVERAGE DELAY FOR QA (DAYS)
L   CUMTQA.K=CUMTQA.J+DT*(QART.JK-TSRATE.JK)
NOTE CUMULATIVE TASKS QA'ED (TASKS)
N   CUMTQA=0
A   ANERPT.K=MAX(PTDTER.K/(TSKWK.K+.0001),0)
NOTE AVERAGE # OF ERRORS PER TASK (ERRORS/TASK)
A   QAMPNE.K=NQAMPE.K*(1/MPDMCL.K)*MDEFED.K
NOTE QA MANPOWER NEEDED TO DETECT AVERAGE ERROR (MAN-DAYS/ERROR)
A   NQAMPE.K=TABHL(TNQAPE,PJBAWK.K,0,1,.1)
NOTE NOMINAL QA MANPOWER NEEDED TO DETECT AVERAGE ERROR (MAN-DAYS/ERROR)
T   TNQAPE=.4/.4/.39/.375/.35/.3/.25/.225/.21/.2/.2
A   MDEFED.K=TABHL(TMDFED,ERRDSY.K,0,10,1)

NOTE MULTIPLIER TO DETECTION EFFORT DUE TO ERROR DENSITY (DIMENSIONLESS)
T   TMDFED=50/36/26/17.5/10/4/1.75/1.2/1/1/1
A   ERRDSY.K=ANERPT.K*1000/DSIPTK
NOTE ERROR DENSITY (ERRORS/KDSI)
A   PERDRT.K=DMPQA.K/QAMPNE.K
NOTE POTENTIAL ERROR DETECTION RATE (ERRORS/DAY)
A   ERRDRT.K=MIN(PERDRT.K,PTDTER.K/DT)
NOTE ERROR DETECTION RATE (ERRORS/DAY)
L   CMERD.K=CMERD.J+DT*ERRDRT.J
NOTE CUMULATIVE ERRORS DETECTED (ERRORS)
N   CMERD=0
A   PRCTDT.K=100*CMERD.K/(CUMERG.K+.001)
NOTE PERCENT ERRORS DETECTED (PERCENT)
A   ERRSRT.K=QART.JK*ANERPT.K
NOTE ERROR ESCAPE RATE (ERRORS/DAY)
L   CMERES.K=CMERES.J+DT*ERRSRT.J
NOTE CUMULATIVE ERRORS THAT ESCAPED (ERRORS)
N   CMERES=0
L   PTDTER.K=PTDTER.J+DT*(ERRGRT.JK-ERRDRT.J-ERRSRT.J)
NOTE POTENTIALLY DETECTABLE ERRORS (ERRORS)
N   PTDTER=0
R   ERRGRT.KL=SDVRT.JK*ERRPTK.K
NOTE ERROR GENERATION RATE (ERRORS/DAY)
A   ERRPTK.K=NERPTK.K*MERGSP.K*MERGWM.K
NOTE ERRORS PER TASK (ERRORS/TASK)
A   NERPTK.K=NERPK.K*DSIPTK/1000
NOTE NOMINAL # OF ERRORS COMMITTED PER TASK (ERRORS/TASK)
A   NERPK.K=TABHL(TNERPK,PJBAWK.K,0,1,.2)
NOTE NOMINAL # OF ERRORS COMMITTED PER KDSI (ERRORS/KDSI)
T   TNERPK=25/23.86/21.59/15.9/13.6/12.5
A   MERGSP.K=TABHL(TMEGSP,SCHPR.K,-.4,1,.2)
NOTE MULTIPLIER TO ERROR GENERATION DUE TO SCHEDULE PRESSURE (DIMENSIONLESS)
T   TMEGSP=.9/.94/1/1.05/1.14/1.24/1.36/1.5
A   MERGWM.K=TABHL(TMEGWM,FRWFEX.K,0,1,.2)
NOTE MULTIPLIER TO ERROR GENERATION DUE TO WORKFORCE MIX (DIMENSIONLESS)
T   TMEGWM=2/1.8/1.6/1.4/1.2/1
L   CUMERG.K=CUMERG.J+DT*ERRGRT.JK
NOTE CUMULATIVE ERRORS GENERATED DIRECTLY DURING WORKING (ERRORS)
N   CUMERG=0
L   DTCERR.K=DTCERR.J+DT*(ERRDRT.J-RWRATE.JK)
NOTE DETECTED ERRORS (ERRORS)
N   DTCERR=0
R   RWRATE.KL=DMPRW.K/RWMPPE.K
NOTE REWORK RATE (ERRORS/DAY)
A   RWMPPE.K=NRWMPE.K/MPDMCL.K
NOTE REWORK MANPOWER NEEDED PER ERROR (MAN-DAYS/ERROR)
A   NRWMPE.K=TABHL(TNRWME,PJBAWK.K,0,1,.2)
NOTE NOMINAL REWORK MANPOWER NEEDED PER ERROR (MAN-DAYS/ERROR)
T   TNRWME=.6/.575/.5/.4/.325/.3
L   CMRWED.K=CMRWED.J+DT*RWRATE.JK
NOTE CUMULATIVE REWORKED ERRORS DURING DEVELOPMENT (ERRORS)
N   CMRWED=0
NOTE
NOTE (D) SYSTEM TESTING SECTOR
NOTE
L   UDAVER.K=UDAVER.J+DT*(AEGRT.JK+AERGRT.JK-AERRRT.JK-DCRTAE.JK)
NOTE UNDETECTED ACTIVE ERRORS (ERRORS)

```
N       UDAVER=0
R       AEGRT.KL=(ERRSRT.K+BDFXGR.K)*FRAERR.K
NOTE ACIVE ERRORS GENERATION RATE (ERRORS/DAY)
A       BDFXGR.K=RWRATE.JK*PBADFX
NOTE BAD FIXES GENERATE RATE (ERRORS/DAY)
C       PBADFX=.075
NOTE PERCENT BAD FIXES (FRACTION)
A       FRAERR.K=TABHL(TFRAER,PJBAWK.K,0,1,.1)
NOTE FRACTION OF ESCAPING ERRORS THAT WILL BE ACTIVE (DIMENSIONLESS)
T       TFRAER=1/1/1/1/.95/.85/.5/.2/.075/0/0
R       AERGRT.KL=SDVRT.JK*SMOOTH(AERRDS.K,TSAEDS)*MAERED.K
NOTE ACTIVE ERRORS REGENERATION RATE (ERRORS/DAY)
A       MAERED.K=TABHL(TMERED,SMOOTH(AERRDS.K*1000/DSIPTK,TSAEDS),0,100,10)
NOTE MULTIPLIER TO ACTIVE ERROR REGENERATION DUE TO ERROR DENSITY (DIMENSIONLESS)
T       TMERED=1/1.1/1.2/1.325/1.45/1.6/2/2.5/3.25/4.35/6
C       TSAEDS=40
NOTE TIME TO SMOOTH ACTIVE ERROR DENSITY (AERRDS)  (DAYS)
A       AERRDS.K=UDAVER.K/(CUMTQA.K+.1)
NOTE ACTIVE ERROR DENSITY (ERRORS/TASK)
R       AERRRT.KL=UDAVER.K*AERRFR.K
NOTE ACTIVE ERRORS RETIRING RATE (ERRORS/DAY)
A       AERRFR.K=TABHL(TERMFR,PJBAWK.K,0,1,.1)
NOTE ACTIVE ERRORS RETIRING FRACTION (1/DAYS)
T       TERMFR=0/0/0/0/.01/.02/.03/.04/.1/.3/1
R       DCRTAE.KL=MIN(TSRATE.JK*AERRDS.K,UDAVER.K/DT)
NOTE DETECTION/CORRECTION RATE OF ACTIVE ERRORS (ERRORS/DAY)
L       UDPVER.K=UDPVER.J+DT*(PEGRT.JK+AERRRT.JK-DCRTPE.JK)
NOTE UNDETECTED PASSIVE ERRORS (ERRORS)
N       UDPVER=0
R       PEGRT.KL=(ERRSRT.K+BDFXGR.K)*(1-FRAERR.K)
NOTE PASSIVE ERRORS GENERATION RATE (ERRORS/DAY)
R       DCRTPE.KL=MIN(TSRATE.JK*PERRDS.K,UDPVER.K/DT)
NOTE DETECT/CORRECT RATE OF PASSIVE ERRORS (ERRORS/DAY)
L       CMRWET.K=CMRWET.J+DT*(DCRTPE.JK+DCRTAE.JK)
NOTE CUMULATIVE ERRORS REWORKED IN TESTING PHASE (ERRORS)
N       CMRWET=0
A       ALESER.K=UDAVER.K+UDPVER.K+CMRWET.K
NOTE ALL ERRORS THAT ESCAPED AND WERE GENERATED (ERRORS)
A       DMPTST.K=DMPDVT.K*FREFTS.K
NOTE DAILY MANPOWER FOR TESTING (MAN-DAYS/DAY)
L       CMTSMD.K=CMTSMD.J+DT*DMPTST.J
NOTE CUMULATIVE TESTING MAN-DAYS (MAN-DAYS)
N       CMTSMD=0
R       TSRATE.KL=MIN(CUMTQA.K/DT,DMPTST.K/TMPNPT.K)
NOTE TESTING RATE (TASKS/DAY)
A       TMPNPT.K=(TSTOVH*DSIPTK/1000+TMPNPE.K*(PERRDS.K+AERRDS.K)
X       )/MPDMCL.K
NOTE TESTING MANPOWER NEEDED PER TASK (MAN-DAYS/TASK)
C       TSTOVH=1
NOTE TESTING EFFORT OVERHEAD (MAN-DAYS/KDSI)
C       TMPNPE=.15
NOTE TESTING MANPOWER NEEDED PER ERROR (MAN-DAY/ERROR)
A       PTKTST.K=CUMTKT.K/PJBSZ.K
NOTE % OF TASKS TESTED (%)
A       PERRDS.K=UDPVER.K/(CUMTQA.K+.0001)
NOTE PASSIVE ERROR DENSITY (ERRORS/TASK)
L       CUMTKT.K=CUMTKT.J+DT*TSRATE.JK
```

```
NOTE CUMULATIVE TASKS TESTED (TASKS)
N       CUMTKT=0
A       ALLERR.K=PTDTER.K+DTCERR.K+CMRWED.K+UDAVER.K+
X       UDPVER.K+CMRWET.K
NOTE ALL ERRORS (ERRORS)
A       ALLRWK.K=CMRWED.K+CMRWET.K
NOTE ALL ERRORS REWORKED ... IN DEVELOPMENT AND TESTING (ERRORS)
NOTE
NOTE **************
NOTE CONTROL SUBSYSTEM
NOTE **************
NOTE
L       CMTKDV.K=CMTKDV.J+DT*SDVRT.JK
NOTE CUMULATIVE TASKS DEVELOPED (TASKS)
N       CMTKDV=0
A       PJBAWK.K=CMTKDV.K/RJBSZ
NOTE % OF JOB ACTUALLY WORKED (%)
A       PJDPRD.K=TSKPRM.K/(MDPRNT.K+.1)
NOTE PROJECTED DEVELOPMENT PRODUCTIVITY (TASKS/MAN-DAY)
A       MDPRNT.K=MAX(0,MDRM.K-MDPNRW.K-MDPNTS.K)
NOTE MAN DAYS PERCEIVED REMAINING FOR NEW TASKS (MAN-DAYS)
A       MDPNRW.K=DTCERR.K*PRWMPE.K
NOTE MAN DAYS PERCEIVED NEEDED FOR REWORKING ALREADY DETECTED ERRORS (MD)
A       ASSPRD.K=PJDPRD.K*WTPJDP.K+PRDPRD.K*(1-WTPJDP.K)
NOTE ASSUMED PRODUCTIVITY (TASKS/MAN-DAY)
A       PRDPRD.K=CMTKDV.K/(CUMMD.K-CMTSMD.K)
NOTE PERCEIVED DEVELOPMENT PRODUCTIVITY (TASKS/MAN-DAY)
A       WTPJDP.K=MPWDEV.K*MPWREX.K
NOTE WEIGHT TO PROJECTED DEVELOPMENT PRODUCTIVITY (DIMENSIONLESS)
A       MPWDEV.K=TABHL(TMPDEV,PJBPWK.K/100,0,1,.1)
NOTE MULTIPLIER TO PRODUCTIVITY WEIGHT DUE TO DEVELOPMENT (DIMENSIONLESS)
T       TMPDEV=1/1/1/1/1/1/.975/.9/.75/.5/0
A       MPWREX.K=TABHL(TMPREX,(1-MDPRNT.K/(JBSZMD.K-TSSZMD.K)),
X       0,1,.1)
NOTE MULTIPLIER TO PRODUCTIVITY WEIGHT DUE TO RESOURCE EXPENDITURE (DIMENSIONLESS)
T       TMPREX=1/1/1/1/1/1/.975/.9/.75/.5/0
A       MDPNNT.K=TSKPRM.K/ASSPRD.K
NOTE MAN DAYS PERCEIVED STILL NEEDED FOR NEW TASKS (MAN-DAYS)
A       TMDPSN.K=MDPNNT.K+MDPNTS.K+MDPNRW.K
NOTE TOTAL MAN DAYS PERCEIVED STILL NEEDED (MAN-DAYS)
A       MDPNTS.K=TSTPRM.K/PRTPRD.K
NOTE MAN DAYS PERCEIVED STILL NEEDED FOR TESTING (MAN-DAYS)
A       TSTPRM.K=PJBSZ.K-CUMTKT.K
NOTE TASKS REMAINING TO BE TESTED (TASKS)
A       PRTPRD.K=SMOOTH((CLIP(PLTSPD.K,ACTSPD.K,0,CUMTKT.K)),TSTSPD)
NOTE PERCEIVED TESTING PRODUCTIVITY (TASKS/MAN-DAY)
C       TSTSPD=50
NOTE TIME TO SMOOTH TESTING PRODUCTIVITY (DAYS)
A       PLTSPD.K=PJBSZ.K/TSSZMD.K
NOTE PLANNED TESTING PRODUCTIVITY (TASKS/MAN-DAY)
A       ACTSPD.K=CUMTKT.K/(CMTSMD.K+.001)
NOTE ACTUAL TESTING PRODUCTIVITY (TASKS/MAN-DAY)
A       PMDSHR.K=TMDPSN.K-MDRM.K
NOTE PERCEIVED SHORTAGE IN MAN DAYS (MAN-DAYS)
A       SHRRPT.K=PMDSHR.K-MDHDL.K
NOTE SHORTAGE REPORTED (MAN-DAYS)
A       MDRPTN.K=MDRM.K+SHRRPT.K
```

NOTE MAN DAYS REPORTED STILL NEEDED (MAN-DAYS)
A   SCHPR.K=(TMDPSN.K-MDRM.K)/MDRM.K
NOTE SCHEDULE PRESSURE   (DIMENSIONLESS)
A   PTRPTC.K=SMOOTH((100-(MDRPTN.K/JBSZMD.K)*100),RPTDLY)
NOTE % OF TASKS REPORTED COMPLETE (%)
N   PTRPTC=0
C   RPTDLY=10
NOTE REPORTING DELAY (DAYS)
A   PDEVRC.K=SMOOTH(MAX((100-((MDRPTN.K-MDPNTS.K)/(JBSZMD.K-TSSZMD.K)
X   )*100),PDEVRC.K),RPTDLY)
N   PDEVRC=0
NOTE % DEVELOPMENT PERCEIVED COMPLETE %
L   UNDJTK.K=UNDJTK.J-DT*RTDSTK.JK
NOTE UNDISCOVERED JOB TASKS (TASKS)
N   UNDJTK=RJBSZ-PJBSZ
N   RJBSZ=RJBDSI/DSIPTK
NOTE REAL JOB SIZE IN TASKS (TASKS)
R   RTDSTK.KL=UNDJTK.K*PUTDPD.K/100
NOTE RATE OF DISCOVERING TASKS (TASKS/DAY)
A   PUTDPD.K=TABHL(TPUTDD,PJBPWK.K,0,100,20)
NOTE PERCENT OF UNDISCOVERED TASKS DISCOVERED PER DAY (1/DAY)
T   TPUTDD=0/0.4/2.5/5/10/100
A   PJBPWK.K=(CMTKDV.K/PJBSZ.K)*100
NOTE % OF JOB PERCEIVED WORKED (%)
R   RTINCT.KL=DELAY3(RTDSTK.JK,DLINCT)
NOTE RATE OF INCORPORATING DISCOVERED TASKS INTO PROJECT (TASKS/DAY)
L   TKDSCV.K=MAX((TKDSCV.J+DT*(RTDSTK.JK-RTINCT.JK)),0)
NOTE TASKS DISCOVERED (TASKS)
N   TKDSCV=0
C   DLINCT=10
NOTE AVERAGE DELAY IN INCORPORATING DISCOVERED TASKS (DAYS)
L   PJBSZ.K=PJBSZ.J+DT*RTINCT.JK
NOTE CURRENTLY PERCEIVED JOB SIZE (TASKS)
N   PJBSZ=PJBDSI/DSIPTK
A   TSKPRM.K=PJBSZ.K-CMTKDV.K
NOTE NEW TASKS PERCEIVED REMAINING (TASKS)
A   PSZDCT.K=TKDSCV.K/ASSPRD.K
NOTE PERCEIVED SIZE OF DISCOVERED TASKS IN MAN DAYS (MAN-DAYS)
A   RSZDCT.K=PSZDCT.K/(MDPRNT.K+.0001)
NOTE RELATIVE SIZE OF DISCOVERED TASKS (DIMENSIONLESS)
A   FADHWO.K=TABHL(TFAHWO,RSZDCT.K/(MSZTWO+.001),0,2,.2)
NOTE FRACTION OF ADDITIONAL TASKS ADDING TO MAN-DAYS
T   TFAHWO=0/0/0/0/0/0/.7/.9/.975/1/1
C   MSZTWO=.01
NOTE MAXIMUM RELATIVE SIZE OF ADDITIONS TOLERATED W/O ADDING TO PROJECT'S MAN-DAY
R   IRDVDT.KL=(RTINCT.JK/ASSPRD.K)*(FADHWO.K)
NOTE RATE OF INCREASE IN DEVELOPMENT MAN-DAYS DUE TO DISCOVERED TASKS (MD/D)
L   TSSZMD.K=TSSZMD.J+DT*IRTSDT.JK+ARTJBM.K*CLIP(1,0,FREFTS.J,.9)
NOTE PLANNED TESTING SIZE IN MAN-DAYS ... BEFORE WE START TESTING
N   TSSZMD=TSTMD
R   IRTSDT.KL=(RTINCT.JK/PRTPRD.K)*(FADHWO.K)
NOTE RATE OF INCREASE IN TESTING MAN DAYS DUE TO DISCOVERED TASKS (MD/D)
L   JBSZMD.K=JBSZMD.J+DT*(IRDVDT.JK+IRTSDT.JK+ARTJBM.JK)
NOTE TOTAL JOB SIZE IN MAN DAYA (MAN-DAYS)
N   JBSZMD=DEVMD+TSTMD
R   ARTJBM.KL=(MDRPTN.K+CUMMD.K-JBSZMD.K)/DAJBMD.K
NOTE RATE OF ADJUSTING THE JOB SIZE IN MAN-DAYS (MAN-DAYS/DAY)

A   DAJBMD.K=TABHL(TDAJMD,TIMERM.K,0,20,20)
NOTE DELAY IN ADJUSTING JOB'S SIZE IN MAN DAYS (DAYS)
T   TDAJMD=.5/3
A   MDRM.K=MAX(.0001,JBSZMD.K-CUMMD.K)
NOTE
NOTE **************
NOTE PLANNING SUBSYSTEM
NOTE
NOTE **************
NOTE
NOTE MAN DAYS REMAINING
A   TIMEPR.K=MDRM.K/(WFS.K*ADMPPS)
NOTE TIME PERCEIVED STILL REQUIRED (DAYS)
A   INDCDT.K=TIME.K+TIMEPR.K
NOTE INDICATED COMPLETION DATE
L   SCHCDT.K=SCHCDT.J+DT*(INDCDT.J-SCHCDT.J)/SCHADT.K
NOTE SCHEDULE COMPLETION DATE
N   SCHCDT=TDEV
A   SCHADT.K=TABHL(TSHADT,TIMERM.K,0,5,5)
NOTE SCHEDULE ADJUSTMENT TIME (DAYS)
T   TSHADT=.5/5
A   TIMERM.K=MAX(SCHCDT.K-TIME.K,0)
NOTE TIME REMAINING (DAYS)
A   WFINDC.K=(MDRM.K/(TIMERM.K+.001))/ADMPPS
NOTE INDICATED WORKFORCE (PEOPLE)
A   WFNEED.K=MIN((WCWF.K*WFINDC.K+(1-WCWF.K)*TOTWF.K),WFINDC.K)
NOTE WORKFORCE LEVEL NEEDED (PEOPLE)
A   WCWF.K=MAX(WCWF1.K,WCWF2.K)
NOTE WILLINGNESS TO CHANGE WORKFORCE LEVEL (DIMENSIONLESS)
A   WCWF1.K=TABHL(TWCWF1,TIMERM.K/(HIREDY+ASIMDY),0,3,.3)
NOTE WILLINGNESS TO CHANGE WORKFORCE (1) (DIMENSIONLESS)
T   TWCWF1=0/0/.1/.4/.85/1/1/1/1/1/1
A   WCWF2.K=TABHL(TWCWF2,SCHCDT.K/MXTLCD,.86,1,.02)
NOTE WILLINGNESS TO CHANGE WF (2) (DIMENSIONLESS)
T   TWCWF2=0/.1/.2/.35/.6/.7/.77/.80
N   MXTLCD=MXSCDX*TDEV
NOTE MAXIMUM TOLERABLE COMPLETION DATE (DAYS)
C   MXSCDX=1E6
NOTE MAX SCHEDULE COMPLETION DATE EXTENSION (DIMENSIONLESS)
NOTE
NOTE **************
NOTE INITIALIZATION
NOTE **************
NOTE
NOTE THE REAL JOB SIZE = 64,000 DSI
NOTE FROM BOEHM PAGE 90:
NOTE DISTRIBUTION OF EFFORT BY PHASE IS:
NOTE DESIGN (39%), PROGRAMMING (36%), INT TESTING (25%)
NOTE FROM BOEHM PAGE 64-65:
NOTE EFFORT = 2.4*(KDSI)**1.05
NOTE= 190 MM
NOTE = 190 * 19 = 3592 MAN-DAYS
NOTE DEVELOPMENT EFFORT = 75 %
NOTE = 2695 MAN DAYS
NOTE GROSS DEV PRODUCTIVITY = 64,000/2695 = 24 DSI/MD
NOTE
NOTE SCHEDULE = 2.5 * (MM)**.38

```
NOTE = 18 MONTHS
NOTE = 348 DAYS
NOTE
NOTE AVERAGE STAFF SIZE = 3592/348
NOTE = 10
NOTE
NOTE GROSS PRODUCTIVITY INCORPORATES: DEV, FOR QA, & REWORKING
NOTE ASSUMING 25% OF EFFORT GOES INTO QA & REWORKING
NOTE 25% OF 2695 MAN DAYS = 674 MAN DAYS
NOTE DEVELOPMENT PRODUCTIVITY = 64,000/(2695-674)
NOTE                             = 31 DSI/MAN-DAY
NOTE
NOTE ASSUME LOSSES IN PRODUCTIVITY = 50 %
NOTE THEREFORE POTENTIAL PRODUCTIVITY = 31 * 2 = APPROX 60 DSI/MD
NOTE DEFINE 1 TASK = 60 DSI
C       DSIPTK=60
NOTE DSI PER TASK
C       RJBDSI=64000
NOTE REAL JOB SIZE IN DSI
C       UNDEST=0
NOTE TASKS UNDERESTIMATION FRACTION (FRACTION)
N       PJBDSI=RJBDSI*(1-UNDEST)
NOTE PERCEIVED JOB SIZE IN DSI
N       TOTMD=MDSWCH*(((2.4*EXP(1.05*LOGN(PJBDSI/1000)))*19)*(1-UNDESM))
X       +(1-MDSWCH)*TOTMD1
NOTE TOTAL MAN DAYS
C       UNDESM=0
NOTE MAN-DAYS UNDERESTIMATION FRACTION (FRACTION)
N       DEVMD=DEVPRT*TOTMD
NOTE DEVELOPMENT MAN DAYS
C       MDSWCH=1
NOTE SWITCH 0 OR 1
C       TOTMD1=0
NOTE TOTAL MANDAYS
C       DEVPRT=0.80
NOTE % OF EFFORT ASSUMED NEEDED FOR DEVELOPMENT
N       TSTMD=(1-DEVPRT)*TOTMD
NOTE TESTING MAN DAYS
N       WFSTRT=TEAMSZ*INUDST
NOTE TEAM SIZE AT BEGINNING OF DESIGN (MEN)
C       INUDST=.5
NOTE INITIAL UNDERSTAFFING FACTOR (DIMENSIONLESS)
N       TDEV=SCSWCH*((19*2.5*EXP(0.38*LOGN(TOTMD/19)))*SCHCOM)
X       +(1-SCSWCH)*TDEV1
NOTE TOTAL DEVELOPMENT TIME (DAYS)
C       SCHCOM=1
NOTE SCHEDULE COMPRESSION FACTOR (DIMENSIONLESS)
C       SCSWCH=1
NOTE SWITCH 0 OR 1
C       TDEV1=0
NOTE TIME TO DEVELOP
N       TEAMSZ=(TOTMD/TDEV)/ADMPPS
NOTE
NOTE **************
NOTE VII. CONTROL STATEMENTS
NOTE **************
NOTE
```

```
SPEC DT=.5,MAXLEN=1000,PLTPER=10
A       LENGTH.K=CLIP(TIME.K,MAXLEN,PTKTST.K,.99)
A       PRTPER.K=LENGTH.K
PRINT TOTMD,DEVMD,TSTMD,TDEV
PRINT TOTWF,CUMMD,CMQAMD,CMRWMD,CMTSMD,CUMERG,CMERES,CMRWET,PRCTDT
PLOT TOTWF=W(0,20)
PLOT PDEVRC=1(0,100)
PLOT PJBSZ=J,CMTKDV=1,CUMTKT=T(0,1500)/CUMMD=C,JBSZMD=D(0,
X       5000)/SCHCDT=S(200,600)/PTRPTC=R,PDEVRC=V(0,100)
PLOT AFMDPJ=F(0,2.4)
PLOT CUMERG=G,CMERD=D,CMERES=S(0,4000)/PRCTDT=P(0,100)
PLOT AFMDPJ=F(0,2.4)/EXHLEV=X,OVWDTH=V(0,100)/MDHDL=H,PMDSHR=P
X       (-500,500)/SHRRPT=1(-500,500)/SCHPR=S(-1,1)/
X       JBSZMD=D,CUMMD=C(0,5000)/SHRRPT=1(-200,200)
```

INDEX

Order Form for the system dynamics project model to accompany

Software Project Dynamics: An Integrated Approach
by Tarek K. Abdel-Hamid and Stuart E. Madnick

Standard Price
  –Copies 1 through 5 (price for each license and package) $200.00
  –Additional copies (each additional license and package) $ 50.00

Educational Price
  –First site license (price for each license and package) $200.00
  –Additional copies (each additional license and package) $ 15.00

All prices are in U.S. dollars. Checks must be drawn on U.S. banks, and must be enclosed.

Tear out or photocopy this page and send to:

    Dynamica
    19 Trillium Lane
    San Carlos, CA 94070
    Tel: (415) 591–3913

Please send the following:

Quantity	Floppy Size (360k/1.2MB)	Unit Price	Total
_____	_____	_____	_____
_____	_____	_____	_____
_____	_____	_____	_____
		Grand Total	_____

Ship to: Name   _____
         Address   _____
         City/State/Zip _____
Special Instructions: _____

Minimum computer requirements: IBM PC or true hardware compatibles with 256K bytes of memory, graphics card and monochrome monitor, one floppy drive, and DOS 2.0 or higher.

Note: The system dynamics model has been written in Professional DYNAMO Plus™, but includes only that part of the system needed for running the model, viewing the results, and changing model parameters for re-runs. You will need the complete system in order to create different system dynamics models. To obtain more information about Professional DYNAMO Plus™, you should write or call:

    Pugh-Roberts Associates, Inc.
    Five Lee Street, Cambridge, MA 02139
    Tel: (617) 864–8880